Re-Imagining
LIFE TOGETHER
IN AMERICA

Re-Imagining
LIFE TOGETHER
IN AMERICA

A *New* Gospel of
COMMUNITY

Catherine Nerney

Hal Taussig

SHEED & WARD

an imprint of the
Rowman and Littlefield
Publishing Group

Chicago

SHEED & WARD
Lanham, Maryland
Chicago, Illinois

Published by Sheed & Ward
an imprint of Rowman & Littlefield Publishers, Inc.
4720 Boston Way
Lanham, MD 20706

12 Hid's Copse Road
Cumnor Hill, Oxford OX2 9JJ, England

Paper: 1-58051-114-7
Cloth: 1-58051-136-8

LIBRARY OF CONGRESS CATALOGING-IN-PUBLICATION DATA

Nerney, Catherine T.
  Re-imagining life together in America : a new gospel of community /
Catherine T. Nerney and Hal Taussig.
      p. cm.
  Includes bibliographical references.
  ISBN 1-58051-136-8 (alk. paper) -- ISBN 1-58051-114-7 (pbk. : alk.
paper)
  1. Community--Religious aspects--Christianity. 2. Christian
life--United States. 3. Community--United States. I. Taussig, Hal. II.
Title.   BV4517.5 .N47 2002
262--dc21
                                                      2002152110

Contents

PREFACE

This book emerged from our long and intense collegiality in the Graduate Program in Holistic Spirituality at Chestnut Hill College. But the roots of that collegial work are both more interesting and significant for the book.

Both of us have been for some three decades deeply committed to an intense combination of local church ministry and scholarship. Although both our academic fields and our Christian denominations differ from one another, our common personal and professional dedication to both church and academy have made for strikingly parallel vocations.

In each of our lives an intense passion for the future of church in America has been the strongest current in this common devotion to both a ministerial and an academic life. This book cannot be understood without our enthusiasm for ministry, church, scholarship, and teaching. Although it strives to provide keen theological, biblical, and sociocultural analysis, our work attempts to be explicitly a part of postmodern consciousness, embracing consciously the limits and advantages of our own engaged social location. We are quite aware of, and ask this book's readers to recognize, our own energy-filled engagement—with all the promise and bias it involves.

Both of us—in strikingly similar ways—have found ourselves over our heads in the likes of developing local church liturgies, shouldering the weight of urban church ministries, counseling students about future church careers, building local church working groups, nurturing new graduate courses and curricula in ministry, challenging rigid church authority structures, developing holistic modalities for the study of religion, advocating for the rights of the oppressed, and burning the midnight oil with student papers.

Both of us have worked most of our adult lives in professional ministries aimed at local church renewal. Cathy Nerney has done this at the local, regional, and national levels. From a high school religion teacher and campus minister, she turned her attention and active ministry toward concern and preparation for the kind of church these young people would inherit. Her direct work in promoting small Christian communities involved more than a decade of ministry in the Pastoral Renewal Office and the Ministerial Development Center of the Archdiocese of Newark, New Jersey, in the Renew Program, and as co-founder of the North American Forum for Small Christian Communities in 1984.

Hal Taussig has been a United Methodist pastor almost continuously from 1974 to the present in the Eastern Pennsylvania Conference. All but three of these years involved the transformation of a dying congregation into a revitalized one.

At the same time we have had major involvement as scholars and teachers in higher education. Cathy Nerney's combination of church and academy has been more serial, and Hal Taussig's has been more simultaneous. While a pastor, Hal Taussig currently teaches graduate biblical studies at Union Theological Seminary, Chestnut Hill College, and the Reconstructionist Rabbinical College. He is the author or co-author of five books and has served in leadership of several Society of Biblical Literature seminars. He is a founding member of the Jesus Seminar. After her two decades of parish ministry, Cathy Nerney now serves as chairperson and associate professor of the Religious Studies Department at Chestnut Hill College. She has taught at St. Mary's in San Antonio, Loyola University in New Orleans, and St. Michael's College in Winooski, Vermont and lectures nationally on church, community, and spirituality. She has authored many lectionary-based booklets for small Christian communities and theological articles. She served in 2002 as member of the theological committee for the national Common Ground Initiative, founded by and in memory of Cardinal Joseph Bernardin.

The idea of the book consciously emerged some time after we co-taught a Doctor of Ministry seminar in "Community and Ecclesiology" in Chestnut Hill College's Graduate Program in Holistic Spirituality. It was also especially fueled by our work in re-shaping the curriculum of that program and in our co-teaching of the terminal seminar of that program's masters degree.

The writing of the book has also been an intensely collective endeavor. The subject matter of "community" has invaded almost every aspect of this book's authorship. We have challenged and supported one another in ways that broke open new levels of friendship, conflict, and understanding.

It is, of course, also true that certain portions of the book are more the responsibility of one author than the other. Since our academic fields are not the same, we have relied on each other's expertise. That has not meant that we did not allow each other to challenge and assist in every aspect of the book.

All of the persons described and cited in this book exist. In all but one case actual names are used. "Jennifer" in chapter eight is a fictional name.

We are grateful to Mary Kay Flannery, S.S.J., and Carolynne Ervin, our colleagues and friends in the Graduate Spirituality Program of Chestnut Hill College, for their keen companionship. We are also deeply indebted to the graduate students of that same program. We want to acknowledge our important, although diverse, intellectual and personal indebtedness to Professor Vincent Wimbush of Union Theological Seminary and Professors Joseph Komonchak, Mary Collins, and Margaret Mary Kelleher of the Catholic University of America. We also want to thank Arthur Brandenburg, Susan Cole, Tom Kleissler, Winifred Grelis, S.S.J., Margi Savage, S.S.J., and Mary Scanlon, S.S.J. for the important ways they mentored us in our own faith life and local church ministries. Finally we are grateful for the myriad of local church communities who are doing the work about which we write here. We are particularly indebted to Renew; St. Vincent's Roman Catholic Church in the Germantown section of Philadelphia; the Roman Catholic Church of the Presentation in Upper Saddle River, New Jersey; the NOVA Community of Northern Virginia; College Hill United Methodist Church in Wichita, Kansas; Lancaster Community Mennonite Church; and Chestnut Hill United Methodist Church in Philadelphia. Their commitment to life together in community is our sure ground and our shared hope.

Introduction

Both Beth and Bill Wolff had been raised with some exposure to church, Beth fitfully in Unitarian and Baptist congregations and Bill formally but infrequently in a geographically distant Albanian Orthodox church. By their late teens they had judged church as unimportant and occasionally offensive, so they dropped out. When they were married, both their mutually unimpressive experiences and their different religious backgrounds reinforced the now established impulse to leave church behind.

The births of their two sons were the occasion to re-evaluate their attitude about church. So they found a local Methodist church they liked and joined it. The boys were baptized and the Wolffs were surprised and pleased at the open-minded, spiritually alive mood of the church.

Shortly thereafter Beth's younger brother committed suicide. This ripped Beth's world apart, threatening directly her mental health, family relations, and spiritual practice. The church responded with compassion, providing pastoral counsel, important companionship, and a safe place to grieve. By designing and performing particular rites of mourning, artists in the congregation worked with Beth to help her process her sorrow and anger. The annual All Saints Day service, which included an explicit invitation for church members to bring mementos of lost loved ones and to light candles in their memory, became a pivotal day for the Wolff family each year. Several years later the Wolffs began to host a church picnic on the deceased brother's birthday.

As the years unfolded, the processing of Beth's brother's death receded in importance, but church involvement did not. Bill became the church treasurer. Beth chaired the fellowship committee and headed up several church fundraisers. The boys became active in the Christian education program and helped anchor the church's annual children's summer camp on environmental issues. Beth's new and successful business became a major funder for the church's projects with Kenyan AIDS victims and a Filipino tribe struggling to hold onto its rain forest home. Beth began to try to formulate for others her strong sense of God as presence that held her each day and the church as her larger family.

This story illustrates this book's central proposal: local church community can rescue Americans from their peculiar isolation and restore a deep sense of wholeness to their lives. The Wolffs did not become world leaders. Nor did they sell all they own and give it to the poor. They did, however, re-imagine their life together through their discovery of church. They connected with a local church community, and the fabric of their lives gradually strengthened in very basic ways. God's presence was much stronger for them than ever before, and what we are calling "a gospel of community" slowly became the way in which they lived their lives and shaped their service to others.

One of the most exciting dimensions of this gospel of community is that it is discernible in a growing number of American situations. Single people lost in the maze of dating games and bar-hopping are finding church groups that help them make sense of their lives and even introduce them to the kind of quality people they want to date. Persons addicted to work, alcohol, or drugs are noticing how a church community can challenge old loyalties and anchor new stability. In certain places church is becoming simultaneously for the wealthy and the disenfranchised an occasion for addressing the huge gap between rich and poor. A wide range of spiritual seekers is learning that Christian community can provide a powerful connection to God. Life is actively being re-imagined by these people, and the result is a clear move toward others and a life together.

This re-emergence of community in the forms of local church is happening at a time of increased isolation for Americans. Robert Putnam's recent *Bowling Alone: The Collapse and Revival of American Community* has fashioned words and provided data for the gnawing feeling of many Americans that they are less and less connected with one another. In his 541-page study, Putnam shows how Americans are voting less frequently, joining fewer neighborhood associations, playing sports together less, letting their connections to synagogue and church drop, forming fewer unions, changing jobs more often, eating dinner together less, watching TV more, and giving less money to charity than forty years ago. Putnam also sees signs that this decline of community in America is having adverse effects. Growing signs of personal stress, major tears in the fabric of social cooperation, road rage, and increasing burdens on the natural environment are all related to the lack of a sense of community in America according to Putnam.

Americans' difficulty in being together is not new. It was noticed almost two centuries ago by the French observer Alexis de Tocqueville, and more recently by Robert Bellah and his colleagues, first in the best-selling book of the 1980s, *Habits of the Heart,* and then in several follow-up studies. Bellah, Tocqueville, and others have pointed out how the heightened sense of individualism fashioned on the American frontier and given full expression in American entrepreneurial ventures brings with it serious handicaps in learning to be in community. Americans, it seems, have been impaired—almost from the beginning—for community.[1] The problem of the last several decades that Putnam describes is not new, it is just particularly acute at the present moment.

THE PROPOSAL

In addressing this major and especially pressing issue, this book, as noted briefly above, has a central proposal: to reveal how and why local churches can help Americans be in community. This proposal is simple and straightforward. We want readers to consider seriously how local church ministry can make important differences in the character and quality of community life for themselves, their friends, and their neighbors. This entire book is a direct invitation to re-imagine how we in North America can live together more thoroughly, lovingly, and enthusiastically through active engagement in local church communities.

Although straightforward, this proposal is not without nuance and complication. It is not just because we two authors have spent cumulatively more than a half-century working on issues of community at the local church level that we make this proposal. Our experience in community building is germane, but there are larger reasons to press this agenda.

Churches in America are strategically located to help Americans claim a sense of community belonging. First of all, as Putnam notes, "America is one of the most religiously observant countries in the contemporary world," (65) placing churches in a central social position from which to influence individuals' relationship to community. Even more germane and again in the words of Putnam, "faith communities in which people worship together are arguably the single most important repository of social capital in America." (66) Putnam's surveys showed that "nearly half of all associational memberships in America are church related, half of all personal philanthropy is religious in character, and half of all volunteering occurs in a religious context" (66).

The range of community building activities in which American churches are already involved reaches into most areas of living. As a particularly striking example, Putnam lists the activities of one week in the life of Riverside Church in New York City: "Social Service Training Session, the AIDS Awareness Seminar, the Ecology Task Force, the Chinese Christian Fellowship, Narcotics Anonymous, Riverside Business and Professional Women's Club, Gulf Crisis Study Series, Adult Children of Alcoholics, and Martial Arts Class for Adults and Teens" (66).

Attending church affects people's general ability to be in community. "Regular worshippers and people who say that religion is very important to them are much more likely than other people to visit friends, to entertain at home, to attend club meetings, and to belong to sports groups; professional and academic societies; school service groups; youth groups; service clubs; hobby or garden clubs; literary, art, discussion and study groups; school fraternities and sororities; farm organizations; political clubs; nationality groups; and other miscellaneous groups" (67) which Putnam dutifully footnotes.

Belonging to a church community also increases one's skills at being in community. "Religiously active men and women learn to give speeches, run meetings, manage disagreements, and bear administrative responsibility. They also befriend others who are in turn likely to recruit them into other forms of community activity" (66). In a time in which life together in families is particularly fragile, relating to church helps particular households develop their own fabric of care.

All of these dimensions of church life[2] that make the churches' location for community building strategic are enhanced by Christianity's dominant religious position in America. Although, as we will see later in this book, Christianity's social predominance is not always spiritually helpful, our proposal that churches provide a strategic place from which to build community in America is made stronger by the numerical dominance of churches in America.

We do not mean to imply that we think Christianity as a religion is superior to Judaism, Islam, or other important American religious allegiances.[3] In this regard, Putnam himself hastens to footnote that "for simplicity's sake I use the term church here to refer to all religious institutions of whatever faith, including mosques, temples, and synagogues" (65). Our point is simply that the vast number of churches in America makes them all the more important as a place where Americans can learn community.

It is not, however, only the churches' crucial and established place as community builder in America that makes our proposal compelling. There are long and deeply held Christian traditions and disciplines that promote and undergird community. These traditions and disciplines present to many isolated Americans a wide set of resources for re-imagining life together by participating in community.

Many of these traditions tie the experience of community directly to faith in God. That is, for a great deal of Christianity, faith in God has less to do with some kind of intellectual rationale than with the dynamics of humans living together and experiencing themselves as part of a greater whole. We will return to summarize these traditions later in this chapter and to explore them directly in the first half of this book.

But it is not only Christian traditions that support community building in America today. Much of Christianity throughout history has developed disciplines by which community can be experienced. Perhaps most dramatically the origins of Christianity are intimately tied to community. The worship and life together in the first several centuries of Christianity assumed and elaborated group life. Similarly and later, the monastic movements of Christianity developed ways of praying, combining economic assets and living under one roof. Many of these community disciplines were extended and elaborated into the congregational life of churches by the Protestant reformers.

Our proposal that churches are crucial to the possibility of Americans learning to be in community rests then on both the strategic social location of churches in America and on the deeply held traditions and disciplines of community in historical Christianity. We are also aware of the irony that in many cases American churches discourage community through a religiously sanctified individualism, a persistent clericalism, and a mindless formalism. Since no proposal can stand without cross-examination, we will look closely also at these anti-community dimensions of American churches in chapter 9.

THE CONTEMPORARY SEARCH FOR COMMUNITY AND THE CHURCHES' POTENTIAL

There is no need for a book to convince Americans that they need community. In a recent survey, over 75 percent of those Americans surveyed said that they lacked a sense of belonging to community, and a sense of community was a primary goal in their lives.[4] Therapy groups, sports leagues, neighborhood associations, community theaters, and the new wave of charitable volunteering all are responses to the American search for community. Nor is it new (to note) that Americans look to churches for community. In another recent church survey more than two-thirds of those seeking a church home said that a primary goal of theirs was to belong to a community.

The thirst for community is also obvious in the massive alienation Americans exhibit. Addiction to alcohol, sex, work, and drugs can be related to the lack of a sense of belonging. Compulsive TV watching and shopping are signs of the loss of people sharing life. School shootings and other noneconomic related violence demonstrates the crippling isolation of many.

No less a student of the American search for community than Robert Bellah has identified churches as critical to the search. He proposes: "I think we have to seriously consider religious community since it is the best community at a local level, provided we can encourage each other through that community to think about the problems that are facing us in the larger society, not at the expense of spirituality, but out of an understanding of who we are as a people of God" (1998, 11). For Bellah, it's not that the churches are perfect, it is rather, as he says, "that I have less confidence in anything else. The local parish or congregation is for many people in this society the only voluntary group that connects them to the larger society. . . ." (10)

Bellah sees the contemporary resources of the churches for community building not only in their being something like a last resort. For him, religious leaders and intellectual traditions also provide strong support. "An enormous amount depends on the minister, the rabbi, the pastor, and the priest. . . .I think there is a tremendous responsibility for religious intellectuals to take leadership in linking religious traditions to the problems of the world in which we live" (10). Such intellectual activity is already occurring within the American church scene, Bellah adds. "I see signs all over the place. There is a lot of sensitivity and awareness. . . .If you read *Christian Century,* or *Commonweal,* or *Tikkun,* you'll see three American journals that are more on top of most of these issues than any other secular or religious journal. . . ." (11)

Robert Putnam illustrates the sustaining power of church attendance in giving people a sense of belonging and even happiness. In examining the leading activities that gave people the most "happiness" (volunteerism, club meetings, entertaining people at home), Putnam found that most activities done in moderation made people happier. He discovered, however, no such trend in churchgoing. There was no limit to the increase of happiness as one increased one's relationship to church. Of those surveyed in the nationally recognized DDB Needham Lifestyle Study, the more one attended church the happier one was. "Churchgoing . . . is somewhat different, in that at least up through weekly attendance, the more the merrier," Putnam concludes. (334)

SPIRITUAL AND THEOLOGICAL PERSPECTIVES ON THE SEARCH FOR COMMUNITY

It would be misleading simply to frame our proposal in a utilitarian manner. We do not, in fact, just think that the people should seriously consider participation in local churches so that American community can be enhanced. Of primary importance to our proposal is the claim that the human experience of community is directly connected to the experience of God. That is, we believe that inasmuch as Americans can experience themselves in community, they—as an inherent part of this social belonging—encounter God. This is why, we believe, a large component of the current search for spirituality intuitively has included a search for community. As the Roman Catholic writer Andrew Greeley has said, "humans are integrated into networks, networks that reveal God." God is not an additive in this proposal, but rather a central component to the very possibility of Americans learning to be in community. To belong to God helps pivotally in knowing how to belong to a community. Conversely, belonging to a social group inherently enhances knowing God.

This way of understanding humans in relationship as a part of their experience of God is what Greeley names "the sacramental imagination" (sometimes he calls it "the Catholic imagination"). "The Catholic tends to see society as a 'sacrament' of God, a set of ordered relationships, governed by both justice and love, that reveal, however imperfectly, the presence of God. Society is 'natural' and 'good,' therefore, for humans, their 'natural' response to God is social."[5]

Bellah, a Protestant himself, praises this "sacramental imagination" and this "idea of the sacred in the world" (1999, 11). He proposes a rediscovery of community for Americans through this "sacramental imagination," even though it will not be easy. "The very concreteness of the sacramental tradition is difficult for free-floating middle-class Americans, even Catholics, to imagine" (13). Bellah quotes parishioners from a largely Puerto Rican Roman Catholic parish in Hartford, Connecticut, to illustrate his assertion that the sacrament of breaking bread and sharing wine as the body and blood of Christ has strong implications for Americans search for community.

One parishioner says:

"'The Eucharist is the living presence of Christ. In sharing that presence, the call is to go out to make that presence operational, living in the world. That going out wears us out, so the Eucharist is both the beginning and the end. It draws us to it, pushes out into the world, and then draws us back. It is an overflow of the Lord's presence. The Mass is a part of the world and the world is a part of the Lord.'"

Another parishioner adds:

"'To become eucharist. I mean to become willing to give ourselves, to be willing to risk all that we have, willing to bring new life to others, willing to break open our bodies. . . . The full sense of the Eucharist would be to understand the totality of our lives as eucharist'" (14).

This book will explore several major traditions about the community of God. The sense that being in community is directly linked to being in God has in various ways been a theme of Christianity since its beginnings. Part 1, the first three chapters of this book, will look at the vibrancy of community in the early centuries of Christianity and how it both inspires us to community in our day and reveals God. In part 1, we identify the particular gifts and genius of those very early churches, examine five particular examples of early Christian community, and discuss the ways early Christianity began to talk about God in community terms. Part 2, the next four chapters, will explore various theological traditions that link the experience of community and God. Specific Eastern Orthodox, twentieth-century European, North American, Latin American, and feminist theologies will be explored as resources for community.

THE PROMISE

St. Gregory the Great, a large parish in Buffalo, engaged in a national Roman Catholic program called Renew in the late 1980s as a part of its diocesan commitment to church renewal. The formation and support of small communities of faith within a larger parish is the heart of this program. Ann, one of the participants in the program, tells the story of her small group meetings during one of the Lenten sessions. The community prayed about Jesus' experience of hunger for forty days in the desert. The conversation easily moved from their own spiritual hungers to the very real, physical hungers of so many in the world today, particularly right there in the city of Buffalo. Joe, another group member, lamented the memory of large events he had attended where food in abundance had been wasted. Others recalled similar experiences. What could this small group of Christians do about this lack of connection, this gap between the rich and the poor in their own city?

Ann volunteered to call the county health department to see if anything prevented them from trying to find a means to transport extra food from one place to the hungry in another. She told the gentleman that she represented a small faith community concerned with bridging the gap between those in want and those tempted to waste. The county health representative understood. In fact, his wife worked for a very large, local bank with a food cart that moved throughout the building each day selling lunch and snacks to its many employees. Daily, the bank had such leftovers. His wife had often mentioned her distress over the thoughtless discarding of so much good food.

Ann presented a sketch for the first food transport operation in her small community. For the coming week, the community recruited members to pick up left-over food daily from the bank and bring it to "Friends of the Night," a large food pantry, located in the poorest section of Buffalo. Seven of Ann's group served as drivers that first week, moving the food from the bank to the needy "Friends" across town. The Food Shuttle of Western New York was born on the Second Sunday of Lent, 1989.

At its tenth celebration a few years ago, the Food Shuttle of Western New York reflected on its simple beginnings in a Renew small group, a community who encountered anew the story of Jesus' temptation in the wilderness. The intersection of faith and life has made quite a difference for the hungry in western New York over the past twelve years. Today, 400 drivers move two tons of food every day from lavish banquet halls, bakeries, hotels, and supermarkets to languishing soup kitchens, food pantries, detention centers, and homeless shelters. The gap between the hungry and the satiated is a little less gaping. Ann admits that she still stands in awe of God at work in their midst. The small faith community continues to meet weekly.

Whether it is Beth and Bill in Philadelphia or Ann and Joe in Buffalo, the promise of community within the framework of local churches looms large for Americans. In part 4 of this book there are many more stories of such experiences of God and community in contemporary American settings. In chapter 11 we examine closely five specific communities of faith, matching the five early Christian communities of part 1. In similar parallel to part 1's study of early Christianity, in part 4 we identify the particular emerging gifts of contemporary Christian communities and develop ways of talking about God in terms of contemporary community experience.

The stakes are high as to whether Americans can learn to live in community. The threats to such a possibility are deeply imbedded and at the moment devastatingly evident. At the same time, the promise inherent in Christian beginnings, traditions, and contemporary efforts beckon. A gospel of community calls. The re-imagination of life together is at hand.

PART ONE

A Gospel of Community in Early Christianity

INTRODUCTION

What we have seen and heard, we proclaim to you as well, so that you yourselves may have community[1] with us. This community of ours is with God and God's son Jesus Christ (1 John 1:3).

W hen one reads these initial sentences of 1 John attentively, the words are quite surprising. That which the writers have "seen and heard" is not an account of the deeds or teachings of Jesus, since the book of 1 John does not contain any. Rather what this early Christian document is proclaiming is community itself (*koinonia* in Greek), which the text says the readers can participate in as it is made known to them by the author of 1 John. The good news is community.

Over and over again this same message resounds in the literature of early Christianity. *Koinonia* is possible on a new and exciting level. It is an experience that brings people together in ways that overcome the harsh fragmentation and oppression of the Mediterranean cultures dominated by the Roman Empire. In places where people had lost a sense of who they were, the gospel of community emerged. As 1 Peter 2:10 put it, "Once you were no people, now you are God's people."

This early Christian community expressed a renewed sense of togetherness, generating with it a powerful commitment to the dynamic of *agape*. Translated in our time as the conventional "love," the *agape* that connected early Christian communities was experienced as a new kind of interaction. *Agape* at that time was not the standard word for "love," and has only become so over the millennia of Christian discourse. For groups of early Christians, *agape*/love was a new sense of connectedness within community.

3

This new sense of connectedness with one another was, as the initial citations from 1 John and 1 Peter illustrate, also a sense of connection with the greater whole, with God. As early Christians began to understand themselves as connected in community, they also understood themselves to be joined in new ways to the cosmos. Their being together as communities was intimately connected to their belonging in God.

This section of the book explores in three separate chapters the early Christian experience of community. In these three chapters we propose that origins of Christianity cannot be understood and claimed without a deep encounter with the dynamic of community. We see early Christianity as deeply rooted in the actual experience of group life. In each chapter we root our own search for community more deeply in this dramatic expression of togetherness of the early Christians.

The first chapter sketches the basic characteristics of early Christian community. In this chapter we illustrate how community was a particularly strong aspect of both the emergent faith and the historical circumstances of early Christianity. This necessitates a review of current notions about the character of Christian origins. In this review we discover the way early Christian communities were part of a larger social revolution in the Hellenistic Mediterranean. And, the issue of diversity in early Christian community receives a closer look. This closer look at the dynamics of early Christian communities means to resource today's readers by showing how foundational realities of community are always part of broader historical and cultural realities. By contextualizing these pioneering Christian communities, we hope to gain a greater sensitivity to the way our own search for community today is undergirded by larger historical and cultural forces.

The second chapter examines in some detail a set of early Christian communities. Extrapolated from careful study of early Christian literature, this chapter presents a portrait of five different communities of the first hundred years of Christianity. In the drawing of these community portraits, the chapter shows that the writings of early Christianity, primarily the New Testament, can be understood best as handbooks for community.

This is explicitly contrasted to viewing these writings as historical records or textbooks on belief. It is our hope that a practical result of this survey of Christian material from its earliest era will lead readers to claim these early writings as resources for understanding how to live in community themselves. Although we do not see these early Christian writings as exact blueprints for community in our American situations thousands of miles and years away, chapter 2 does want the scriptures to be appropriated as a major heritage and resource for communities in our time. The five early Christian communities to be examined are those of the Congregation of Israel, the "Christ cult," Corinth, Matthew, and Luke.

The third chapter of this section will take a more theological approach to early Christian community. It will study the central notion of *koinonia* in early Christianity. Surveying the writings of five different thinkers throughout the first several centuries of Christianity, it will open the window to a way of thinking that very explicitly connected community and God. Derived from a developing understanding of church, called an "ecclesiology of communion," chapter 3 encourages our contemporary striving for community by establishing some basic theological components.

Part 1 on community within early Christianity then grounds the larger quest of this book in some of the most basic movements of Christian faith itself. It lays a foundation for the contemporary re-affirmation of community that is the hallmark of *Re-Imagining Life Together in America*. The vibrancy of early Christian community formations makes this foundation much more than an inert building block. Like the foundations of twenty-first century buildings, the foundation contains networks of power from below the surface, which pulse energy upward into the main structure, making all kinds of complex connections possible.

Chapter One

THE EMERGENCE OF CHRISTIAN COMMUNITY IN THE HELLENISTIC MEDITERRANEAN

That early Christians were excited about their life together in community encourages us in our efforts to learn to live together today. The Acts of the Apostles, written around the end of Christianity's first century, expresses this excitement: "The whole group of believers was united, heart and soul; no one claimed private ownership of any possessions, as everything they owned was held in common" (4:32). A closer look at the way early Christian groups emerged reveals even more promise. Not only is the early Christian affirmation of community resonant. The way these groups came into being can be examined in enough detail to help identify some instructive hallmarks of their existence. Although no models from one historical era can be completely transposed to another time, the study of early Christian communities' development has advanced enough to make certain patterns from that time available as exciting examples for our time.

The very earliest documents we have from Christians are the letters of Paul in the early 50s C.E. to a variety of groups in what is now Turkey, Rome, and Greece. Although we know that Jesus of Nazareth lived in the northern territories of colonial Israel prior to these letters and that there were probably some written documents at least from the same period as Paul, the letters of Paul to those groups are our earliest complete testimonies to some kind of Christian movement. In the letters Paul makes clear that some of the groups already existed before he knew them, some of them he was instrumental in founding, and some of them he has not yet even met. From this, scholars have concluded that these first Christian groups in Turkey, Greece, Syria, and Rome most likely came into being in the 40s and early 50s C.E.

A closer look at these earliest Christian documents surprises the reader with their interest in community. Paul's letters contain only one very short story about Jesus and only one paragraph of teaching reported as coming from Jesus. In all of Paul's correspondence with these groups there seems to be little interest in the deeds and teachings of Jesus of Nazareth.

Instead, the letters brim with messy negotiations about the groups' social dynamics. They are full of debates and reflections on how the group members relate to one another. The letters discuss extensively who should talk when the group gets together (e.g., 1 Cor. 11–14); how Jews and gentiles should act toward one another (Gal. 2 and 3; Phil. 3, Rom. 14); how slaves and masters should relate in the group (Philem.); the character of male-female relations (1 Cor. 11, 14); what joining the group means (Rom. 6:1–11); where the group should shop (1 Cor. 8 and 10); who should be leaders in the group (1 Thess. 1, 3; Rom. 1; 1 Cor. 2–4); sexual conduct (1 Thess. 4; 1 Cor. 6, 7); and what the groups should do with their money (Phil. 1; Rom. 15). The letters make constant reference to various personalities in the respective communities, cajoling some, greeting others heartily, and contesting with still others. Who God in Christ is for them is inseparable from their particular community dynamics.

An underlying and central agenda of these letters is the character and quality of people's life in community. In the back and forth of Paul's rhetoric one can see group identities being forged and negotiated, as the communities work painstakingly on issue after issue. And although Paul's perspective often pushes each community to be in agreement with him, the way Paul writes also reveals both that his viewpoint did not always prevail and that the communities were often quite different from one another. What the correspondence has in common is the conviction that the character of community life matters greatly both for Paul and for those to whom he writes. Paul and these communities cannot conceive of an abstract, noncommunal message about God.

So the terms with which Paul's conversations pursue the subject of community are also striking. The letters show that everyone concerned saw their communities' dynamics through a kind of cosmic and religious lens. The communities being together are regularly referred to as their being "in Christ." "Alive or dead, we belong to the Lord," Paul writes (Rom. 14:8). Although American individualist piety has tended to make these references of belonging into personal statements about single individuals, Paul always uses the plural "we" and "you" (in Greek there are two different words for *you*, one singular and one plural). The communities coming into being understand themselves therefore as having major significance. The way they live out their "in-Christ-ness" matters on a cosmic level. "The whole creation itself might be freed from its slavery to corruption and brought into the same glorious freedom as the children of God" (Rom. 8:21).

Since these groups were neither widespread nor large numerically, the juxtaposition of their communitarian intentions and their cosmic perspective is at first jarring. Why would such a nascent movement of small groups have such an overblown vocabulary about the significance of their social formation? The facile psychological answer of many of our contemporaries—that this jarring dissonance between the group's real size and their ambitions means they were crazy—is probably insufficient. Rather, a growing number of scholars studying early Christianity are tending to see this dissonance as an indication that these groups, to whom Paul wrote, saw themselves as what we might call "social experiments."[1] That is, their grandiose religious vocabulary, applied to their tiny movement of little groups, suggests that they were trying to forge communities that would have a larger social significance for the Hellenistic world. When they compared their small groups to the groaning of all of God's creation, they were proposing that their life together could serve simultaneously as both an entrance into God's very being and a model for the way the rest of society should be.

What were these groups like? What did they actually do? Here too the letters of Paul are rich with description. Although it is important not to take Paul's word as necessarily an objective description of the situations, they—even with their particular biases—give an amazingly detailed picture.

It is likely that these groups assembled between several times a week to once a month. They seemed to have gathered almost only for meals. Those meals were long and lively. They sang songs to the Christ. They read the Hebrew scriptures and letters from Paul and perhaps others. They—at least in some settings—provided food for one another. They paid some kinds of dues, and used the money for various purposes. And they discussed and debated among themselves.

These groups were fairly diverse (a topic to which we will return both later in this chapter and in chapter 2). In at least some of them there were both men and women, slave and free, Jew and gentile. This mix was experienced as a contrast to the way men and women, slave and free, Jew and gentile in general related to one another outside of the community meal.

The leadership of these groups was relatively fluid and sometimes in debate. As noted above, it was not always clear who was allowed to speak and to whom the groups owed allegiance. Some groups sent emissaries to other groups, and there were some persons—like Paul, Timothy, and Barnabas—who seemed to float from one group to another.

So the vitality of communities at the core of early Christianity, as we can know it through the earliest literature, resonates throughout the letters of Paul. In his clarion celebration of how being "in Christ" brings together Jew and Greek, slave and free, male and female (Gal. 3:26–28 and 1 Cor. 12:13), we have a sense of the way community resonated for a wide spectrum of early Christians.

Once one sees the prevalence of community issues in the letters of Paul, the rest of early Christian literature can also be seen as throbbing with excitement and debate over the shape of new Christian groups. Many scholars now tend to study the Gospels as story expressions of particular Christian communities. Documents such as the turn of the first century Didache turn out to be instruction manuals for such communities. Despite its historical unreliability, the description of early Christian community in Acts 2:42–45 mirrors a similar spirit (probably derived not so much from an actual community that Acts purports to describe as a more general idealization of this larger process):

> These remained faithful to the teaching of the apostles, to the *koinonia*, to the breaking of bread, and to the prayers . . . .And all who shared the faith owned everything in common; they sold their possessions and distributed the proceeds among themselves according to what each one needed.

How could the groups of early Christians have emerged so readily over a curiously wide and disparate geographical area? Even the later gospel accounts of Jesus' teachings do not contain any instructions for followers of Jesus to form such groups. How can we account for their appearance—with at least some common forms of life—in the 40s and 50s?

There are two keys to understanding the rapid emergence of these early Christian communities: 1) the existence of what are called "voluntary associations" throughout the Greco-Roman world of that time; and 2) the growing popularity of Jewish communities among gentiles throughout the Roman Empire. In order to understand the power and character of early Christian groups, both phenomena need to be described in some detail.

EARLY CHRISTIAN COMMUNITIES AND GRECO-ROMAN VOLUNTARY ASSOCIATIONS

In the twentieth century scholars of the history of early Christianity have uncovered a wide range of documents about a particular kind of social group in the Mediterranean area from approximately the second century B.C.E. to the fourth century C.E. These groups have now received the designation of "voluntary associations."[2] The term comes mainly from the fact that these groups constituted themselves through individuals choosing to associate together. That is, these groups were not constituted by familial, tribal, or national loyalty or obligation, nor did they originate from political, social, or cultural pressure. Neither were they groups fashioned by the necessities of production, defense, or geography. They formed by virtue of the voluntary association of individuals together in these units.

For contemporary Americans, that many groups form through voluntary association goes without saying. This, however, was not the case during the Hellenistic era in which Christianity emerged. Indeed, voluntary associations appear as a culture-wide phenomenon for the first time in western civilization during this period. Thus, voluntary associations were dominant, unusual, and innovative in the Hellenistic era in contrast to the earlier periods of Mediterranean cultures.

This culture-wide innovation of voluntary associations was precipitated by the long-term dominance of imperial rule in the Mediterranean. Tribal and national cohesion and identity entered a dramatic period of decline after Alexander the Great conquered so much of the Mediterranean and Near East and the subsequent invasions and rule by the Seleucids, the Egyptians, and, then most ambitiously, the Romans. These centuries of imperial domination dealt mortal blows to many of the ways extended families, clans, tribes, and nations gathered people together. The oppression of the various empires seriously undermined the ways people gathered in traditional associations based on blood and geography.

Many of the empires attempted to replace traditional social groupings with their own organization. There were constant attempts to impose new kinds of social organization on the conquered peoples. Perhaps the most dramatic example of this in the long Roman rule of the Mediterranean was the wildly ambitious attempts of Rome to build complete new cities, based supposedly on the ideals and values of classic Greece and imposed on almost every area by conquest.[3] These imperial attempts to replace many traditional groups of kinship and nationality with their own constructs had limited success.

The combination then of the destruction of traditional groups and the resistance to imperially imposed institutions resulted in a lack of social cohesion and identity among the populace throughout the Roman Empire. In the wake of these combined forces of social chaos, a new kind of social association emerged. This was the voluntary association, in which an individual chose to belong to a group in contrast to being forced by the empire to be a part of some grouping or being able to claim a decimated extended family, tribal, or national social grouping.

In this Hellenistic period a wide variety of these associations blossomed. There were associations formed around work roles, such as associations of shipbuilders, craftspersons, and farmers. There were associations organized around entertainment and music. There were groups gathering for teaching and philosophy. There were many different new religious groups, most fashionably gathering around the discovery and/or honoring of a foreign deity. Jewish synagogues most likely also belong to this phenomenon. Of perhaps the greatest popularity were what were labeled "funeral associations." These groups gathered ostensibly for the purpose of guaranteeing a decent burial for each of its members. But the actual activities of these "funeral associations" were only marginally related to funerals, and functioned mainly as a way a variety of people assembled socially.

The primary way all of these voluntary associations met was at meals. Sometimes weekly and often monthly gatherings were primarily in the manner of the Greco-Roman banquet. The associations made various kinds of provisions for how the food was to be provided. Sometimes the banquet was held in the vicinity of a local temple, where banquet rooms could be rented and meat could be obtained from sacrifices. Sometimes a patron would host such a meal in an aristocratic home. When the Greek literature of this time refers to a wide variety of voluntary associations, the terms often used are, in fact, *koinoinia* or *koine*, meaning "community," "that which is held in common," "friendship," or "fellowship."

Of particular surprise and delight—both to the writers of literature and to us today—is the very mixed character of these voluntary associations. Slaves could be leaders in such groups. The mix of slaves and free in this protected environment was frequent. Similarly men and women associated in these settings far more than in public. And, of course, the general family and ethnic loyalties of former times were breached in the associations' acceptance of many different individuals. While these groups were an occasion for joy, one interesting side effect of their diversity is that the accounts of how they functioned include stories of conflict among those who are not so used to being together.

Both the joy and stress around this new mix of people and traditions evident in the Hellenistic literature indicates that the voluntary associations were places of social experimentation. Whereas in the larger outside world, both Roman control and residual customs mitigated against mixing men and women, slave and free, foreign and local religious practice; in the voluntary associations there was a lively atmosphere in which these mixes could be tried out and experienced without threat of larger social catastrophe or consequences. How much freedom to be granted in such experiments, what rules should and should not be established to control the variables, and what responsibilities each individual had for the maintenance of the group all are explicitly addressed in these associations' minutes and inscriptions.

It is in this larger cultural context that the early Christian associations emerge. The cultural readiness and modeling of individuals gathering voluntarily to explore new identities and a sense of belonging within a religious frame allowed the early Christian groups to form. The larger context of voluntary associations provided a cultural pattern in which nascent early Christian community could come into being. In other words the notion of a diverse group coming together for the sake of a special sense and spirit of belonging was already going on in many different ways. That early Christians did this fits the larger social momentum of the day.

To identify this cultural model and framework into which emergent Christian communities fit does not prevent the assertion that the formation of Christian community is from God. Rather, one can see the emergence of voluntary associations under Roman imperial domination as part of a larger action of God in this time. Early Christian communities are a part of a larger redemptive pattern for the peoples of the Mediterranean, in which new senses of belonging to a greater whole are discovered in voluntary association. That the early Christian groups to which Paul converted were gathering "in Christ" parallels closely the way other groups around the Mediterranean invoked the names of the "new" gods of Isis, Mithra, Eleusis, and Adonai.

The early Christian literature shows sustained evidence of voluntary association-like structures and relational dynamics. We have already detailed the ways the letters from Paul and John address groups very much like this. In the Acts of the Apostles the narrative—again not to be taken as historically accurate in its details—pictures both Peter and Paul relating to groups that act very much like the above portrait of voluntary associations. The book of Revelation sends messages to seven different assemblies, and the messages address voluntary association-like issues. The early Christian document, the Didache, is an instruction book for something like a voluntary association that gives instructions on which visitors to welcome, what behavior is acceptable in its group, what meat to buy, and how to host a meal.

Early Christian communities need to be seen then as a kind of voluntary association. Their quick and strong development rides on the momentum of the larger Hellenistic momentum of the associations. Their interest in social experimentation is in keeping with the way the associations developed. The early Christian focus on meals is a part of a larger picture of these voluntary groups, getting together within the protective and creative framework of the Greco-Roman banquet.

THE DIASPORA SYNAGOGUE AND EARLY CHRISTIAN COMMUNITIES

The Jewish synagogue developed in the places around the Mediterranean where Jews lived at too great a distance to be a regular part of the Temple life in Jerusalem. The synagogues (literally in Greek, "meetings") were the ways Jews in this Diaspora (dispersion) had a life in common. These "synagogues"—sometimes just as gatherings, sometimes as buildings—emerged within the Hellenistic age. As suggested above, it is probable that the synagogues were thought of by gentiles as yet another voluntary association. It is also quite possible that the voluntary associations served as a model as Jews developed the synagogue as an institution.

In Jewish, early Christian, Greek, and Roman literature there is a large amount of evidence that many gentiles were attracted to the synagogues. Most likely because of the new philosophical popularity of monotheism in the Hellenistic Mediterranean, the high ethical standards of Judaism, and the ways the synagogues resembled voluntary associations, gentiles attended synagogues in substantial numbers. Some gentiles actually converted to Judaism, but many more became "god-fearers," that is gentiles who did not become circumcised but had a secondary status in the synagogues.

The book of Revelation refers to several of its Christian "assemblies" as synagogues. Paul and the book of Acts refer to his visits to synagogues. So it is safe to assume that many early Christian communities originated in, were confused with, and/or overlapped with the synagogue life.

In the Hellenistic world brand new institutions were not prestigious. In some contrast to our day, "new" was not good. If a group was worth one's attention, it needed to be attached to an ancient tradition. It is quite clear that as the early Christian communities began to claim credibility ("honor" in the terms of the day), one of the major ways they did so was to attach themselves to the tradition of the people of Israel.

Since there were Jews all over the Mediterranean, these synagogues along with their recent gentile followers were ideal locations for the early Christian movement. By attaching themselves to synagogues, the early Christians had an immediate network around the Mediterranean.

That early Christian communities were by and large a part of or thought of as synagogues around the Mediterranean is shown by their tradition of reading the Jewish scriptures at their meetings. We know that many emergent Christian groups saw the Hebrew scriptures as authoritative because their literature so often cites these scriptures as the basis for their values. Paul grounded himself in metaphors related to Adam and Abraham. The book of Revelation quotes from these Scriptures regularly. The Gospels' picture Jesus in the mold of earlier Israelite epic figures such as Moses, Elijah, and David. From the outside that these early Christian communities were thought of as Jewish seemed logical since their main figure, Jesus, was a Jew.

So the combination of the existence of voluntary associations and the network of synagogues made early Christianity a quickly spreading phenomenon of community. Although not always distinguishable from other voluntary associations and synagogues, communities of early Christians had spread from Galilee to as far away as Egypt, Rome, and Greece within fifty years after Jesus' death. The communal character of this movement is striking in that we have no record of solitary "Christians" at all within that period. It may have been possible to follow the teachings of Plato as a single individual, but the following of Jesus necessitated engagement with socially experimental communities.

DIVERSITY IN EARLY CHRISTIAN COMMUNITIES

As noted at the beginning of the chapter, one of the main characteristics of early Christian communities was their diversity. Although perhaps not every group had striking diversity in its constituency, the earliest Christian literature lends major attention to the variety of people within the Christian associations.

Such attention is evident in a very early baptismal formula that scholars have found embedded in Pauline literature. This formula associated being "in Christ" with being "neither Jew nor Greek, slave nor free, male and female" (Gal. 3:28).[4] The diversity of these early groups can be seen then in terms of ethnicity, economic status, and gender. It is probable that other differences also existed, such as those related to cultural codes of honor and shame. But the ethnic, economic, and gender differences were dramatic and difficult to overlook. They also are very available categories for consideration of contemporary American differences and their relationship to the gospel of community in our day. In any case, the ways early Christian communities engaged diversity as a way of enlivening and defining their life together calls us to look carefully at what they have to teach us.

Ethnic Diversity. Very early in the formation of early Christian communities the association of Jews and Greeks was both an attraction and a problem. Paul speaks about an incident that happened at Antioch sometime in the 40s, a time substantially after Jesus lived and markedly before any books of the Christian scriptures were written:

> When Peter came to Antioch, I opposed him to his face, because he was at fault. Before James and those with him arrived, Peter ate with the gentiles. But when the others came, Peter withdrew and separated himself, fearing those who were circumcised. And the other Jews also dissembled as well, so that even Barnabas joined them in their separation. But when I saw that they were not walking according to the truth of the gospel, I said to Peter in front of everybody: If you, being a Jew, live like the gentiles and not as a Jew, why do you force others who are gentiles to live like Jews (Gal. 2:11–14).

Paul addresses similar issues in his letters to the Romans and Philippians. Likewise references to problematic and inspiring ethnic mixes occur in all of the four canonical gospels, ranging from Jesus' encounter with the Samaritan woman to his healing of the Syro-Phoenician woman's daughter. Although the Acts of the Apostles picture of Peter's position about ethnicity in the following of Jesus is at substantial odds with the picture presented in Paul's letters, Acts as well reflects communities sorting out and holding up the mix of Jews and gentiles as exemplary. The Revelation to John emphasizes the way the early message applied "to the ends of the earth."

So the early Christian literature practically throbs with excitement and controversy occasioned by Jews and gentiles gathering in the same communities. It is important not to idealize this trend, since almost all of the literature reveals disputes about the ethnic mix as well. At the same time it is clearly the possibility of bringing together ethnic worlds that contributed great energy to the communities themselves. In their small gatherings they experienced the crossing of boundaries that in the broader Roman Empire only rarely were unproblematic. This gave the members of these early Christian communities a sense that God was present to them in a special way and that something of cosmic significance was occurring in these tiny gatherings.

Gender Diversity. Gender was another major diversity that characterized these early Christian communities. Like the association between Jew and Greek, men and women eating together was not at all unproblematic. Although it was not only the early Christian associations that had a mixture of men and women and not all early Christian groups allowed women in their associations, the first century literature of these "churches" is filled with negotiations and disputes about the inclusion of women in community and in leadership.

There is some indication that many of the so-called Jesus movements in Palestine from 30 to 60 C.E. were either characterized by women's presence and leadership or at least in debate about it. The leadership of both Mary Magdalene and Mary, the mother of Jesus, is difficult to deny in the generation after Jesus. As we will see in chapter 2, the Jesus movement scholars refer to as the "congregation of Israel" seems to proclaim its inclusion of marginalized women. The Gospel of Thomas, which has much material from that very early period, refers to the problems created by women at the Jesus movement meals and in their leadership.[5]

Paul's letters refer to a number of women leaders in the communities. Some of these references—especially those in 1 Corinthians—indicate that Paul was one who opposed this gender diversity. Points of dispute in Corinth appear mostly to be about what kind of leadership women were taking. That Paul needed to write about this topic at all is sure indication that there were such early Christian women leaders.

The Gospel of Mark includes women in its narrative in very striking ways. The stories about the Syro-Phoenician woman, the woman with a hemorrhage, the woman who anointed Jesus, and the women at the tomb all trade on issues in which women are in one way or another a problematic presence. Especially pointed is the way Mark removes the command to have Jesus' meal "in memory of me," and transfers it to the anointing woman whose deed is to be "proclaimed throughout all the world in memory of her" (14:9).

That gender diversity was intensely debated becomes even more obvious in the generations after Mark. The post-Pauline letters go out of their way to exclude women from leadership and certain kinds of participation, while the Gospel of Luke inserts women into its story to make sure there are as many women as men relating to Jesus. Similarly the relatively newly discovered Gospel of Mary (Magdalene)—written most likely around the same time as the Gospel of Luke—presents Mary as a disputed leader of the disciples.

Prior to the advent of feminist scriptural scholarship there was a curious acceptance of the picture that early Christian communities were dominated by men to the general exclusion of women. Both church authorities and most scholars seemed to take at face value Paul's command that women not speak in the assembly (1 Cor. 14:35) and the gospel lists of twelve men as Jesus' followers. The closer look at early Christian documents that has occurred in the past thirty years and is summarized here has changed that impression. It is now clear that the diversity of early Christian communities had much to do with women and men together.

Economic and Class Diversity. Finally, the diversity of class and economic status in these early Christian groups has also come into obvious focus. The affirmation of "slave and free" together in community cited in Galatians 3:28 is reinforced by Paul's letter to Philemon. In that letter Paul appeals to Philemon, a member of a Christian community, on behalf of Onesimus, a slave belonging to Philemon. This letter has been controversial in the history of the Christian church and in today's society in that Paul does not really ask Philemon to free Onesimus from slavery, but to take him back "as a beloved brother" (Philem. 1:16). Paul's implicit acceptance of the institution of slavery and his lack of resistance to the injustice of slavery may be understood today as morally objectionable. But for our purposes here they also reveal that slaves and free formed early Christian communities together, and thought of each other as brothers and sisters.

Similarly noticeable and not without problems are the economic differences that seem to have existed in the Corinthian groups to whom Paul wrote. In 1 Corinthians 11 and 12 Paul is very concerned with the way people who have different amounts of food and different degrees of prestige are treating one another within the community of Christ. Again here this indicates that these communities did have substantial economic and class differences, which were both difficult to negotiate and acclaimed as "the body of Christ" (1 Cor. 12:27).

The Lukan communities also seem to have consisted of a wide range of economic abilities. Although Luke's vocabulary is that of an aristocrat and Luke's story introduces wealthy women into the story of Jesus, Luke makes an explicit point of portraying poor people in the circle of Jesus in ways that the other gospels do not. This leads many biblical scholars to think that the Lukan milieu itself was in debate about the way its own members should relate to one another economically. For instance, it is only in Luke that the "rich are cursed" (6:24), "the hungry are filled with good things and the rich sent away empty" (1:53), and the rich man and the poor man Lazarus have a conversation after they die (16:20–24).

Similarly in the Lukan-authored Acts of the Apostles there are images of both the wealthy and the poor sharing and not sharing. In 2:44–45 the community is reported to have sold all their belongings and held everything in common. In 4:34, thirty-five rich members are said to have sold their houses and distributed the wealth to the community. And, in 5:1–10 a couple who falsely claimed to have shared all is struck dead for its deception.

So like the diversity of ethnicity and gender, the differences of class and wealth were central to the identity of these early Christian groups and at the same time highly volatile problems. These social experiments in diversity were consistently remarkable and unfinished in character.

THE RELIGIOUS DIMENSION TO EARLY CHRISTIAN COMMUNITIES

We have already alluded to how early Christians saw their tiny supper club-like gatherings as very significant for their whole society, for the entire Roman Empire, and the universe itself. We know this because they kept referring to their groups as founded by God and earth-shattering in their effect on human history.

This sense of having cosmic significance is resonant from the very beginnings of Christian community. An early hymn, written before any of the letters of Paul and quoted by him in his letter to the Philippians, sees the purpose of "everyone pursuing not selfish interests but those of others" "so that all beings in the heavens, on earth, and in the underworld should bend the knee at the name of Jesus" (Phil. 2:4, 10). Paul writes of the importance of these early communities as "the whole of creation waiting with eagerness for the children of God to be revealed" (Rom. 8:19).

In our day social experimentation and religious expression are—at least in most traditional Christian settings—polar opposites. That is, most religiously established groups are slow to examine new social forms and expressions, and religion is used to resist rather than encourage social experimentation. But it is important for this presentation that the bold communal experiments of early Christianity be understood also as enthusiastically religious. As they celebrated and negotiated their ethnic, gender, class, and economic diversity, they were inventing songs about their sense of God's fullness and the way the whole universe was being changed. In the midst of their new experience of "Jew and Greek, slave and free, male and female" together, they were bursting with a sense of "God with us" (Matt. 1:23).

Because American culture has privatized religion and caused most people to assume that religious expression is about individual inner experience, it is not easy to take in the essentially social character of early Christian religious expression. Religion for those early Christians served primarily to assert and celebrate what they saw as the universal significance of their small groups. The hymns they composed, the Hebrew scriptures they read and commented on, the mystical visions they ecstatically experienced together, and the stories and letters they wrote for their communal gatherings were religious expressions of the cosmic importance they saw in their own social formations.

On another count it is also crucial not to misunderstand these grandiose claims of the early Christian communities. There is a pervasive and errant reading by contemporary Americans that takes away much of what they have to teach us today about community. This mis-reading of the cosmic claims of these small early Christian groups goes something like this: Those communities predicted the rise of Christianity as history has witnessed it, and western civilization's current cultural and economic domination of the world is the proper result and culmination of the early Christian communities' vision.

Without denying some connections between the early Christian values and contemporary western culture and religion, the basic suggestion that our society today is the logical working out of early Christian communal values does not do justice to those values. Perhaps the easiest illustration that western civilization is not at all the natural result of early Christian cosmic hopes is the clash between the inspired early Christian communal connections and current American insistence on the priority of the individual person and the United States as a privileged, individual nation. This illustration also underlines how much contemporary American culture has to learn from early Christian communities.

CONCLUSION

What then does this overview of the emergence of early Christian communities have to say to the search by twenty-first-century America for viable forms of living together? This question needs to be asked explicitly, given the nature of this book. But the way it is answered needs to reflect the delicate processes of inheriting tradition, critically evaluating history, and honoring the ongoing dynamic of history.

Most significant is the baseline affirmation that early Christianity was a deeply communal phenomenon. The most deeply generative dimensions of Christianity were fundamentally tied to questions of how people shared each other's lives.

Similarly some of the major characteristics of early Christian communities can serve as value-beacons for our day. The way so many of those early communities dared to engage questions of diversity within their membership calls us today to see such diversity as a primary value in the building of life together. The advocacy for the outsiders within many of the early communities points us to similar actions within our own groups. The social experimentation that was characteristic of early Christianity challenges tradition-bound Christian churches to loosen up and trust similar dynamics. The role religion played for those early groups both reinforces the value of such expression and beckons us to make our own religious expressions part of social experimentation, not retrenchment. The way enthusiastic God language blended seamlessly with early Christian social experimentation pushes pious groups today to break out into new social adventures and encourages communitarian movements in our day to open their hearts to God.

But early Christianity, even in its New Testament forms, cannot function straightforwardly as models. The way these traditions are received by our day must be nuanced with an appreciation of the relative historical perspectives that their time and our time exhibit. In addition, the differences both among various early Christian groups and among particular cultural settings today dare not be overlooked. Inasmuch as some modeling from early Christianity for twenty-first-century America can occur, delicate attention must be paid to which particular early Christian community can serve as an example for which particular cultural setting in America today. So, the two edges of such learning must be observed. First, the hope that there is one model from early Christianity for our day must be abandoned. Neither the diversity of early Christian communities nor the many interesting differences among Christian groups merit reducing search for community to one model. Second, the valid hope for some models from early Christian communities for some particular situations must be honored. In fact, it is the multiplicity of community models from early Christianity that provides powerful impetus to the possibility of new and energized Christian communities today. Early Christian diversity actually encourages us to appropriate these traditions by examining the ways particular models from the past may inform and inspire specific communities.

In order to facilitate this nuanced learning from early Christianity the next chapter will profile five different samples of early Christian community emerging from contemporary biblical scholarship.

Chapter Two

FIVE EARLY CHRISTIAN COMMUNITIES

Biblical scholars of the last thirty years have begun to produce portraits of the communities that composed the books of the New Testament. We can now much more easily imagine who the people were who wrote and inspired the New Testament. Using the methodologies of anthropology and sociology alongside more traditional New Testament disciplines, scholars are attempting to draw rather accurate initial pictures of what these early communities looked like.

This research is so widespread and complicated that even a cursory review is impossible for this book. Three striking book-length portraits of early Christian communities do, however, serve as examples of this major new dimension to New Testament scholarship. The Roman Catholic biblical scholar Raymond Brown produced in 1979 one of the first such books, *The Community of the Beloved Disciple,* a nuanced description of the several different groups that composed the Gospel of John and the three Epistles of John. Making deft use of what is known as rhetorical criticism, Antoinette Wire less than a decade after Brown was able to draw a portrait of the Corinthian community to which Paul wrote in her *The Corinthian Women Prophets.* Most popular and at the same time most sophisticated in methodology is *The Lost Gospel: Q and Christian Origins* by Burton L. Mack (1995), which pictures how some of the first generation of Galileans after Jesus lived and worked together. Although these portraits cannot be seen as definitive, neither the attractiveness of their historical sketches nor the sophistication of their research methodology can be denied.[1]

This chapter will not, however, concentrate on the scholarly dimensions of these community portraits. Rather, it will winnow the relatively prosaic biblical scholarship into straightforward descriptions of the ways these groups most probably constructed their life together. For those interested in the more technical scholarly basis for these portraits of early Christian communities, a footnote summarizing works to be consulted for each community is included. Nor will this chapter be comprehensive in its description of the many different early Christian communities, exhibited in the first one hundred years of literature. Rather, this chapter will sample five of these communities in order to give some sense of the diversity and similarity within early Christianity. Even though this selection will be limited, it will demonstrate the sparks of new community as Christianity came into being.

Luke: The Community of Breaking Bread

Sometime between 85 and 125 c.e. in either Syria or Asia Minor a group or set of groups thrived in a sophisticated city setting.[2] This was a community of mostly gentiles, although many of the community knew and studied the scriptures of the Jewish people, most probably in Greek translation.

These people lived in relative safety compared to many of the traumatized populations of the Roman Empire. In contrast to so many groups, families, and entire nations that were torn apart by military intervention, poverty, and major social changes, this group—perhaps by virtue of some wealth—was not falling apart. This assembly, which we shall call "The Community of Breaking Bread,"[3] gathered in the homes of several aristocratic women at least once a week. Even though in their immediate vicinity a local Jewish synagogue was thriving, relatively new groups worshipping the Egyptian goddess Isis and the Persian-based Mithra were making new converts, and several older temples for Greco-Roman gods still claimed many adherents, this particular Christian community did not seem to feel itself in competition with them. Nor were they persecuted in any explicit way by the Roman governmental officials in their city.

The community gathered mostly for meals and occasionally for small business gatherings. At the meals there was much laughter, singing, and conviviality. After the eating portion of the meals there were usually readings, speeches, singing, and discussions. These more formal parts of the gatherings mixed stories about Jesus with discussions about economics, politics, God, and each other's lives.

It was rare that everyone in the Community of Breaking Bread was at the same meal. Rather, meal gatherings often would occur in one of the women's villas, attended by a portion of the whole community. To a certain extent those who attended the meals at a particular villa would also go on another occasion to another villa, but some would attend mostly at one specific residence.

These gatherings were astonishingly diverse in terms of social status. Since the patrons of the community were aristocratic women, a good number of the community were their household members. This included aunts and uncles, cousins and nieces, as well as slaves and servants of the patron/matron's estate. So to a certain extent the diversity of the Community of Breaking Bread had to do with the range of classes living at the villa. What was different about Breaking Bread groups' meal gatherings was that there was a certain level of mutuality between master and slave, and men and women, which did not occur outside the gathering.

These meals, of course, also included the slaves and masters, and women and men from several other villas. In addition, there were some people from beyond the orbit of the villas, mostly tradespeople, but some slaves as well. Crucial to this mix were a few Jews. That the patrons/matrons of the Community of Breaking Bread were women attracted some other women from the city. Many of these women would come with a husband, a male cousin, or a nephew. To attend the meals, a few single women violated the general taboo against being in public alone.

At least one of the community's patrons was a widow. She not only hosted the meals regularly, but was also the owner of her villa. Like some of the other unmarried women—either those accompanied by other men or those not—she had declared her allegiance to the Community of Breaking Bread by renouncing other attachments. This amounted to both a declaration of celibacy and a mutual economic commitment between them and the community. In the case of the patron(ness), her celibate commitment accompanied her sharing much of her wealth with the community. In the case of other committed—but less wealthy—women, they were often dependent on the community for some economic support.

The community was led both by the wealthy who hosted the suppers and by several individuals whose ability to compose songs, teach others, pray deeply, or administer gatherings propelled them into leadership roles. The cohesiveness of the patron(esse)s' estates helped the community stay somewhat unified. The excited character of participants from different walks of life often provided fresh energy for the group. The astounding way that they came together across social boundaries inspired them to sing and speak of God's powerful actions in their lives.

This mixture of men and women, slave and free, celibate and married, did not shape itself easily. The Community of Breaking Bread had many disputes about who should be leader in which regard, about what the relationship between the wealthy and the poor should be, about the status of women and celibacy, and about what the relationship between Jewish scriptures and their story of Jesus should be. There were so few Jews in the community that controversies about circumcision and Jewish dietary rules did not exist. The Jewish members of the group did hold some special places of honor by virtue of their knowledge of their scriptures.

In general there was an energized commitment in the Community of Breaking Bread. Although the rough edges of the experiment were obvious, the eagerness to participate in this set of overlapping supper societies was contagious. Originating in some irregularly scheduled supper gatherings, the community lasted for almost two generations. It disappeared not because it was unsuccessful, but because it merged with several other similar Christian communities toward the middle of the second century.

THE CONGREGATION OF ISRAEL

Living in the northern part of Israel called Galilee a good generation after Jesus, a relatively small and loose-knit group of Jews emerged in the several villages.[4] This community went almost unnoticed in its environs. It neither made many waves nor promoted itself broadly. The few people outside the group who were aware of them hardly cared one way or the other about them.

The community itself was quite enthusiastic about the new kind of life experienced together. Probably the most exciting aspect of the community for those who belonged was the character of its constituency. This was a veritable rag-tag gathering. It was as if a magnet had collected most of the social outcasts in the village.

There were four or five severely crippled individuals, two of whom had been forced to beg for substantial portions of their life. There were a good half dozen persons who were considered crazy or possessed. That there were a number of women in the community made it odd in village settings where women did not associate much with men outside of their families. And then there were the very marginally employed, those who had lost some of their extended family connections which sometimes might have provided some work and those whose physical stature or mental ability made them less valuable workers.

The primary way this community came together was at very simple meals. Because they had so few financial resources, their meals often looked rather pitiful in terms of what was eaten. Different persons were able to bring a little bread, fish, or vegetables.

But the spirit of this marginal group of people continually astonished their own members. It was as if their own resources expanded exponentially when they gathered. At their gatherings, they mostly told stories. Some were about their own struggles. Some were about observations they made of others. Some were about Jesus. The stories these people told about Jesus were about him as someone who healed the sick and the outcast and who had great power. They saw him as walking on water and feeding vast numbers of hungry peasants.

This community understood itself as uncovering a deep strand of its own Jewish heritage. They thought of Jesus as their central spiritual marker, and consciously compared him to Moses, Elijah, and Elisha. Their stories made him look like these great heroes of Israel. They were especially aware how Moses and his Torah spoke so powerfully of the way the outcasts are to be included. They remembered many of the Elijah/Elisha traditions in which those great prophets befriended the marginalized. They did not think of Jesus as belonging to the Davidic line with its royal and messianic promises for the big city. Rather they understood themselves and Jesus as belonging to a Congregation of Israel that was centered in the rural peasantry.

In the tumultuous years of the 60s and early 70s when Israel first successfully revolted against Rome and then was finally brutally recaptured and punished, this Congregation of Israel disappeared. Their failure to survive seemed to have little to do with the merit or lack thereof of their own community. Rather, they, like so many other small groups in northern Israel, simply fell apart in the midst of the horrible trauma of the revolt and its aftermath.

CORINTH: THE COMMUNITY OF THE CHRISTSPIRIT

Many days journey away from Galilee where the Congregation of Israel met, a very different kind of community gathered in Corinth, Greece.[5] This group that began its enthusiastic gatherings in the late 40s had hardly any Jews in it at all. In this commercially thriving metropolis, the community claimed a good number of relatively wealthy members. They hosted meal gatherings in their homes and sometimes rented a dining hall for the group.

This community had a sense of spirit that infused all creation within their gatherings. They were wildly celebratory of this feeling of God with them. Many times they felt that the Spirit was speaking through them, and these expressions were ecstatic and full of joy. *Christ* was the term they used most to characterize this Spirit with which they felt anointed. They would compose and sing songs to the ChristSpirit, who united them to the power in all things.

The Community of the ChristSpirit produced spin-off groups as its enthusiasm spread. There was a good deal of communication among these groups, and often members of one attended the celebrations of the other.

One of the hallmarks of this community was the leadership of women. Women led their celebrations regularly, and were often some of the more ecstatic and expressive participants. Typical of their new Greek city, these women were breaking out of some of the restrictive molds of a male domi-nated society. This women's leadership did not always sit well with some others in the community.

There were opponents to the Community of ChristSpirit from the outside. Among them was the roving emissary of Christ, Paul of Tarsus. Although Paul showed some affection for this community, he was mostly a vocal critic. He sent at least three letters to them, counseling ways they should change their behavior. According to Paul, many of the members of the community were so enthused about their unity with the ChristSpirit that their behavior was not nearly as moral as it should be. He reprimanded them for their lack of attention to some less wealthy members, for some of their sexual behavior, and for the way they allowed women to be in leader-ship roles. The increasing antagonism of Paul to the Corinthian groups exhibited in the later letters seems to indicate that the Community of ChristSpirit for the most part rebuffed Paul's advice.

The Community of ChristSpirit grew steadily for many generations. It parented more and larger gatherings of Christ people. Most likely Corinth was a center for inspired, women-led communities for more than a hun-dred years.

THE GOSPEL OF THOMAS: MYSTICAL COMMUNITY

One of the most self-conscious communities of early Christianity seems to have carried the name of the disciple Thomas as moniker.[6] This group, living most likely in the eastern part of Syria,[7] worked hard at distinguish-ing itself from a broad range of other religious options, both Christian and Jewish. Indeed, they saw themselves as having the mystical key to life in the "realm of the Father."

Although this sectarian dimension to their self-understanding sepa-rated them socially from other groups, their own mystical consciousness gave them a sense of belonging to Jesus and the universe in an intimate way. "I am the light that is over all things. I am all: From me everything has come forth, and to me all returns. Split a piece of wood: and I am there. Lift up a stone, and you will find me there," says the Jesus of the Gospel of Thomas (77).

This union with everything and with Jesus seems to have involved both intense intellectual reflection and an enthusiastic ritual practice. The Thomas community both studied and produced sayings of Jesus. The Gospel of Thomas is one of the earliest collections of sayings attributed to Jesus, and its parallels with canonical gospels demonstrate that this community took seriously the collection and study of the sayings of Jesus. But they also understood themselves as able to hear Jesus directly. They saw Jesus as the expression of divine Wisdom/Sophia, who speaks in every generation through the friends of God (Wisd. of Sol. 7:27). As friends of God they heard and spoke the words of Jesus Sophia, which came to them.

Like many other early communities, the Thomas group ate together regularly. It was most likely at these meals that the sayings of Jesus were studied, elaborated, and heard anew. These gatherings were strikingly inclusive of women. The Gospel of Thomas has a generally negative view of the named disciples of Jesus, except for Mary Magdalene and Salome, who are pictured as full participants in the meal and mission. Curiously for contemporary readers, the way the Thomas community expressed this insistent inclusion of women was to say that they had "been made male" (114). Most likely, this indicates that the women leaders and participants in the Thomas community were celibate.

Baptism was especially important to the Thomas community. They experienced baptism as an overcoming of divisions. In Thomasine baptism, the two became one, the male and the female, and returned to an original unity (22:4–7). This celebratory return to an original oneness was consciously different for the Thomas community than the expectations of some other Christian groups who looked to the end of time for an apocalyptic culmination. From the way sayings in the Gospel of Thomas differ from those in the sayings gospel Q, scholars have been able to detect an explicit rejection by the Thomas community of the idea of the end of time. The Thomas people strove for a return to the beginnings of the cosmos, where they were bathed in a unifying light.

The Thomas community thrived for at least several centuries. It spawned an array of other groups throughout Syria, Asia Minor, and Egypt. Many of these other communities were sectarian, mystical, and celibate. By the fifth century this larger movement, of which the Thomas community was an instrumental precedent, wilted under active pressure and persecution of less mystical versions of Christianity.

COMMUNITY IN MATTHEW: INSCRIBING THE LAW ON THE HEART

The groups that eventually produced the Gospel of Matthew in all likelihood did not have a special name or identity because they saw themselves as belonging to the greater community of Israel. They were Jewish, and worked hard on shaping their communities within the imagination and categories of Judaism.[8] Although conscious of some of their differences with other, non-Jesus related Jewish groups and movements, these "Matthean" people most likely simply thought of themselves as belonging to their local synagogue.

These groups, perhaps located within the large Jewish population in the Syrian city of Antioch[9] in the last two decades of the first century, were gripped by the call to deepen their living of the Torah. They saw in the images and teachings of the Jesus traditions the possibility of inscribing that Law on their hearts, as the book of Deuteronomy had urged. They devoted themselves to a spiritual internalization of the Torah, which made them more dynamic and responsible. Instead of just avoiding the explicit evils of murder, adultery, and injustice, the Matthean movement challenged its members to examine their motives and inner thoughts of hatred, lust, and revenge. Instead of harboring judgments against one another or letting some outside authority prescribe behavior, the members of these groups urged one another to talk through their disputes and differences before they worshipped.

The power of this shared inner life was so evocative that these groups not only made the Law more internal, they changed their inherited sayings of Jesus to make them more spiritual. No longer was it the physically poor who were "blessed," but rather the "poor in spirit." No longer were the hungry blessed, but "those who hunger and thirst for justice."

As was the case with many synagogues outside of Israel, there were a few gentiles who associated with the "Matthean" groups, but the overwhelming majority were Jews by birth. It is not clear what the role of women was in the "Matthean" groups. There is substantially less evidence of women's full participation and leadership in Matthew than in some other early Christian communities.

More important—and problematic—to this part of the Antiochene Jewish community was the fairly constant incursion into their gatherings

Kanuga

CONFERENCES, INC.
AN EPISCOPAL
CENTER

Chapter 1 — What are terms: to leave for VA?

1) Was the voluntary associations permitted by Rome or did they meet in secret? (12)

2) Did Paul convert an expatica V.A. or were they all newly formed? (13)

3) Diversity today : Theological

POST OFFICE BOX 250 • HENDERSONVILLE, NORTH CAROLINA 28793-0250
TELEPHONE: 828-692-9136 • FACSIMILE: 828-696-3589
e-mail: info@kanuga.org • web site: www.kanuga.org
Printed on Recycled Paper

of wandering "prophets," seeking to give teachings about the life of the spirit, morality, and/or Jesus. There were many itinerant teachers in the eastern end of the Mediterranean of that day. Although the practice of wandering from place to place and offering one's teachings to anyone who would listen in the marketplace or at someone's banquet preceded the Jesus movements, this custom of semi-homeless teachers had caught on throughout Palestinian and Syrian "Christianity" as well.

The Matthean community seems to have received them so regularly that it sometimes became a problem. The judgments of these teachers were often so sharp that the households who hosted them had second thoughts. On the other hand, these sharp teachings also seemed to help the Matthean community in its own self-critical spiritual journey. Overall the Matthean community welcomed them as speaking for Jesus, even if they gritted their teeth sometimes when they saw the "prophets" coming.

This very Jewish spiritual community, focused on Jesus as the key to what it meant to belong to Israel, had major opponents within Judaism. The most violent anti-Pharisaic teachings in early Christianity come from the Matthean community. Both the Matthean community and the Pharisees saw themselves as having the key (different keys) to what it meant to be Jewish after the Temple in Jerusalem had been destroyed in 70 C.E. This intra-Jewish rivalry brought both groups to curse the other.

But the rivalry with the Pharisees did not seem to be at close range. Overall the Matthean community was at peace with itself. It continued to hear new teachings in the name of Jesus and to experience itself as a part of Israel's exodus from bondage. It spawned other groups, and it or its successors lasted well into the second century.[10] Eventually the much stronger success of gentile Christian communities and the more embattled state of Judaism caused this set of Jewish-Christian communities to die out, but not before a good one hundred years of life together.

CONCLUSION

Contemporary Christian communities can learn a great deal from these portraits of early Christianity. This more complicated picture could at first blush be disorienting.[11] The diverse character of early Christian community could be jarring and disappointing in that it deflects the possibility of a simple and unified formula for community emerging from early Christianity. On the other hand, it points to a deeper well of resources and a stronger, broader energy for community in its obvious diversities.

It is at this deeper level where we suggest the importance of early

Christian community for the vital tasks of social belonging and group nurturing in current day America lies. The various pulses of people coming together observable in first century Corinth, the Congregation of Israel, Thomas movements, Matthean synagogues, and Lukan "Christianity" provide a spectrum of models for our day.[12]

For instance, the different ways new women's participation and leadership were negotiated in the early Christian communities of Corinth, Luke, and the Congregation of Israel can inspire particular contemporary groups in different ways as they work to recognize and promote women in their settings. Some communities today may look assertively to the Corinthian women prophets for the way they modeled strong and expressive leadership in first century Corinth. Such a Corinthian model might prove helpful for communities today in which strong women's leadership is being challenged by influential men such as Paul. It is, of course, quite telling that there are many Christian communities today whose powerful women leaders are being confronted by male authorities. These communities and women can claim the early Corinthian Christian communities as ones who successfully rebuffed their male authoritarian challengers.

On the other hand, the more subtle and complex negotiations of women's power within the Lukan community may serve other contemporary groups more strategically. The way Lukan women used their wealth and a particular emerging model of celibacy to maintain participation and leadership in their groups in the face of challenges to female leadership could help some twenty-first-century groups maneuver useful constellations of women's influence. Here it is not so much the motifs of wealth or celibacy that may be the most strategically useful in affirming women's participation today. Rather, two more general strategies for women's empowerment can be deduced from the Lukan situation.

First, strategic assessment of where women have influence on others in the community (as Lukan women's wealth did) can often help promote women's leadership, even if below the surface. For instance, family connections to men in authority, professional prestige accumulated by women outside the church, or existing women's subgroups can be used strategically to enhance the status and place of women within some church communities with inherent male oppression. Second, development of innovative social roles (like the innovation of celibacy in the Lukan movement) can also lead to important women's leadership in some communities. Many Roman Catholic laywomen have in the past two decades received graduate theological degrees and obtained ministerial employment by virtue of the radical decline in the number of priests. These new social roles, resulting to a large extent from women's initiative, have produced parishes with strong women's leadership because women do many roles previously reserved for priests.

Or the Congregation of Israel might be a model for yet different contemporary situations. That women's leadership did not seem to be a problem within the congregation relates to those communities today in which women's leadership is openly celebrated without opposition. The way the formerly marginalized women formed creative bonds within the congregation with other formerly marginalized people such as the crippled and ritually impure can be an inspiration for emerging and uncontested women's leadership today.

This one example of how the diverse community strategies for women's empowerment within certain early Christian movements provide a spectrum of models for could be multiplied. It is not yet even clear how many models there are and how many ways they can be applied to our need for community. The intense communal focus of these various early Christian communities makes for both an astonishing set of examples and an overarching exemplary momentum toward community.

Chapter Three

COMMUNION: MEANINGS OF COMMUNITY TAKE ON UNIVERSAL SIGNIFICANCE

Early Christians associated their strong experiences of community with their experiences of God. As we have seen in chapters 1 and 2, it was in the rough and tumble of community that various groups found a powerful sense of God-with-them. Their enthusiasm for God was inseparable from the ways they treated each other as Jews and gentiles, women and men, slave and free. To be in God implied being in community, and vice versa. It is not at all clear that the first seventy-five years of Christian communities had much interest in the connection among the various communities around the Mediterranean. Indeed the New Testament evidences at least as much tension between certain communities as it represents connection.[1]

But as Christianity grew into its second century, the communities' awareness of one another also increased. This set of connections beyond the local churches found them thinking about this connection as also deepening their sense of God. God was not just present in the local community. God was present in the dynamic that sought to hold these communities together as a larger organism.

It is this larger exploration of more-than-local community in the subsequent but still early Christian movements that chapter 3 addresses. It will do so by surveying the thinking of five church leaders in the second through seventh centuries to see how they negotiated these larger connections among the communities and the emerging sense of God as a part of this larger process. Chapter 3 will introduce some theological categories used by twentieth-century theologians who have returned to these early centuries as resources for interpreting contemporary issues facing church as community. These categories will help accent important insights from early Christianity applicable today, and will provide a strong foundation for reflection later in the book on the promise and challenge of community *being offered.*

A matter of vocabulary emerging from this theologizing about early Christianity needs to be clarified at the outset. This goes directly to the issue of how to talk about community as a local phenomenon and community as something larger than just a particular group. For the purpose of this study, we want to clarify from the beginning our understanding and use of the terms *communion* and *community* (both translated from the Greek, *koinonia* and the Latin, *communio*) as we retrieve, interpret, and apply them to our contemporary situation.

When we differentiate these terms, we understand *communion* to mean that invisible disposition or attraction toward others, even toward all others in an experience of oneness and interconnection, claimed as gift. This gift of communion was, early on in the reflections of the churches, associated with the presence of the Spirit, the felt awareness that Christ continued to be there, drawing persons together wherever two or three gathered in his Name. This connection between communion and Spirit was emphasized in the thought and writing of patristic thinkers from the time of Ignatius (108 C.E.) who understood that "where the Spirit is, there is communion."[2] Through the twentieth-century contributions of theologians like Yves Congar and John Zizioulas, whom we will meet in chapters 4 and 5, we have access once again to this core, theological insight. Though we will not explicitly reference the Spirit every time we talk about communion, divine activity, as well as human, will be intended throughout our study.

Indications abound that human persons intuitively know, even when that knowing remains at an unconscious level, that we are somehow vitally linked together. A good visual example might be to picture the spontaneous response of passengers riding a crowded bus, when suddenly a standing passenger begins to fall over. Before on-lookers can even think about what they're doing, they gravitate toward the falling person, as if they themselves were in danger. Only a deliberate withholding seems to prevent this "natural" response. We understand communion as this invisible thread, binding us to one another. Communion is this leaning toward the other's well-being. A recent event of dramatic proportions makes this invisible thread even more conceivable. In late July 2002, nine Pennsylvania coal miners were trapped forty feet under the earth for several days while rescue teams worked day and night to reach them. The nine men leaned so convincingly into one another's keeping that they shared together one ham sandwich because all were hungry and they could not imagine only some being able to eat. "Forseeing death, they tied each other together so that they would be one body when found; no one would be lost." Amid the jubilation of their rescue, the governor of Pennsylvania, Mark Schweiker, remarked that these men "weren't concerned about saving themselves but about saving each other."[3] Communion is the word we use for this simultaneously human and divine reality.

We will differentiate this unseen bond from its embodiment by the term *community*. In other words, in our usage, communion, as the Spirit's gift, needs to be lived out in the work of forming and sustaining community, a responsible way of shaping life together, even when the felt awareness of communion is not present. The term *community*, then, as the concrete, living out of communion, will, like its unseen counterpart (communion), always and at the same time be a word about life in God and life in and for one another. We will try to avoid reducing community to either a theological or a sociological category alone, but will always intend both simultaneously. As the Eastern Orthodox theologian, John Zizioulas insists,

> The Church is the community that results from the communion of the Spirit and of the basic structure of that community—the structure that emerges from the vision of the eschatological community as the complex of the specific relations in and through which the Spirit constitutes this community.[4]

The two terms, *communion* and *community*, will interact in this way. The word *communion* will designate both the larger interconnections among communities and the intangible dynamic present within local communities. In some contrast, we will reserve the term *community* for the actual group life of specific people. By this distinction we mean to preserve that more elusive aspect of community that is beyond specific interactions but intends the realization of that vision of God's dream, the eschatological community (Zizioulas). This aspect of community—now designated *communion*—can be apprehended as much larger than just a particular group of people. It can refer to what people really live for. For instance, a person who lives alone can say that her/his guiding principle for life is that of *communion* without this necessarily being hypocritical. As *community* takes on this less localized character, it also becomes a term that asserts itself as authoritative. With deep connections to the Spirit, communion becomes a claim on how to live and who to follow.

But by making this kind of distinction between *community* and *communion*, we hope that the connection between the two remains both obvious and central. Neither can be full conceptually without the other. *Communion* can easily become either a mere abstraction or an excuse for authoritarian supervision of local groups, if it is not rooted in the actual life situations of particular individuals in particular *communities. Community,* on the other hand, can be too easily reduced to a matter of sociological and psychological strategies, if the intangible and internal rigors are overlooked and/or the broader connections and responsibilities among communities ignored.[5]

This chapter examines some of the basic structures of that communion as they developed in a complex of relations. Through these patterns of relating, the early churches sought to actualize their vision of community. Our study of how the meaning of community expands in both scope and authority during the next several centuries will allow us to ground, in these foundational centuries of church, the book's larger proposal that community itself is a powerful category of Christian meaning and authority for today. And it will illustrate the ways community/communion became a crucial part of a larger vocabulary of faith.

The expansion of what community signifies from actual groups in Christianity's first one hundred years to a fundamental category of Christian meaning and authority is key to this book's thesis. We see community both as historical people living together in concrete groups and as a vision of the ultimate character of life itself, capable of leading persons toward God and each other. The ways the first seven centuries of Christianity made community into this larger message about God and life are exemplary.

In the last forty years, a significant number of theologians have paid close attention to the way the early Christian centuries saw community as central to life's meaning and God's presence. With their insistence on returning to the sources, (the French scholars called this insistence *ressourcement),* these scholars have proposed that the early Christian centuries' understanding of community is very closely connected with the early Christian vision of God. Indeed, the highpoint of patristic theology may be seen in the great Cappadocian insight that "the very nature of God is communion."[6] God is not first One (Substance) and then Three (Persons), not Three and then One, but simultaneously One in Three/Three in One, a relationship of intimate belonging one in the other. This core trinitarian belief is, for these theologians, key to understanding how the community called church is one and many, universal and local simultaneously. This is so because the church lives in the communion life of God through the Spirit who constitutes it. The point of this contemporary return to an earlier ecclesiology of communion is not simply an interest in early Christianity. The core of this emerging ecclesiology has to do with the conviction that today also the nature of God and the character of community are intimately connected.

For these thinkers, early Christianity's affirmation of the communion of God proclaims a central possibility for today: to be in community points to God, and conversely, to be in God necessitates community. Several of these twentieth century theologians will be discussed at some length in chapter 4. At the same time, their investigation of communion as a core, theological category for early Christianity forms much of the backdrop for this chapter's portrait of early Christian theologians' thinking about the community called church. We believe that much more critical scholarship remains to be done on these early sources. We acknowledge the fragmentary character of the following portrayals, but hope that they serve to demonstrate one main point: community's meaning expanded and deepened during this period, extending beyond the local and temporal to embrace the universal and eternal—even the very being of God.

On the other hand, we will see how the structures and authority early Christian community took on demonstrates both the limits in trying to express the vision of communion meaningfully and the dangers of using it as a means of coercing unity. In the period to be studied in this chapter, communion not only served as a goal and gauge for finding meaning, God and authority in one's life. During these formative centuries of Christianity, concern for the unity of the community became a way, at times, of suffusing differences, imposing uniformity, and exploiting authority.

During this critical juncture, the church had to come to terms with how the particular, local communities were in relationship to the larger whole. This need held the potential for greater meaning and arbitrary authority. Both appeared clearly and sometimes simultaneously. When this chapter describes communion as a way of talking about Christian self-understanding, we will also note ways this central term became an agent for oppression as well. It is our opinion that this ironic and counterproductive tendency in the early church is inherent in the very tensive character of community. Its gift and task dimensions require that a primordial unity-in-difference be safeguarded; that the one and the many be understood as definitive of community itself. The achievement of a common life together where unity honors diversity has proven itself at every period of history to be flawed and graced at the same time.

IGNATIUS OF ANTIOCH

As the first century turned into the second, Ignatius was a leader of the churches in the Syrian community of Antioch. As an early Christian theologian, he thought about communion as more than life together in one concrete, local community. Indeed, it was the way different local communities associated with one another that was a major concern of Ignatius. This concern, coupled with how each community in its own diverse circumstances manifested the same reality of life in God and one another, preoccupied him. These issues surfaced for Ignatius as he traveled in exile from his home church in Antioch. They are evident in the letters he sent to churches he visited. It is important to notice that Ignatius includes in his thoughts on how communities ought to relate to other communities the care members show to each other in the same community. "Hold no grudges against one another" (Trallians 2). In a personal letter to Polycarp, bishop of Smyrna, he wrote, "Suffer together, struggle together, run together, labor together. Be long-suffering with one another in gentleness as God is with you" (6:1–2).

Little is known of Ignatius' faith community of origins. But his writings after he was sent away from Antioch provide an important picture of the issues around communion at the beginning of the second century. Perhaps the most important realization concerning Christian communities at that time is the substantial number that existed. On his way to martyrdom in Rome, Ignatius encountered and sent correspondence to communities in Ephesus, Smyrna, Magnesia, Tralles, Philadelphia, and Rome. His writing exudes a sense of the Christian churches as numerous and disparate. Coming directly out of his experience of intense dispute at Antioch, he constantly appealed to a unity among the communities.

Although it would be a mistake to think of Christianity at the beginning of the second century as either influential or pervasive in the Mediterranean world, Ignatius' writings are so expansive in their visionary address to allow Christians at least to imagine themselves as co-extensive with the vast Roman Empire. This vision of Ignatius certainly does suggest that the individual Christian communities had grown enough to raise two central questions: 1) can Christian community eventually contest in scope with the claims of the Roman Empire? and 2) what is to be done about the substantial diversity in practice and belief among the growing Christian communities?

In grappling with the possibility of an actual empire-wide Christian community and in worrying about disunity among the churches due to their diversity of practice and perspective, Ignatius asserts two unifying dynamics of Christian community: a common meal (see discussion of early Christian meals in chapters 1 and 2) and one bishop. Although it is questionable whether all the communities Ignatius addressed even knew what the terms *eucharist*[7] and *bishop*[8] were, Ignatius' effort to begin to construct a notion of Christian community that extended beyond the local circumstances of each group was pioneering. Clearly gripped by his expulsion from his own Antioch community and by the vision of his pending death in Rome, at the place where the whole empire directed its gaze, Ignatius held up a way for the various Christian groups to think of themselves as part of a larger communion.

This larger communion could be experienced, Ignatius proposed, through each community practicing the common meal[9] together in similar fashion with similar meanings, all presided over by a bishop. The larger community of Christ is convened, he suggested, in this common meal under the direction of a common leader whose scope of authority extended beyond the individual groups. As we have seen in chapters 1 and 2, although the practice was somewhat diverse, almost all early Christian communities did regularly have a common meal together. It was in these meals that the communities experienced and celebrated their new sense of belonging to each other and to God. So Ignatius' assertion of a "community beyond the local community" expressed in a common meal practice had both precedent and resonance.

The Roman regional system of governance provided him with a model of overseers who verified that local bodies followed Roman law. Based on this Roman government model, the bishop emerged then in the thought of Ignatius as a possible guarantor of such a meal held in common by various communities. He wrote to the community of Smyrna: "Where the bishop appears, there is the community, just as where Jesus Christ is, there is, the catholic church. It is not permitted to baptize or to hold an agape (one early Christian word for a common meal) independently of the bishop" (8:4).

Even though bishops and common meals are the actual experiences of "communion beyond the local community," Ignatius refers this unity to two other unifying notions, which are less immediate, but intended to make his proposed unity in community authoritative. These two supports for unified community are the oneness of God and the authority of Rome. God is one, therefore the community beyond the local community needs to be one, "for Jesus Christ, our inseparable life, is the will of the Father, even as the bishops, who have been appointed throughout the world are by the will of Jesus Christ" (Eph. 3:2). Rome is the place where the known world is centered. As the capital of the empire, the Roman church is "the church presiding in love." Ignatius signaled a major new consciousness of community that is not just local. Meals held in like manner by Christians in diverse locales, bishops who oversaw the common meal experience and its interpretation, God's own unifying self, and the authority of Rome over the world were linked by Ignatius so that community explicitly and practically became something bigger than one group of people. The structures of communion beyond particular communities emerged.

We cannot, however, simply celebrate this advance in the understanding of Christian community without also noting some of the loss that occurred at the same time. Ignatius' assertion of the unifying role of bishops and his attempt to unify Christian meal celebrations were among the foundational gestures by which formalism and authoritarianism crept into Christian communities' authority. Ignatius did provide some important initial insights into how various Christian communities might see emerging connections among them as both divine and effective. But these very ideas set precedents for the communion among churches to be defined over time as the authority of the bishop alone without the community in which she/he presides and the right form of the meal rather than the divine/human interconnectedness that Ignatius also invoked.

For Ignatius and much of the tradition that followed his lead, a primary safeguard against an empty formalism or an external authoritarianism lay in the power, simultaneously human and divine, of the Christian meal itself. Though these meals varied greatly at the time of Ignatius, nonetheless, in all of them, a gathered community enacted its own communion-life and opened itself to a reality of communion, shared with other communities, beyond itself, but living too in the one body of Christ. The primary role of the bishop, as Ignatius saw it, was to preside at that common meal, to represent the one among the many that constituted communion.

THE SHEPHERD OF HERMAS

Sometime in the late first or early second century an imaginative set of writings were written by one or several early Christian visionaries. These writings came to be known as those of someone called "the Shepherd of Hermas." We know very little about the author(s) of these writings. And these writings—perhaps because they did not claim any special authority for the recognized leaders of early Christianity—have only in the last century begun to catch the attention of a larger audience.

There are striking similarities and contrasts between Ignatius of Antioch and the Shepherd of Hermas. For our purposes, the most important similarity in both is the consciousness of the burgeoning of connections between the growing number of Christian communities of the early second century. In both, the growth of Christianity seems to prompt thought about another level of community beyond the local one. Another similarity lies in our lack of any knowledge of either's local community. All we have are the writings themselves, which do not refer to any specific historic, cultural, or geographic particularities of either the Shepherd or Ignatius' faith community.

The differences between the Shepherd and Ignatius are as noteworthy. In contrast to Ignatius' episcopal letters, the Shepherd is a curious mix of fantastic visions and exhortation. Many scholars think that the visions and exhortations may be originally from different hands. But both differ substantially from Ignatius' authority-laden instructions. The Shepherd's visions are much more mystical, and his exhortation much more relational and ethically interested.

It is in the visionary and relational character of the Shepherd that we find his description of communion. Here we see—often in fantastic imagery—the faith and hope that the various Christian communities participate in a larger reality of connectedness. "The church of God will be one body, one understanding, one mind, one faith, one love, and then will the Son of God rejoice and be glad in them," he wrote (Similitudes 9:18).

The Shepherd's hope for communion beyond the local community represents a movement in early Christianity that proposed a larger unity of Christianity through faithfulness to this prophetic imagination. For the Shepherd it is not a unity of practice, interpretation, or bishop's instructions that join all Christians together. Rather it is a dedication to a spirit of interiority, righteousness, and a heartfelt hospitality. It is the common character of this spiritual receptivity and openness to others that constitutes the greater Christian community. For Hermas, this spirit of receptivity is a gift often received by fasting, always in an attitude of self-emptying and repentance.

The underside of his vision of a shared, universal communion is also in retrospect apparent. Although the more implicit and interior qualities of the Shepherd's connectedness elicit self-generating relationality, they also open the door to Christian practices in different quarters that can be in tension, even in contradiction, with one another. The more explicit (and visible structures) of Ignatius do not run this risk.

The Cappadocian Contribution

These second-century concerns to extend the idea of Christian community beyond particular, local churches to the vision of a worldwide communion continued even as the church grew numerically and spread geographically. The invisible bond of communion now required additional "external criteria and social patterns for organizing and realizing" community beyond the local level.[10] Besides the unifying role of the bishop and the centrality of the eucharist, a concern for unity in "orthodox doctrine" or right belief took center stage.[11]

By the fourth century, the greatest dangers to church unity came from factions within the community whose teachings denied the unity of God as Trinity. In the articulation and defense of the Christian community's faith in the Tri-unity of God, a new way of assessing the "communion" or catholicity of many disparate communities became possible.[12] This period of serious reflection and discernment by the Christian community on its central beliefs about the nature of God provided the foundations also for a radical renewal of the community's practice. With the contributions of several, but in a most profound way, by the Cappadocians, the intimate connections between what we believe about God and how we live our lives became clear once again.

Named for their common place of origins, the three bishops Basil of Caesarea; Gregory of Nyssa, Basil's brother; and Gregory of Nazianzus are often referred to as the Cappadocians. For the purpose of our study, the contribution of the individual Cappadocians will be both restricted and extended; restricted in that we will have Basil speak for the other two, and extended because we will introduce Macrina, the usually silenced fourth member. We do so to promote our conviction that from the earliest Christian centuries, the presence and actions of women helped to form and inform the character of life together. The power of re-imagining life together is, in many ways, linked with the creative work of re-imagining our Christian origins that has been going on for the last several decades in the scholarly world. Recognizing the presence of women in our day is critical to the emergence of renewed communities in our churches.

Macrina was the oldest sister of Basil and Gregory of Nyssa. Gregory acclaims her as their most formative "teacher"—at a time when women were not allowed to be called teachers. Born into a noble and esteemed Christian household, Macrina illumines for us the meaning and value of Christian community in at least two ways. Her lessons integrate the contributions of both Hermas and Ignatius. Like the Shepherd, she advocates for an interior disposition of humility and self-renunciation as a prerequisite for receiving the gift of communion. With Ignatius, she insists on concrete conditions for its growth by laying out structures for a Christian community's life.

To foster an interior attitude of humility and receptivity, Macrina believed that Christians must submit themselves to one another in mutual support and correction. She did not shy away from the practice herself, even when it came to admonishing her brother, Basil, for a puffed-up pride in his own oratory after he returned from studies in Athens.

Macrina assumed responsibility for the care of the household after the death of her father. She persuaded her mother to sell their home in Caesarea and found a small monastery in Annesi with their entire household. The community devoted itself to a life of charity and the celebration of God.[13] For Macrina, an awareness of life in God and others required concrete practices to demonstrate it. She prevailed upon her mother to treat the slaves as equals, since all of them shared equally in God and were all called to serve each other as members of community. For Macrina, community required mutuality and equality and was incompatible with divisions created by rank or status.

The monastic community founded by Macrina, along with others begun by women at this time, though not directly related to this study, is nonetheless instructive. For example, in these communities, Basil saw clearly how one's communion in God and one another was lived out. Mutual support and mutual correction were integral to shared life together. This was in radical contrast to the fiercely independent lives of the desert anchorites he had visited, to the contemporary structures of the Greco-Roman model of the *pater familias* (father as head of the household), and to his own experience of living in seclusion. His evaluation of the superiority of community life over a patriarchal, hierarchical one or over life alone impacted all his subsequent pastoral judgments.

Macrina's influence led Basil to found a community of monks close by, for whom he wrote a rule, still in use today. At the heart of Basil's rule is each one's need of the other. "I know perfectly well," he wrote, "that I stand more in need of the help of each one of the brothers than one hand does of the other."[14] Evident also is Macrina's lessons about mutual correction. Basil explains, "Furthermore, a person living in solitary will not readily discern his own defects, since he has no one to admonish and correct him with mildness and compassion" (Ques. 7).

Basil was ordained to the priesthood in 362 at the age of 32 and was made bishop of Caesarea eight years later. The character of Basil's service to the church of Caesarea combined a deep mysticism, inherited from his family spiritual tradition, and a practical understanding of the community's needs. Both as priest and bishop, Basil was committed to the project of reforming the church on the pattern of the apostolic community of Jerusalem. It is not possible to assess adequately how much factual information Basil had available to him on the pre-Constantinian house-church model of Christian community. But he was convinced that only in genuine and concrete Christian communities could the injunction of

Jesus not to separate love of God and love of one's neighbor be realized.

Communion for Basil required a corporate lifestyle. This condition assumes greater importance when we focus on the urban character of Christian life in the fourth century. In the midst of many factions and disordered groupings of Christians, the temptation to escape into some idealized version of communion in seclusion was great. By succumbing to it himself, Basil found that his own sinfulness was impossible to escape. He realized that "the only path to communion in God is discovered in the Holy Spirit and in the brotherhood" (Letter to Eph. 133).

His own noble birth made him able to converse with wealthy citizens of Caesarea and make demands on them as members of Christian community. During a terrible famine that struck the city in 368, Basil demonstrated connections he saw between one's communion in faith and in service. He sold the little property he had to feed the poor. He asked a concrete response from the rich, as well. "There would be neither rich nor poor if everyone were taking from his wealth enough for his personal needs, then gave to others what they lacked" (In Famem 68E).

For Basil, there is no "idea" of community outside of the concrete, historical one being built up daily by the Holy Spirit and human persons who compose it. However, the geographical and physical limits of concrete communities did not determine the boundaries of life in communion. Ongoing communication, especially through letter-writing and meetings, were a requirement for unity in this wider community. Over 330 letters of Basil, 250 of them written as a bishop, testify to his commitment to communication, as a concrete demonstration of communion everywhere in the world. As bishop of Caesarea, Basil's letters to his fellow bishops evidence his lament over the many ruptures in the community. They attest to the mutual interconnection he saw between the local and universal church. In letter 243, Basil expresses great disappointment in the churches of the West who had seemingly cut themselves off from responsibility for the suffering churches in the East.

> Do not think of yourselves being moored in a safe haven, where the grace of God gives you shelter from the tempest of the winds of wickedness. Reach out a helping hand to the churches being buffeted by the storm, lest if they be abandoned they suffer complete shipwreck in the faith (4–5).

In another letter, Basil calls upon the churches of the West again to transcend geographical boundaries and "inasmuch as we are united in the communion of the Spirit, to take us into the harmony of one single body"

(Epistle 90:2). In assessing the communion work of Basil, Hans Von Campenhausen concludes that

> It would have been comparatively easy for Basil to keep to his own Cappadocian circle. . . . but he would have regarded that as a betrayal of the common cause of all Christians. Basil required an ecumenical outlook of all bishops (95).

Because of a personal grudge, a new bishop of Neocaesarea, Artarbis, refused to send Basil a copy of his "enthronement letter." Basil, the elder, broke the ranks of custom to reach out to the younger bishop, admonishing him to expel the thoughts that he can live without the bonds of communion with others. Solidarity and mutual cooperation were distinctive marks of life in community, a community not limited by physical boundaries. Only human refusal to cooperate with the gift of communion in the Holy Spirit caused division. In writing to maritime bishops, Basil warned them:

> Let not this consideration influence you, "We live on the sea, we are exempt from the sufferings of the generality. We need no succour from others; so what is the good to us of foreign communion?" The same Lord who divided the islands from the continent by the sea bound island Christians to those on the continent by love. Nothing, brethren, separates us from each other, but deliberate estrangement. We have the same Lord, the same faith and the same hope (Epistle 203:3).

Communion cannot be reduced to some inchoate feeling of well-wishing in Basil. To communities suffering from poverty, material resources were to be shared, to those communities in conflict and doctrinal confusion, instruction and correction were to be offered. Basil frequently asked others in his letters to assist him in his responsibilities by their prayers, visits, good advice, and sympathy. Basil's understanding of community was clearly grounded in a dual bond fostered by the Holy Spirit, drawing persons to life in God and in neighbor. This life is translated into mutual care and sharing in the goods of one another, whether material or spiritual. Basil expressed his dependence on the Holy Spirit in a eucharistic prayer he wrote that asks that "the Spirit may unite all of us to one another who become partakers of the one Bread and Cup in the communion of the Holy Spirit."[15]

At the same time, Basil's theological formulations of trinitarian faith, especially the role of the Holy Spirit, flowed directly from his pastoral and liturgical experience. His understanding of the social nature of the Christian life provided the experiential grounding for reflecting on and articulating the communion nature of God. It would be wholly inadequate to study trinitarian theology as it was formulated by the fourth-century Cappadocians without situating it in the ecclesial concerns, local and universal, that preoccupied Basil and his theological partners.

Because of subsequent institutional developments, Basil's teachings on community were later applied more or less solely to monastic/religious institutes. But a careful study by George Fedwick, *The Church and the Charisma of Leadership in Basil,* concludes that: "Any attempt to limit the scope of Basil's projected reform of the church of his day to one small portion of it should be dismissed as ill-founded and anachronistic" (22).

AUGUSTINE OF HIPPO

By the time of Augustine (354–430 C.E.), the established church strove to conserve unity through its doctrines and preserve it through its institutional design. It had successfully articulated and defended the doctrine of God as Trinity, particularly through the contributions of the Cappadocians. Out of this core belief, responsibilities for communion behavior flowed. But the church's practice of communion was legally structured by this time, not always in close correspondence with the central beliefs it sought to embody.

As bishop of the church of Hippo, Augustine inherited these structures and understood himself to be the primary mediator of communion within his local church and within the college of bishops for the larger church as well. For Augustine, synodal meetings, letter-writing, and the sharing of eucharistic communion demonstrated and furthered the universal communion of the one Church of Christ. How did Augustine's theology or practice make a difference in his day and what might it contribute to our understanding of community today?

For the purpose of this study, we will look to Augustine's eucharistic instructions and his actions and decisions as bishop for the clearest expressions of his thinking on community, rather than to his highly speculative and psychological analogy of the Trinity. Augustine's homilies to those learning about Christian faith and to those newly baptized present his Pauline theology of the eucharistic assembly as the body of Christ. As a pastoral theologian, he wrote and preached passionately about the interconnections between community and life in God. Augustine writes in Sermon 272:

If you wish to understand the Body of Christ, listen to the apostle's words, "you are the Body and the members of Christ" (1 Cor. 12:7). If you are the Body and members of Christ, it is your mystery that is placed on the Lord's table; it is your mystery that you receive. It is to that which you are that you respond "Amen" and by that response you make your assent. You hear the words "the Body of Christ" and you answer "Amen." Be a member of Christ so that your "Amen" may be true.[16]

For Augustine, the "becoming one body" is the manifestation of the church's mystery, the living out of communion in community. The tasks of communion behavior, of building up the one body of Christ in its infinite variety of members, are undertaken as a response to the eucharist. Love for the unity of this many-membered body is Augustine's compelling exhortation. He describes love as fire that alone can meld the many into one. For Augustine, this love for the unity of the church has practical consequences at the local level. He insists that the gift of table-fellowship entails bearing with one another in faith. Rather than abstract loving, it is concrete love for the person who embraced the cross, now present in the ecclesial face of many sisters and brothers in Christ.[17]

To fully appreciate the complexity of Augustine's theology of church, it is necessary to move beyond his pastoral instruction on the eucharist. In his treatises, he offers an interpretation of church that is both temporal and eternal. To grasp his pastoral decisions as bishop of Hippo in North Africa, it is critical to notice how he reasons theologically concerning an eternal Church. For him, God sees the Church as it will be one day and eternally, not only as it is at any one historical juncture. This insight ought to render the church humble, since at no time can the church say for certain who is inside the Church and who is outside. For God alone sees what will eventually be. Nonetheless, this caution against certainty cannot impede the church from acting in history, which for Augustine is the only place in which the church can come to be in time what it will one day be in God's eternity. The church is impelled to make judgments about communion behavior here and now.

With his brother bishops, Augustine understood a certain responsibility he bore for the unity of the church, dispersed throughout the world. He appealed to the Manichaeans, an influential, religious sect with considerable success within the Roman Empire, who taught "an absolute dualism, a conflict between light and darkness, good and evil."[18] Having earlier subscribed to their tenets, Augustine now urged them "to return to the bosom of the catholic church, the true mother of Christians."[19] The intimacy of communion, described in Augustine's feminine imagery, was mediated by the institutional office of bishop. His letters and his actions as bishop of

Hippo make it clear that the bishop of Rome held a special place of honor and authority in this communion of the churches.

Augustine found in the canonical scriptures (especially the letters of Paul) and in apostolic tradition (in Ignatius, Irenaeus, and Cyprian) the vision of a church consisting of the communion of the whole world. In this vision, he searched for wisdom to respond to the needs of his times. Seeing himself as a bishop in this worldwide communion was but a part of his self-understanding. He also believed himself summoned by a future Church, where for him the fullness of communion resides. This future Church called him to become a more faithful member in the present. At the same time, the church of which Augustine was a member was simultaneously local and universal:

> I am in the church whose members are all those churches which as we know from the canonical scriptures were born and strengthened by the labors of the apostles; with the Lord's help I will not desert their communion either in Africa or everywhere (Epistle 93:23).

The summons to which Augustine sought to be faithful was the Spirit of God at work, he believed, only in the communion of this catholic Church, even though some did not profit from the Spirit's activity. Augustine's interpretation of communion is for him clearly linked with the life of the Trinity. Through the Spirit what is common to the Father and Son becomes a communion between and among us and with the triune God. This leads Augustine to say that "Whoever has the Holy Spirit is in the Church, which speaks with the languages of all peoples. Whoever is not in the Church does not have the Holy Spirit. . . . For if a member of the Body is cut off, doesn't the spirit pass?" (Sermon 268:2). The communion we share with one another is rooted in this shared participation in trinitarian communion. The more we are in God, the more we are in one another.

Three criteria guaranteed the catholicity or universal communion of the church: the apostolic tradition, the apostolic episcopate, and the apostolic scriptures. Augustine's argument for any one of these criteria was always the other two, and he argued his own position in fidelity to the teaching of his predecessors. His capacity to explore further and extend or revise the tradition lay in his understanding of the "eternal Church" in God. Even though this concept of the eternal Church may have served occasionally for Augustine as a way to trump his opponents, it also provided his ground for critiquing all historical attempts to embody the life of trinitarian communion in concrete communities and institutional structures.

In Augustine's homilies on baptism, one can find at least ten references to the Ephesians' image of the Church "without blemish or wrinkle." Yet in his refutation of the Donatists, he insists that this blemish-less Church does not describe the church in history. The Donatists had appealed to Cyprian, bishop of Carthage, for support in their separation from those bishops they considered *traditores*, those who had handed over the church's sacred books to be burned during fourth-century Roman imperial persecutions in North Africa. Throughout the fourth century, Donatists argued that priests guilty of such cowardice at the time of persecution were not worthy to administer sacraments in the community. This Donatist response is especially understandable when one remembers that they, as North Africans, had been persecuted by the Roman Empire for more than three hundred years.[20] In response to the *traditores* handing over their sacred books to be burned by Roman authorities, Donatists separated themselves from any communities that included such weak presbyters. As a movement, the Donatists achieved the upper hand in fourth-century North Africa, appointing a bishop in every city. They insisted that the holiness of the church depended upon the holiness of its ministers and where holiness was tainted, the church's unity was broken.

Not until Augustine did an alternative position find a convincing spokesperson. As Augustine reasoned, the church's holiness is not dependent on the holiness of an individual minister but on its universal unity, as the body of Christ, established in the Holy Spirit, the bond of peace (Eph. 4:3). He argued that if persons withdraw from the church, they cut themselves off from the source of holiness that the church will attain in eternity and on which it depends in history. This historical church for Augustine means, at least in part, the governing authority of communion that comes from Rome. Linked to Augustine's position, in 411 the government launched a sustained and persistent coercion to force the Donatists back into catholic unity. Only scattered Donatist groups continued to survive in North Africa until the Arab conquest. In the Roman church's dealings with the Donatists, we see once again that the goal of communion came at a high cost.

Like Ignatius centuries before, we find in Augustine further reason to question the success of the norms, determined by early church councils to prevent division. Despite Augustine's attempt to draw the circle of communion broadly by his recommendation that in essentials the church seek unity, in non-essentials—diversity and in all things—charity, the boundaries were more often than not drawn too narrowly. As the church moved through history, the vision of a universal community did not always impel church authority to discern more and more concrete gestures of hospitality and inclusion. On the contrary, the safeguarding of unity often fostered a fear and distrust of conflict and differences, which led to confessional isolation, sacramental exclusion, and pronouncements of anathema.

Within this historical record marked by sin and grace, Augustine leaves us with the reminder that the communion life we seek here and now will always be tinged by human sinfulness, his own and each of ours. The church will never be able to image fully in history the trinitarian communion that is its source and goal. Consequently, institutional expressions of communion will always be in need of reform. But the potential for reform is always present in the historical church attentive to God's summons.

MAXIMUS THE CONFESSOR

More than a century separates Maximus (580–662) from Augustine. The age of the great "patristic thinkers" is drawing to a close. Yet, several reasons persuade us to include Maximus in this conversation on communion/community. First, like Hermas in the second century, Maximus does not represent an official voice of authority in the church. He is in a unique position as a layman and a monk to speak out of another experience of responsibility for church life. That responsibility flows from Maximus' intense life of mystical prayer, ascetical struggle, and assiduous theological study. In complex and nuanced ways, Maximus introduces new understandings of the role of the human in mediating communion. This mediation takes place within the human will and its exercise of freedom, a freedom that manifests itself in each person's ecstatic movement toward others in the deliberate creation and nurturance of agapic communities.

Each community receives its mandate for and model of life together in the Christian liturgy, especially in the eucharist. The eucharistic liturgy is for Maximus the ritual enactment of divine, human and cosmic communion *par excellence*. The liturgy is cosmic in its scope, calling on heaven and earth and drawing all creation into its prayer of praise and gratitude. It is, nonetheless, concrete in its demands, enacting a sacred drama where the divine speaks to the human "I am for you" and the human is moved to respond with the same self-offer. Communion is made liturgically present, seen and heard, touched and shared.

In Maximus' cosmology, the whole created order emerges within the embrace of trinitarian activity as the direct result of God's free decision to move out in love. This ecstatic act of Goodness overflowing itself has brought about creation in all its infinite variety. God's movement in the cosmos is reflected in a pre-eminent way in the human as "the movement of the will" (Thunberg, 31–49). As God-established, the human will is directed toward communion with God or deification. Maximus often uses the term *deification*, interchangeably with the word *communion* to suggest the divine/human gift exchange. God took on a human nature so that humans might take on the divine nature, which is life in communion. The process of deification, in Maximus, never takes place in isolation from the entire creation, but is intended to lead all of creation back to its original communion character (38).

Though all of creation emerges as a trinitarian event, humankind shares a privileged place in God's design. The Christ-event reveals the intention of God for communion in human life and history. The plan of salvation as divine/human reciprocity continues throughout history as humankind cooperates with the Holy Spirit in furthering the scheme of love to bring all things into the unity of communion in the Trinity. The role of church in Maximus' synthesis is to serve as an icon of this trinitarian activity "by accomplishing the same unity among believers as God." This unity consists primarily in a shared faith, a response of the will in love, experienced in a pre-eminent way as communion in eucharist. Maximus continues in his commentary on the eucharist, *Mystagogia*:

> However different people are by their characteristics and their differences of places and ways of life, they find themselves unified in the Church through faith. It is God's nature to work this unity in the substance of things, without fusing them. God softens down the diversity in them and unifies them . . . through their relationship of communion in God as their cause, ground and goal (14).

By its mission of unity, the church exists to continue the liberation of humankind from all forms of isolation and divisions brought about by sin, the disruption of communion. For Maximus the role of humankind as a whole, and the church in particular, is to unite all things in God, and thus to overcome the evil powers of disintegration, division, and death that were threatening the seventh century Byzantine world. The exemplar for this human and ecclesial mission of unity and reconciliation is the person of Jesus Christ. In Christ, and through his incarnation, Maximus argued, the divine will and the human will conformed totally in a free and mutual self-gift. Jesus Christ shares totally a divine and human nature without confusion. By refusing to submit to the thesis of one will in Christ (monothelitism), Maximus contributed breakthrough understandings to the meaning and value of human freedom in the achievement of full personhood.

Though Maximus insists that the natural movement of the human will is toward communion, he does not disregard human freedom. In fact, it is precisely his regard for human freedom that is at stake in his argument against the Monothelites' interpretation of one will in Christ. Because Christ's human will remains fully itself and free in its self-gift to God, Christ represents the fullness of communion between the human and the divine. Maximus held with Gregory of Nyssa that true human freedom does not consist in autonomy but in communion. To the extent that human persons are separated from God, they are enslaved to their passions, to self-concerns and ultimately to evil itself. In Maximus' anthropology, human persons are truly free when they live in God in cooperation and communion. But life in communion with God and in community with others is a decision that human persons freely make by intentionally giving themselves over to the care of one another. Growth in genuine community, then, requires a process of continually freeing one's self of self in order to receive another.

Maximus never permitted his own or others' mystical experiences of communion to transcend these concrete, existential consequences. His life as a monk was dedicated to the practice of spiritual disciplines and liturgical prayer intended to purify and move the will toward communion with God and others. He spoke of this as the ascetical struggle. He understood this work to consist of a lifelong process of discarding those selfish attachments and self-interests that prevent one from entering into communion with others, with the whole cosmos and with the God of communion, whose nature we share with all creation.

Ultimately it is love that liberates the natural powers of the human will, freeing them to grow in the likeness of God for which the human is destined. The human "will for communion," made visible in concrete communities, represents both a microcosm of the relationship inherent in the whole universe and functions at its center as the mediator of this God-established communion (Thunberg, 54). The breakthrough contribution of Maximus to our conversation on patristic understandings of community rests in his determinations about the role of human freedom and intentionality in furthering God's design for communion. This seventh century Byzantine monk and mystic may yet have significant insights for us to ponder today—we, who must wrestle with questions of freedom and autonomy and with the responsibility of the "liberated" human person in relationship to others, to God, and to the cosmos.

CONCLUSION

The community we experience in life together forms a continuum with the longings and intuitions of our inner selves as well as with the ways groups reach out to connect with each other. Community and communion are the same reality viewed from different vantage points. When humans try to account for this continuum of connectedness, references to God abound. The inner connections sensed intuitively among people evoke a bonding shared in God. The ways small groups become a part of a larger whole invite people to give a name to the largest whole. This is the dynamic, often called Spirit, which has emerged in our reading of early Christian theologians.

As the relatively independent early Christian groups flourished and became more aware of each other, their theological leaders spoke of God. This helped fill out a vision of how the diversity about which early Christians were so enthusiastic was held within a larger oneness. Language of communion expressed the passion for genuine connection across differences within each person and among diverse communities through linking it with the very unity in diversity of God. And, this same evocation of oneness also served the powerful as they required unity in God from those weaker. Communion as the invisible component of community confirmed the emerging Christian world.

The emergence of early Christian community, as we have seen in chapters 1 and 2, points the way toward our own chance to belong to one another in the twenty-first century. The ensuing development of communion language examined in this chapter allows us to see that the ways we belong to each other is a part of belonging to God's greater wholeness. The grace and grit of each historical attempt to live this communion out in concrete, structured ways in the church's early centuries encourage us today to do our community building work in self-critical but innovatively hopeful ways. The re-imagining of life together is now our pressing task.

PART TWO

THE COMMUNITY OF GOD: TWENTIETH-CENTURY THEOLOGICAL AND PHILOSOPHICAL CONTRIBUTIONS

INTRODUCTION

R*e-imagining Life Together in America* must take direct account of the enormous difficulties in doing so. In this book's introduction we have already examined some of these difficulties, and in chapters 8 and 9 we will review various ways Americans resist life together in our time.

Because of massive resistance to community in the American psyche and major cultural ways of life which encourage competition and individualism over cooperation and mutuality, all those who endeavor to build community in this situation must be equipped with both perspective and staying power. Part 2 of this book means to provide some of both.

The chapters that follow in part 2 are intensely theoretical. They present in some detail the thinking of at least nine different theologians and social philosophers of the twentieth century. At some points part 2 may feel to the reader like a textbook in theology and philosophy rather than a handbook for community. We present these theories about Christian community not out of some perverse pleasure or academic myopia, but out of concern that the long process of building community in America will not survive without very sturdy theoretical bases.

The heart of part 2 proposes that God and community are completely entwined. The thinkers presented in these chapters all link who God is with what community can be. The nature of the divine for these thinkers and for this book is itself communal.

Americans question the call to community from so many different angles. There are countless distractions that undermine the task of learning to live together. These challenges and distractions are sure to confuse and even discourage the leadership of community building in contemporary churches. It is our hope that the foundational material of part 2 can provide those interested in Christian community in America today with a sense of purpose as well as perspective. This theological presentation is motivated by a growing desire in American church life to break through the barrier between academics and ordinary church leaders. Although part 2 does employ an explicitly theological vocabulary, it tries to represent the thinkers in question in an accessible manner—in conversational rather than dissertational style, in order that some of the important Christian ideas about community over the last century might be available to church leaders today. These chapters are meant to show how some of the deepest strains of Christian faith point toward disciplined and enthusiastic life with and for others. As such, these chapters can furnish a staying power for the long process of learning to live together in church settings.

Chapter 4 examines three twentieth century Roman Catholic theologians who broke through some encrusted layers of Christian tradition to discover beneath it an abiding interest in social life. Their theological work had a dramatic impact upon the Roman Catholic Church during the Second Vatican Council (1962–1965). Chapter 5 presents the work of the Eastern Orthodox thinker, John Zizioulas, whose pivotal work on community and communion has already been mentioned in chapter 3. Chapter 6 departs slightly from theology to study the works of Josiah Royce, a Protestant social philosopher, and Bernard Lonergan, a Roman Catholic philosopher and theologian who together offer a comprehensive method for thinking about and assessing Christian community. Chapter 7 summarizes the energized work of a number of recent liberation and feminist theologians who are concerned that any effort to re-imagine life together takes seriously the gospel call to justice and inclusive love.

Part 2 grounds the quest for community in an understanding of God. God's own inexhaustability makes this a deep and intense task. But such a foundation can provide the perspective and staying power needed for the exciting challenge of building community in America in our time.

Chapter Four

A CHURCH CALLED BACK TO ITS ROOTS

W here have we come from and where are we headed? The last fifty years within the Roman Catholic Church have witnessed an amazing response to questions such as this. At least in its documents, it has begun to re-claim a vision of community and the notion of communion as the church's source and goal. This has been all the more astounding, since the Christian linkage between God and community had slipped into the background for much of the period between 1000 and 1930 C.E. This chapter charts this dramatic re-emergence of the importance of human community in recent Christian understanding of both God and church.

We begin with an acknowledgement of loss. Multiple factors contributed to the church's loss of its core identity as communion during the second millennium. More and more the church became identified with the empire in ways that militated against its gospel character of community. Church as communities of disciples gave way to institutional forms that more closely resembled the ruling powers of its day. As centuries passed, political and sociocultural factors continued to influence ecclesial reflection and church structures. Of major significance to the Roman Catholic Church's self-understanding was the definition of church formulated by Cardinal Robert Bellarmine (1542–1621). In refuting the Reformation's claim that the true church remained invisible in human history, Bellarmine argued for a church in visible and concrete forms. He defined this church as a *societas perfecta*. This *perfect* society was "indeed a community of men, as visible and palpable as the community of the Roman people, or the kingdom of France or the republic of Venice."

This move by the Roman Catholic Church to assert visibility in such a definitive way seems to have overlooked the sacramental nature of the church, whereby invisible and visible, divine and human mutually co-exist. For all practical purposes, the kingdom of God, as invisible reality, collapsed into the visible Roman Catholic Church.

In this chapter we describe a retrieval of the early church's notion of communion that took place during the twentieth century. By highlighting the work of three particular theologians, we hope to offer some theological resources to assist church leaders in understanding the nature and mission of the church in the world. By so doing, we want to strengthen our appeal to the North American churches. They, too, can assume greater responsibility to nurture life in community. As we outline this appeal, it will be important to keep in mind the deep, intrinsic relationship between church and world. We will hold that the church is in the world and the world is in the church.

THE SECOND VATICAN COUNCIL AS DRAMATIC TURNING POINT

The Second Vatican Council stands out as the watershed event of the twentieth century for the Roman Catholic Church. So great has been the impact of the Second Vatican Council on this church's self-understanding that it has been described in terms of a "Copernican revolution."[1] It is important to investigate at least a few of the stirrings that caused such a dramatic shift.

In the opening paragraph of one of the core documents of the Council, the Dogmatic Constitution on the Church, *Lumen Gentium*, council members stated their duty to "set forth as clearly as possible . . . the Church's nature and universal mission" (*Lumen Gentium*, 1). They explained the "greater urgency of this duty" in light of "the conditions of the modern world" where people are drawn ever more closely together by social, technical and cultural bonds, while it still remains for them to achieve full unity in Christ" (LG, 1). That the church exists to draw all humankind together in unity springs from a renewed understanding of the church's identity as "a sign and instrument of communion with God and of unity among all" (LG, 1). A theology of communion emerges in recurring documents of Vatican Council II. What was not achieved at the time of the Council or subsequently is a design for community. Communion's appropriate structures and behavioral practice have not been worked out, even though the Council proclaimed that it is only in and through concrete communities that the church realizes its own identity and plays its role in the transformation of society (LG, 23).

In appraising the achievements of the Council fifteen years later, the

Synod of 1985 named communion "the central and fundamental idea of the council documents."[2] Though this synod likewise failed to identify the concrete means needed to achieve communion, it acknowledged that "communion must be put into practice more and more and made to conform to a more perfect rule" (450).

VISIONARY PRECURSORS OF A RENEWED THEOLOGY OF COMMUNION

In an attempt to understand better some underpinnings of this "theology of communion" and the demands of its practice, we will go behind the texts of Vatican II to some of the core thinkers whose theological work on communion informed them. Their theology was significantly shaped by patristic sources where the idea of communion is a dynamic and concrete prescriptive for the church's self realization in history.

For decades prior to Vatican II, a group of theologians had summoned a call to *ressourcement*—a return to the sources of church life in the early centuries of its formative history. But what was it that these pioneer theologians were seeking in their journeys back to the first millennium of Christianity? A glimpse at a few of these thinkers' work reveals their dissatisfaction with the prevailing, static, and exclusionary view of the church that had dominated Roman Catholic thinking for at least 150 years.

With patristic sources in hand, Yves Congar, O.P., Henri DeLubac, and Karl Rahner, S.J. were among the theological consultants at the Second Vatican Council, whose influence provoked a cataclysmic shift in the Roman Catholic Church's self-understanding. This movement was from a juridical view of the church, inherited from Robert Bellarmine and the Council of Trent (1545–1563),[3] to a renewed, patristic understanding of church as "a Mystery of Communion that comes into being from the unity of the Father, Son and Holy Spirit" (LG, 4). Throughout the documents of Vatican II, the voices of these theologians of *ressourcement* are recognizable. Their own thoughts resonate with the patristic writers' deep conviction that the church lives in history as a communion of life between the triune God and those devoted to Christ. As historical, social bodies explicitly aligned with the divine, churches must be dynamically engaged in their concrete, social situations. But the reality of the Roman Catholic Church prior to the Council was, to a great extent, disengaged from its social context, claiming some divinely ordained status, which rendered the church more and more removed from and irrelevant to a world in need and in flux.

By returning to the patristic sources, these theologians discovered several core ecclesial characteristics that had become central to an ecclesiology of communion. These characteristics have immense social and communitarian implications for us today. For the development and limits of our thesis, we will discuss three:

1. Theology emerged from practice. Pastoral needs shaped the questions that theology sought to illumine. Life in communion required concrete communities where reflection on life together and larger pastoral needs took place.

2. Amid tensions and disagreements, the early churches struggled with their perceived call to catholicity. By this was meant a radical inclusivity, which defined the church as a universal communion in the design of God.

3. Salvation was social. The church shared a radically corporate understanding of God's desire to save a social body or whole people in which each unique individual plays a part.

HENRI DELUBAC

So committed was Henri DeLubac to the retrieval of the social mission of the church that he subtitled his great programmatic work *Catholicism* "the social aspects of dogma" and he warned the church of 1942 that "if we no longer live from this teaching, the fault is our own."[4] The church of the early centuries found the realization of its social vision in the eucharistic action. DeLubac explains:

> True eucharistic piety . . . is no devout individualism . . . With one sweeping, all-embracing gesture, in one fervent intention, it gathers together the whole world. . . . It cannot conceive of the action of the breaking of the bread without fraternal communion (1950, 48).

The early church to which DeLubac looked for the means to nourish the church of his day was a church fully aware that "prayer was essentially the prayer of all for all" (xv–xvi). The invasion of the spiritual life by the "detestable I" that occurred with the development of the Enlightenment's spirit of individualism coincided with the demise of medieval Christianity, as DeLubac saw it. Like many of the twentieth century theologians of *ressourcement*, DeLubac credited the nineteenth century school of Tübingen under the leadership of Johann Adam Mohler with the seeds for reviving the catholic, social vision of the early church. DeLubac claimed as his own agenda the desire to elaborate the fact that "fundamentally, the gospel is obsessed with the idea of the unity of human society" (xv).

As an appendix to *Catholicism,* Henri DeLubac attached translations of ten of the fathers of the church, East and West. In the eastern fathers, DeLubac found over and over again a contemplation of God's delight in the creation, not only of individuals but in the creation of "humanity as a whole." He explains: "For Irenaeus . . . as indeed for Origen, Gregory of Nazianzen, Gregory of Nyssa, for Cyril of Alexandria, Maximus, Hilary and others, the lost sheep of the gospel that the Good Shepherd brings back to the fold is no other than the whole of human nature . . ." (1950, 1–2).

Girded with the pastoral methodology of the patristic writers, Henri DeLubac was able to move beyond the narrow-minded confines of the early twentieth century dependence on neo-scholasticism.[5] For him, the Catholic spirit embraced the mystery of communion in a paradox that refuses to reduce the truth to anything that is manageably one-sided and partial.[6] As Hans Urs Von Balthasar has pointed out "it is precisely the power of inclusion that becomes the chief criterion of truth" in the ecclesial vision of DeLubac.[7]

DeLubac's historically-conscious methodology enabled him to promote a renewed vision of the church as a communion, not on some lofty, metaphysical plane but in the concrete and practical arena, where it is constituted by both historical and spiritual dimensions, realizing its own identity in the face of the many challenges posed by the modern world. The spiritual identity of the church cannot be bypassed in DeLubac's historically conscious ecclesiology. The two dimensions are radically interdependent.

In his treatise on *The Motherhood of the Church*, he explains the Spirit's role in birthing the church.

> The Church has a vital principle, a soul, and this soul is the Spirit of Christ. Visible and invisible at one and the same time, organized society and mystical participation, institution and communion, unfolding in history and already breathing within the Eternal, she is the stem in the midst of our universe, as Peguy said, or the axis, the axial current, as Teilhard liked to say, charged with channeling in order to liberate our miserable and sublime humanity, not only nor in the first place from its thousand historical bondages but from its congenital bondage, from the evil that leads it to death (1982, 20).

For DeLubac, one of those evils threatening humankind in the twentieth century was a positivist conception of the church, one that systematically confined itself to its external aspects without linking the church's structure to its "underlying nature" constituted by the Spirit of Christ. DeLubac feared a theological community that no longer dared to "plunge into the Mystery of God" which is "in fact the intimate homeland into which all men [sic] whether they know it or not, dream of being admitted" (1982, 23). DeLubac's intense study of the patristic theologians convinced him that they "understood profoundly" the Mystery of the Church as communion, a truth, which they experienced intensely. "She [the Church] is in their eyes the reality at once historical and mystical that embodies everything, the universal place outside of which they would be in exile, lost" (1982, 23). DeLubac challenged the Christian community of his day not to lose its heritage but to breathe new vigor into it.

Joseph Komonchak described the contribution of DeLubac as that of bringing the depth of the Catholic tradition into a critical encounter with the pressing issues of his day. He achieved this by his strong resistance to a prevailing view of the supernatural, which had created for so long a Catholic subculture, existing in relative detachment from the rest of the world. DeLubac's inclusive understanding of Catholicism rejected anything that promoted a sectarian view as truth.

YVES CONGAR

Henri DeLubac's practical vision of communion was written in response to a request by his friend, Yves Congar, for a series entitled, *Unam Sanctam*. Congar had written the inaugural volume for this series, *Divided Christianity*, which bore the subtitle, "Principles for a Catholic Ecumenism." Congar, like DeLubac, found in the patristic sources the spirit and guiding principles to revision the nature and mission of the church in his day. For several decades, Congar had worked under a dark cloud of suspicion from Rome, but at the time of the Second Vatican Council, he was able to forge a path that opened up a new direction for the church in the modern world. This direction included a more encompassing vision of Christian tradition, an awakening to the scandal of division that had for almost a millennium separated the one Church of God. Beginning with ecumenical concerns, Congar became a pioneering voice calling the churches to "return to the sources" in which he found "the grand lines of a concrete program for a catholic ecumenism" (330–33).

But Congar's concern for the unity of the church long preceded his

1937 inaugural work, *Divided Christianity*. While studying for ordination as a Dominican friar in the 1920's, Congar had a profound and formative religious experience. When praying with the seventeenth chapter of John's gospel, which includes Jesus' prayer that "all may be one," he recognized his life's work to labor for the communion of all who believe in Jesus Christ. Throughout his long life and professional pursuits, nothing interfered with this vocational decision. He was convinced that deep-seated prejudices and long-standing divisions could be overcome where people open to the stirrings of the Holy Spirit, who draws humans together in communion. By living and acting as if divisions are inevitable, we become co-responsible for the separations that breed mistrust, misunderstanding, rivalry, and injustice, Congar reasoned. To this extent the attitudes and behavior of every individual Christian matter. Congar reminds us that "the whole Church is answerable for the ecumenical effort. To a tiny and yet very real extent, the issue is in the hands of one parishioner in some remote village" (1967, 125).

The call to unity served as a methodological lens in all of Congar's theological investigations. With it, he analyzed in a sustained way the destructive character of longstanding division among Christians. When separation becomes more and more the taken-for-granted way of life, people no longer sense the sin involved in such exclusion of the other. The climate of isolation creates an environment where prejudice can grow. Unchecked by personal interaction and dialogue, fear and suspicion replace the possibility of co-operation and mutual enrichment. The disunity of the church has weakened its mission to the world, has prevented new insights and correctives from being received in church tradition, and has made distortions of truth inevitable. Congar's keen interpretation of the destructive character of separation, as a taken for granted way of life, has implications beyond church boundaries to every other level of social interaction.

Within the priestly prayer of Jesus, Congar perceives the vision of a church of fullness, a unity preserved in diversity. "The unity which Jesus asks for the Church in his high-priestly prayer is that of a unity of plenitude, the image of unity existing between Father and Son. It is not a union woven by poverty, by reduction to a single element. Pluralism will find a place there"(1939, 63). Throughout the church's history, Congar discovered church at its best when it was struggling to find appropriate ways to incorporate diversity into its unity. But, of utmost importance to our study, Congar refused to romanticize any period in the church's history of "wretchedness and grace" (21) or to speak about "rediscovering" some unity that had been "lost."

As he studied the patristic period, he saw clearly that tension and differences have always accompanied the movement of the church through history. For Congar, church unity is bonded by faith in the Lordship of Jesus and confidence in the Holy Spirit. This confidence chooses to preserve rather than break the peace of Christ. He painstakingly reviews events throughout the early Christian centuries that support his call for greater diversity in the church's communion.[8]

Yves Congar's influence at the Second Vatican Council can be most clearly recognized in the Decree on Ecumenism, the decree that Emmanuel Lanne equates with the "most precise locus" of the "Copernican revolution" in Roman Catholic self-understanding.[9] Here the Catholic Church chose a "communion optic" as its lens for looking at other Christian churches. Instead of beginning with things that divide and separate the churches, "this decree has resolutely opted for a positive approach expressed in terms of communion, subsisting in spite of divisions and obstacles" (121).

For decades, Congar committed himself to healing the divisions that for centuries had prevented the churches from seeing the greater unity they shared in the communion of God's own life. To extend this optic of communion to the church's relationship with the world became a necessary consequence of listening to Jesus' prayer in John's gospel in light of the contemporary situation. In its pastoral constitution, The Church in the Modern World (*Gaudium et spes*), the Roman Catholic Church embraced a new vision of catholicity.

> In his fatherly care for each of us, God desired that all should form one family and deal with each other in a spirit of brotherhood [sic]. All in fact are destined to the very same end, namely God himself. . . Furthermore, the Lord Jesus, when praying to the Father, "that they may all be one . . . even as we are one" (Jn. 17:21–22) has opened up new horizons closed to human reasons, by implying that there is a certain parallel between the union existing among the divine persons and the union of the sons and daughters of God in truth and love. It follows then that if humans are the only creatures on earth which God has wanted for their own sake, humans can fully discover their true selves only in a sincere giving of themselves (GS, 24).

That Congar's prayer for unity should incite such an inclusive vision of oneness with all of the world's people at Vatican Council II testifies to persevering faith. Of Congar, Joseph Komonchak has said: "There is no theologian who did more to prepare for Vatican II or who had a larger role in the orientation and even in the composition of the documents" (1983,

402). As we continue to struggle through and move beyond concerns of the Council, Congar's findings provide psychological and spiritual principles, such as, "an optic of communion" as an intentional stance toward life, that have implications far beyond divisions among Christians. They challenge us to ask deeper questions about God's desire for the oneness and diversity of all creation.

Congar claimed that the best way to understand the church is as the mystical body of Christ, a communion rooted in the Trinity, but with concrete, historical structures. It is at one and the same time convoked by God and constituted as a social body by human persons. As such, Congar was interested in moving the church beyond the static ecclesiology of the neo-scholastic manuals. But to be faithful to this mystery of divine/human communion, Congar was committed to the ongoing need for the structural reform of the church. Archbishop John Quinn referred to this insistence of Congar when he wrote:

> He [Congar] believes that any true and effective reform must touch structures. . . Most of those in the Middle Ages who wanted reform, he said, were prisoners of the system, incapable of reforming the structures themselves through recovery of the original vision, incapable of asking the new questions raised by a new situation (1996, 13).

For Congar, it was this dialectic between mystery and history that enabled him to protest against a certain mystification of the historically conditioned structures of the church, imposing on the present, social arrangements some absolute, divinely ordained character. He spoke of the dangers of "a creeping infallibility and hierarchology" that neglected the development of collegiality and reduced the church to its hierarchy. To the Holy Spirit, Congar turned for confident assurance that in every generation the church is called to reform itself. It does so, in light of newly emerging social conditions and the companioning Spirit, who is alive in and working through particular, historical agents and events. Congar appealed to the Eastern fathers, particularly Athanasius and Irenaeus, whose use of theandrism, the divine/human, provided a non-dualistic way of seeing God at work in human persons, their social constructions, and their history itself.

Like his patristic mentors, Congar remained focused on and concerned about the historical reality of the church but never in a way that separated ecclesiology from spirituality. To be the mystical body of Christ, as the church is called to be in history, requires nothing less than conformity to Christ in the everyday demands of self-giving love.

. . . The Mystical body does not consist in exterior manifestations or ceremonies, however valuable or striking they may be. But it is when a small child, a humble lay-sister, a working mother whose life is taken up with ordinary daily chores, when people like this unnoticed by the world, love God with all their heart and live a life of ardent charity, then the mystical body is realized and increased in stature. Such persons grow in holiness and bring about the kingdom of God to the profit of all, for it is only as Christ's members that we grow in him by charity, so that the whole body benefits from the advance of each (127).

For Congar, one's personal holiness is never individualistic. It is intimately tied up with the whole body of Christ, the corporate, ecclesial body of which each Christian is a part.

In the work of Henri DeLubac and Yves Congar several dimensions of the early church's self-understanding take center stage again. These include concern for the concrete, historical situation in which the church is called to make present the mystery of divine/human communion; an openness to a radical inclusivity as core to Catholic identity; and an understanding of the social nature or community component of Christian life. Through the presence and influence of these theologians at the Second Vatican Council, these dynamic, pastoral and theological components of the early church have returned to illumine the church of our time.

KARL RAHNER, S.J.

Karl Rahner is a third theologian whose influence at the Second Vatican Council we highlight as exemplary for today. Rahner was fundamentally a pastoral theologian, one who has been called by Harvey Egan, his student and foremost biographer, the "father of the Church of the twentieth century." By pastoral here, we suggest with Egan, that Karl Rahner understood theology as an integration of prayer, theory, and practice. Prayer often intersperses his most profound, speculative thoughts. His theological treatises often "begin and end in prayer and explicit prayer and penetrating reflections on prayer punctuate his entire theological life" (Egan, 24).

A synthesis of prayer and practice was a taken for granted method by many patristic writers, to whose contributions these twentieth century theologians turned for new insight. Like his patristic forebears, Rahner sought to stay connected and respond to needs of specific people in his theological reflections. Most of his works originated as occasional writings, written to address specific topics suggested to him by diverse audiences.

This pastoral agenda provided a context for Rahner's personal prayer and theological reflections, as he reasoned his way through contemporary concerns with light gleaned from the church's long, theological tradition.

Karl Rahner addressed concerns similar to Congar and DeLubac. He attests that holiness is never a private matter. Since the human person is not simply an individual but a social being, holiness must express itself socially. Genuine human faith forms community, has a history, and finds expression personally and publicly. For Rahner, Christianity is necessarily ecclesial. He insisted:

> If the comparison between a Christian and the Church and that of a child to its parents bothers you, then disregard it. Ecclesial language often refers to "mother church." It is a custom that goes back to earliest Christianity. What it affirms is something that really makes sense: The Church is the mediator and guarantor of my life in unity and solidarity with God. To this degree I can call the Church my mother (1990, 16).

And for Rahner, this unity with God is unity with neighbor and must therefore be related to church and society. The communion life we share with God makes concrete demands on us. It never remains a vague, abstract feeling. He insisted that unity with our neighbor required loving them in practical ways; such love must be concerned about the things of this world. But, at the same time, it cannot reduce human existence to human needs. For genuine love of neighbor is called to initiate human persons into a community of faith, hope, and love, which Rahner saw as an introduction into the life of God's very self.

To understand the mutual correlation that exists between these two related but distinct terms, communion with God and communion with neighbor, it is essential to understand the methodological starting point of all Rahner's theology. That point of departure is the divine/human drama unfolding because of God's free, self-offer to the human person. The deepest human meaning is in being an addressee of that divine self-communication. To say something about God is to say something about the human and to say something about the human is to say something about God. To say that God's self-communication is at the heart of human existence is to summarize Rahner's entire theological project.

Because of the absolute gratuity of God's self-offer, the human person, precisely as human, is coded for the experience of God, for communion, even if it takes place in hidden and unreflected ways. To open oneself to this primordial experience of God's genuine self-communication is what Rahner spoke about as the mysticism of ordinary life. Rahner was fond of saying that "the Christian of the future will be a mystic, (he/she will experience something) or will cease to be Christian at all" (1971, 115). This mystical approach to life is a practical one, an essential condition for meaningful human living. Because of this, the church

> . . . must teach us in the concrete to maintain a constant closeness to this God; to say "Thou" to him [sic], to commit ourselves to his silence and darkness. It must be made intelligible to people that they have an implicit but true knowledge of God—perhaps not reflected upon and not verbalized; or better expressed, they have a genuine experience of God, ultimately rooted in their spiritual existence, in their transcendentality, in their personality or whatever you want to call it (1990, 15).

To recognize in every human person the bearer of divine communication and to affirm their absolute self-worth, despite their finitude and sinfulness—through self-forgetting love, this is authentic, earthy mysticism. It is this everyday mysticism that provides the conditions for genuine, human community in the life of the Trinity to be realized. It is not ahistorical or abstract communion but a divine/human relationship experienced in the daily and the mundane.

> The launchpad, if we may so call it, may be flimsy and narrow, and rise so scarcely above the flat plain of the everyday as to be hardly noticeable at all. But these trivialities—the biblical glass of water to someone thirsty, a kind word at someone's sickbed, the refusal to take some small, mean advantage even of someone, whose selfishness has infuriated us, or a thousand other everyday trifles can be the unassuming accomplishment by which the actual attitude of unselfish brotherly and sisterly communion is consummated. And this communion is life's proper deed (1983, 103).

For Rahner, the divine/human drama provided the two mutually conditioning components (one transcendent, the other historical) of all his theologizing. It is not surprising then to learn how consonant his understanding of the church is with Vatican II's description of the church as a sacrament, a sign and instrument of communion with God and the unity of the human race (LG, 4). This sacramental character of the church is explained further as a mystery with both a human and divine component. These components cannot be thought of as two separate realities, but rather the divine/human forms one complex reality (LG, 8), neither of which begins where the other leaves off. Rahner had long held that to speak about God at all is to implicate the human and vice versa.

The mutual conditioning character of these pairs provided Rahner with the conceptual tools for explaining that the concrete church in history is integrally a divine/human partnership. It is incarnation going on through the Holy Spirit's presence in the people and structures that constitute the community called church. In speaking of this divine/human partnership, Rahner explained how "it is possible for the Church to be seen as the Body of Christ, as the People of God, and for the Church to be understood as the people of God on their journey. It is possible to recognize that the Church itself is still seeking to find her goal through history" (27). For Rahner, viewing the church in this light of "both/and" is an achievement of "more than a one-sided view of the Church as an authoritative institution of salvation" (28). The decision to take responsibility for the church as a human community is never done in isolation from deep trust in the companioning presence of the Spirit of Christ moving in its members. From this vantage point, Rahner believed that "the Church appears not primarily as one who acts upon us, but rather as the one who we are, in virtue of the fact that the grace of God has moved and inspired us and bound us together into a unity" (28).

How to reflect critically on ever-emerging, concrete situations and pressing concerns, to which the church must respond, requires multi-disciplined skills and commitment. Rahner acknowledged learning more and more about these skills of critical reflection from his students. One of those insightful students, Johann Baptist Metz, developed Rahner's mutually conditioning pairs by insisting that the church best understands itself as a mystical/political community. Rahner agreed.

> I believe that what Metz says is true. That Christianity particularly today has to have a mystical and social component. Because without the mystical component, a merely external indoctrination does not do justice to the existence of God, Christianity or its content. And a social component is particularly significant because the person of today will not find true love of neighbor that comes from God if it is limited to an intimate, little sphere (Vorgrimler, 127).

Rahner recognized the difficulty in refusing to separate the mystical from the political, the divine from the human, the historical reality from its eschatological goal. In an essay, entitled "Why Am I a Christian Today?" Rahner is particularly autobiographical.

> Every true Christian naturally suffers from the social and historical structure of the Church. In its empirical reality, it always lags behind its essence.

It proclaims a message by which its own empirical reality is always called into question. We can do our part to remove its meanness, only if we help to bear the burden of its wretchedness, for which all of us too bear some guilt (1986, 15).

Between 1972 and his death at 80 in 1984, Rahner wrote more and more about the church of the future growing up from below in small communities. He watched the movement in Latin America with deep pride and hope, as he listened and advised some young Jesuits and students. A true, catholic theology of liberation must exist, he believed, for the unity of love of God and love of neighbor needs to be worked out in a more radical way. "The Church has a task toward society that is political in the strictest sense of the word" (Vorgrimler, 126). That concrete communities were central to Rahner's vision of the faithful church of the future is clear.

I am of the opinion that a basic community church can only be a basic community if over and above the strictly religious, the abstractly religious, it molds an actual community of human beings who really feel that they belong to each other, who are in a true sense a community of love, a unity in which genuine Christian love is not only theoretically proclaimed but concretely practiced (1986, 69).

CONCLUSION

At a time when the church of the West, particularly in North America, was beginning to experience a breakdown in cultural Christianity and community life, the Roman Catholic Church gathered in its most authoritative body, a worldwide ecumenical council, presided over by the bishop of Rome. One major result of this ecclesial event has been a re-appropriation by the Roman Catholic Church of its very nature and purpose as a "sign and instrument of communion with God and of the unity of the human race" (LG, 1). This chapter has traced the conditions that made possible this renewed ecclesial self-understanding to the work of key theologians at the Council, who themselves had found this dynamic view of church prevailing in the earliest centuries of the Christian tradition. By introducing some core theological claims of these twentieth century Roman Catholic theologians—Henri DeLubac, Yves Congar, and Karl Rahner—common resources have surfaced.

Each has a thorough appreciation for the church as a mystery of communion, originating from its communion life in the Trinity. Such an understanding resists all efforts to reduce the church to a mere administrative organization or sociological construction. At the same time, the sacramental character of the church requires that it have visible, historical embodiment, concrete social structures and systems of administration. One of the greatest contributions we sense in these theologians is their persuasive insistence that the human and divine, the individual and community, the particular and the universal do not contradict or exclude the other. Rather they simultaneously and mutually condition each other. In other words, communion provides a core category for understanding how the church is to make visible in human history the presence of the divine life in whom "it lives and moves and has its being" (Acts 10:10). Or in the words of Karl Rahner, "Communion is life's proper deed" (1983, 103).

This spirit or gift of communion makes possible not only tangible care for a genuine life together in concrete groupings. The pressing point, made in various ways by these theologians, is the social nature of communion in and of itself. In other words, it is in community, as this entire book proposes, that God's love is poignantly and directly experienced. And community is expansive. In a genuine spirit of catholicity, communion requires a radical openness to and concern for all, not simply in theory but in practice.

Since the close of the Second Vatican Council in 1965, the category of communion has become the primary theological starting point for all dialogues among the Christian churches. From this point of departure, the churches acknowledge their earliest self-understanding emerging in the Gospels and the communities resulting from them. Likewise, communion or shared partnership in the triune life of God, describes a common understanding of the mission of the churches in the world and toward all creation.

By recognizing that this early and sacred dimension of communion has a cultural and social counterpart, joined at the hip as we described them, churches must claim anew the responsibility to determine and provide the kinds of structures needed to nurture "life in communion." This re-claiming of the church's roots in community needs to occur here and now where existing American social structures often militate against life together. That the church has been shaped by its social situation cannot be denied. That the churches can assume some role in reshaping these social situations is the hope that underpins and directs this project. It is time to re-imagine church for the sake of God and life together in America.

Chapter Five

AN EASTERN ORTHODOX CONTRIBUTION TO UNDERSTANDING COMMUNION: THE WORK OF JOHN ZIZIOULAS

A passion for the possible incites us to make available to more and more church leaders—lay and clergy—critical and creative, spiritual and intellectual resources not yet fully tapped in the church's long heritage of community. Good theology, rooted in life, must be the undergirding foundation, energy source, and reflective companion for decisions we make as people of faith. Saying something about the character of God is imperative to the kinds of lives we live. Adult Christians deserve appropriate, critical tools to think theologically.

The work of community-building, in and of itself, helps constitute the church's very identity and is integral to its mission in the world. At a time when theology has become suspect, as to its relevance in everyday, "real" life, this chapter, like the last, presses our case for the practical and the concrete as the starting point for and the arena to which all theology must return. What does not matter ultimately for the life of the world, so loved by God (John 3:16), does not ultimately matter.

The unlikely guide for this chapter speaks to us from his Eastern Orthodox tradition. John Zizioulas, metropolitan bishop of Pergamon, addresses our western culture on the theology of community as a scholar of the patristic sources. When the Second Vatican Council was finishing its sessions and documents in the fall of 1965, this young, thirty-one-year-old, Greek Orthodox priest was just finishing his doctoral dissertation at Oxford University on "The Unity of the Church in the First Three Centuries." His theological and pastoral work since then has demonstrated an ongoing devotion to expanding and deepening those initial investigations. Having been discovered in the ecumenical arena by Yves Congar, not long after his theological career began, Congar introduced him to a Roman Catholic audience with glowing acclaim. He described Zizioulas as "one of the most original and creative theologians of our epoch" (1985, jacket cover). We share much of this same enthusiasm for the contribution of Zizioulas.

For our purposes, John Zizioulas provides a further understanding of the notion of community by reading a whole set of traditional Christian categories from a social perspective. In his comprehensive and synthetic explanation, he can find no other valid reading of the churches' early life. Deeply rooted in the world of Greek thought, Zizioulas does not easily fall into neat, divisible, theological categories. For him, each theological truth is implicated in a greater whole, where they mutually interact and interdepend. To understand one theological concept, one must appreciate its relationship to another. His emerging synthesis produces his clear, theological position. Because God exists only as a God in relationship, everything that is, is related to everything else that is. All are "corporate beings," because all live in one another since all live in God. We deny this truth at our own peril and to the peril of the social and cosmic order. However, before drawing out this thought, Zizioulas invites his readers to place core meanings of God, the human person, the person of Christ, and the eucharist in explicit conversation with social questions. He refuses to see any of these doctrinal categories as simply abstract truth. So, for instance, the eucharist cannot be thought about theologically without explicit consideration of actual gatherings of people.

This chapter briefly outlines Zizioulas' development of several distinct doctrinal categories while being aware that to separate them is no more possible than it is to isolate an individual from her relationship to everything else. Beyond doubt, Zizioulas' social reading of patristic theology provides important grounding for taking human community seriously.

At the heart of Zizioulas' project and central to the theological reconstruction of community is his claim that God's very nature is relationship. The "essence" that makes God be God is not some abstract "divine substance" but a communion of persons, a dynamic life in relationship. Here, oneness is not sacrificed to diversity nor are differences swallowed up by unity. Such a social understanding of God's trinitarian life has huge implications for all whose self-understanding is shaped by Christian tradition. Inherent in this tradition is the claim that humankind has been created in the image of God and is called to grow in this divine likeness.

Baptism and Corporate Identity

Zizioulas serves, perhaps more dramatically than any theologian discussed thus far, to underscore the non-individualistic nature of the Christian life. His interpretation of Christian tradition leaves little room for doubt that we belong to one another and our common destiny is forged in corporate self-appropriation. He provides the foundations for such unequivocal judgment in his interpretation of the social nature of the ecclesial person. In a rather unprecedented way, Zizioulas distinguishes an "ecclesial being" from an individual, a distinction that results from the meaning of Christian baptism. From the ritual waters of baptism, one emerges, no longer an isolated individual, but a member of the body of Christ. This identity of "personhood," (being for another) in Christ is graphic and literal in Zizioulas' theological understanding. He is clear in stating that we live only in and as members of one another. Christ is the many-membered body, of which each of us is a part. The baptized Christian, this ecclesial being, is corporate just as Christ is corporate. Both of these theological categories, the baptized person and the person of Christ, merge and flow in Zizioulas' integrative system to provide key principles to recast thinking about the church's social mission.

John Zizioulas' theological clarity adds depth, as well as fresh perspective, to this book's portrait of why North American churches are so well positioned to help reshape the social fabric. As authors we do not intend to reduce the mission of the church to a social task alone, but we do ask if the church can faithfully participate in God's saving mission in Christ through the Spirit without assuming some of this work as its own.

Throughout his theological project, particularly as a participant in many ecumenical dialogues, John Zizioulas has consistently argued for church reform from a patristic starting point. This is not because he sees in the early centuries some preconceived blueprint for how church is to function throughout human history, but because patristic sources demonstrate clearly just how critical history and culture, politics and social location are to the ongoing growth and theological development of the churches. In the years since his doctoral dissertation, Zizioulas has been painstakingly careful and boldly constructive in making links between the patristic theological synthesis of the fourth and fifth centuries and social responsibilities confronting the churches today.

We Are Saved by Belonging to One Another

In Zizioulas' opinion, the greatest error committed by the Christian churches in modernity sprang from a malaise called confessionalism. The result has been overwhelming confusion between "the idea of the local church," the only sense of church known in the early centuries, and "the idea of a church as a confessional body." This confessional body looks at truth as a matter of propositions and sees a church that acquires its identity on the basis of these propositions. Tradition then becomes the handing down from generation to generation of the original faith of the apostles mainly in the form of creeds and theological statements. Divisions among the churches have hardened around some of these confessional propositions. Zizioulas believes that a study of the early church reveals a far different understanding of saving truth. "We are not saved by belonging to a confessional body but to a concrete ecclesial community, to the Church." We are saved, in other words, by belonging to one another. Within this fundamental relationship of communion, the faith, hope, and love of the living body of Christ is passed on from one generation to the next. This simple declaration has theological underpinnings that need elaboration.

Eucharist as the Rejection of all Dualism and Divisions

For John Zizioulas, it is a matter of life or death that the churches come to understand their life together as a network of concrete communities, finding their identity and mission in eucharistic self-giving for the life of the world. His vision of eucharistic life is at the heart of understanding a life of communion. Into the eucharist, Zizioulas gathers all of creation. Not only does the eucharist make visible human connections within the body of Christ, but the inherent connections between matter and spirit themselves. As Paul MacPartlan, a British scholar of Zizioulas, reflects on his theological synthesis, he emphasizes the non-dualistic character of all Zizioulas' thinking and finds in it a remedy for so many of the dichotomies that have sprung from the separation of spirit and matter. Zizioulas provides for the healing of this split in his keen explication of eucharist, where matter and spirit are the heart of worship and life.

> A vision of the world derived from the experience of the eucharist leaves no possibility for dissociating the natural from the supernatural, a dissociation in which western theology has imprisoned humans by setting

them in front of the dilemma of choosing between the two. The eucharist underlines the fact that nature and creation viewed as a whole must not be rejected on the pretext of some kind of supernatural. The eucharist accepts and sanctifies all of creation recapitulated in the One Body of the "first born of all creation." In the eucharist, the human acts as priest of creation, in the name of and because of the priesthood of Christ, the high priest par excellence. The human person has to become a liturgical being before he can hope to overcome the ecological crisis (131–32).

The eucharist (what some Christians call the Lord's supper or communion) is the event, par excellence, for breaking down the division that much western, Christian thought has established between the natural and the supernatural. This new unity of God's realm and the human realm that the eucharist realizes is demonstrated because the eucharist focuses on the natural elements of bread and cup and proclaims these very common, material things as Christ's body. For Zizioulas also, reverence for creation flows from humankind's awareness that nature (material creation) is holy, filled with spirit. The spiritual and material dimensions of life are gathered together (recapitulated in Christ) as celebrated in eucharist.

In studying the centrality of the eucharist in the theology of Zizioulas, it is important to understand also the meaning of the eucharistic *synaxis* (or gathering) for the early church. Since eucharist has taken on many, varied, and sometimes static interpretations in our day, it is critical to point out that, in Zizioulas understanding of the early churches, eucharist is not something that takes place within a gathering or in the context of communion. Rather, the eucharist is this gathering and communion itself. The eucharist is not something that the church does; it is who the church is; where the church is the church. When the church is living communion, it is offering and communicating in the body of Christ. It is most perfectly representing the church in the world. Saving grace comes in the communion of persons with one another and with all creation (bread and wine represent all visible matter), to become again and again, more and more, the body of Christ. For Zizioulas, the gathered assembly around the table is the *eikon* of the "kingdom in its glory made visible." Each time we speak about eucharist in the context of a community's life, we intend this dynamic and inclusive meaning.

Zizioulas is concerned to see the eucharist not as a distraction from history, something that takes us out of time, but rather as that which brings about the sanctification of time and history. In Zizioulas' sustained study of the early church he saw that the bishops of this period, pastoral theologians such as Ignatius of Antioch and above all Ireneaus and later

Athanasius, approached the being of God through their experience of the church community, of ecclesial being. This experience revealed something very important: the being of God could be known only through personal relationships and personal love. Being means life and life means communion.

THE "SIMULTANEITY" OF THE ONE AND THE MANY

It is difficult to convey the full import of Zizioulas' anti-individualistic interpretation of life without referring again and again to its paradigmatic enactment in the eucharist. It is the eucharist that the church must offer the modern person "who lives everyday under the weight of the opposition between the individual and the collectivity, and whose social life is not communion but societas" (1985, 88–89). In the liturgy, one is not subordinated to the many, nor the many to the one; the one and the many are simultaneous. This concept of simultaneity was reiterated in the program of DeLubac, Congar, and Rahner. So central is it to Zizioulas, that we clarify it as a pattern of unity here. He makes his case by interpreting how the human person is uniquely one and differentiated and at the same time, one's very particularity embodies that which constitutes the many. In other words the whole of who humankind is (its nature), is instantiated in each unique person. His argument is as follows.

To see someone as a person is to see in her/him the whole of human nature (1985, 106). Human nature is not some vague resemblance that members of a species universally have to one another. In the Cappadocian fathers, Zizioulas found the key for understanding personhood. There he made the assertion that nothing exists in a naked state, without some *hypostasis* or "mode of being." These technical Greek philosophical terms are translated by Zizioulas into a key assertion of the necessary communality of human beings. For Zizioulas, these Cappadocian terms mean that human nature exists, therefore, as a universal term, only because there are some particular human beings, who exist only as these particular human beings. There is no such thing as abstract humanity. Humanity is always a specific group of particular human beings. Likewise, Zizioulas understands the Cappadocian insight into the divine nature in much the same way. The triune God, Father, Son, and Holy Spirit make possible the existence of a divine nature only because they exist as this relationship of three persons, each of whom in freedom and love bears the whole divine nature. What takes place spontaneously in the very life of God, this freedom and love to embrace and express the dynamic oneness/wholeness of the Divinity, must be willed by each human person in freedom and love. To live this decision of dynamic oneness/wholeness without losing particularity or diversity is Zizioulas' explanation of "catholicity." For him, catholicity and communion are interchangeable as the Spirit's gift and the mission entrusted to the church. He seeks to bring all into oneness, make communion happen in history, live as one community in God.

LIFE IS COMMUNION

Zizioulas believes that several centuries later Maximus the Confessor took this important thesis of the Cappadocians and developed it in his understanding that "the catholicity (wholeness) of the church is to be found in each member personally." So that, each member can genuinely claim that "I am in the church and the church is in me." The thought that underlay this teaching of Maximus is that "in the Spirit, the very structure of the church becomes the existential structure of each person." Now the structure of the church is communion. This is what the Spirit makes of the church. Relationship is the very fabric of the church's existence. Every person, born of the Spirit, is likewise constituted by and for communion. Each is created as person-in-relation, as being-for-others. Nothing exists in isolation from anything else, or as Maximus declared in the seventh century, "Every human person is a microcosm of the universe" (Thunberg, 74).

To be a member of the church is to bear within oneself the life of the whole. The baptized person lives now no longer for himself but in and for the whole body of Christ. Zizioulas explains this baptismal change in ontological terms, in other words, as a change in one's very being. The individual exists no longer in isolation but as a person in relationship, a relationship to the whole and to each of its parts.[1] This relationship or life in communion is realized again and again in the eucharistic liturgy and lived out in "the liturgy after the liturgy," an Orthodox expression for the daily enactment of one's eucharistic life. This gift enables us to live in communion with others and all creation in such a way that we give and receive life from one another and become authentic persons in communion. For Zizioulas, life is communion.

THE GOD OF LIFE IS COMMUNION

Little of John Zizioulas' conviction about the centrality of communion as the fundamental character of all life would be possible without his even deeper faith in a God of Life who is communion. Zizioulas never tires of saying something about the nature of this God as he interprets it in the Cappadocian fathers. It is from these patristic thinkers that articulation of Christian faith in a trinitarian God comes.

Central to this doctrine of the Trinity is the understanding of relation or person as the primary mode of God's Being, which allowed the Cappadocians to speak of the unique personal identity and distinction within God "without postulating a difference in substance between the Divine Persons" (Mowry-La Cugna, 243). For Basil of Caesarea, Gregory of Nyssa, and Gregory of Nazianzus, personhood was not an addition to the nature of God. It is how God exists. If God were not personal, God would not exist at all (244). God's very being originates in love, *ekstasis*, self-gift, and fecundity.

The Cappadocians departed from the dominant Greek cosmology of their day that thought of God as creating the world out of necessity. By predicating personhood rather than substance as the ultimate principle, they were able to talk about a world created by a personal God in freedom and love. Because the Greek fathers made relationality coefficient with existence itself, it becomes difficult to speak about any existence in and of itself, especially the existence of God. This God, whom Christians have come to know in Jesus Christ and through the Spirit is One God, distinct in three persons, but undivided in unity. This being from another and for another constitutes genuine personhood and was made incarnate love in Jesus Christ. The Johannine gospel portrays Jesus as God's anointed, the Christ, who has come from God (being from another) and who lives "for others" ("My body . . . for you."). The heart of Christian theology, as John Zizioulas reads it in his early Greek sources, is this life in relationship; it is communion. Simply put: we have come from communion and are destined for communion. In the meantime, we are saved by and for one another.

Chapter Six

Social Philosophers as Conversation Partners about Community

For many of us living in North America today, the individual provides the cultural starting point for any idea of community that subsequently develops. This cultural code, lauding the triumph of the "rugged individual," has been among us as a nation from our beginnings. A spirit of individualism has so permeated the American psyche that it serves as a two-edged sword cutting into our self-understanding, leaving many of us with ambiguous feelings of both attraction and resistance to the idea of community.

This chapter will shift our focus a bit from theological perspectives on community to a focus on the topic through theories provided by two social philosophers—Josiah Royce and Bernard Lonergan who help make the idea more exact. Both of these thinkers lay out what they see as basic components of community so that the term *community* is not used to refer to simply any group arrangement. By introducing the theory of community developed by Royce and another sketched by Lonergan, we will have some tools available to critique the quality of community life operative in our concrete social situations. This, in turn, will allow us to envision a design for life together using these criteria as guideposts for the constructive work ahead.

Josiah Royce's Theory of Community

From his earliest roots in Grass Valley, California, to his endowed chair of philosophy at Harvard University, Josiah Royce used the experiences of his life to deepen the convictions that ripened into a fully developed philosophy of community. Born in 1855 in a small mining town of the Sierras, Royce graduated from the University of California in 1875. After studying

German idealism (Kant and Hegel) in Leipzig and Gottingen, Royce returned to complete his doctoral studies at Johns Hopkins University in Baltimore in 1878. While teaching English back in California (1878–82), Royce became increasingly aware of his need for a philosophical community to test his ideas. He wrote to his future colleague at Harvard, William James, of his feelings of "being in this wilderness with nobody to talk about it."[1] James arranged for Royce's appointment at Harvard as Instructor in Philosophy in 1882, where he was ultimately appointed Alford Professor of Philosophy, a post he held until his death in 1916. Though deeply immersed in academic life, Royce's thoughts reach down into the depths of human life—into the most practical social, religious, and ethical concerns of his day.

Throughout the early years of the twentieth century, Royce believed that good thinking was needed to help "lost and isolated individuals" live "for some cause that binds many lives as one" (Clendenning, 347–48). Through intense philosophical study and sustained reflection on his own religious experience, Royce was convinced that the vision of Christianity, particularly as it was articulated in the genius of Saint Paul, held the key for rescuing individuals of his day from the moral burden of their lostness.

Almost a century later as we reflect on the crisis of community facing twenty-first century North Americans, we too are looking to the churches for a leadership role in helping us overcome the dehumanizing isolationism that threatens the American experiment. Our goal in introducing the work of the American social philosopher Josiah Royce is two-fold: First, we believe that his responses to the religious and ethical questions he investigated provide us with criteria for formulating a practical notion of community. Second, we look to his theoretical analysis of community for a structure to aid in the constructive work to be undertaken in our own day if genuine life in community is to have a chance.

Toward a Practical Notion of Community

In his study of the Christian doctrine of life, Royce found that the early Christian churches had from the beginning incorporated into their understanding of Jesus' vision of the "kingdom of God" some idea of community. The form the vision took in each age depended upon its being fashioned anew. Royce believed that the gap between the vision of Christianity and its concrete expression constituted Christianity's "problem." As a social scientist, the concept of problem suggested an opportunity for creative resolution and he understood this challenge as the one faced by the churches at each period of its history.

Royce grounded his understanding of human persons in their need for membership in the universal community in order to attain their life's goal. Royce used this root metaphor of "universal community" to encompass the source and goal of human desiring. He found in his reading of the early Pauline communities a vision that responded to this core universal longing. In Royce's estimation, the vision of Jesus, which placed love of God and love of neighbor side by side, needed time to mature and disclose itself. Its next mediation came through the power of Christ's Spirit working in the community. He claimed that the apostle Paul, fully aware of his dependence on the Spirit's presence, interpreted the next phase of the Christian doctrine of love. What Paul did was crucial to the practicality of the Christian idea. Through Paul's interpretation of love of God and love of neighbor, a "new third being" was introduced into Christian self-understanding. This new being seemed novel in its type even to Paul, who called it a "mystery" (91).

To express the mystery, Paul used metaphors that have become classic, with the powerful symbol of the "body of Christ" becoming a paradigm for early Christian communities' self-understanding. Royce contended that it was genius to conceive of the "body of Christ" as a corporate entity. This new corporate entity did not make love more abstract but rather insistently clearer. The community was the body of Christ that one was to love. Daily life was bound up with the Spirit of its crucified and risen Lord but it had a practical concreteness and common sense about it. The Christian community existed as a fact of human experience and as a divine creation. "In Christ's love for the Church, Paul found proof that both the community and each individual member were the object of infinite concern which glorifies and unites them both" (95). Royce called one's love for the community "loyalty" and defined it as "a thorough, practical, loving devotion of a self for a united community" (109).

This Pauline community was for Royce a genuine, universal community because its embrace included the whole world. In Paul's vision everyone was a member of this community or was intended to be. The idea of a universal community, understood as the "body of Christ," represented for Royce the first essential element in Christianity. Its psychological basis lay in the social nature of humankind and met the genuine human need of every individual for a saving community. Its ethical challenge was concrete; one was called to love not only every unique individual but also the community that was also a person, the body of Christ. This raised human love to a new level.

In addressing the reasons why the idea of community had not been more fully realized in human history thus far, Royce coined the phrase "the moral burden of the individual" to describe just how far persons were weighed down in their individual efforts to attain the goal of life. Royce's theory of the "lost individual" explained the incapacity of the unaided person to save her/himself. Looking at the concrete situations of his own day, Royce pointed to the conflicts between individualism and collectivism that were breeding moral unrest and discontent within people. The modern, advanced, industrialized culture of the early twentieth century spoke of personal, moral independence as if it were a spiritual ideal. This social training was responsible for creating the moral individualist, self-reliant and independent, a "divided self" who submitted externally to the social will while rebelling inwardly.

The remedy Royce saw for this warfare between the individual and collective wills was the "voluntary devotion of the fully conscious individual to the cause of the community" (156). So different was this from the pressures of social compliance that Royce saw it as a new level of living. It involved a new type of self-consciousness, the conscious decision of one who "loves the community as a person." Only the miracle of love, not social training, created this new type of self-consciousness, one capable of devotion to the community.

The reality of community was for Royce beyond the natural; its membership was human but its source was divine. The initiative for participating in this level of life needed to come from the spirit of a saving community. In his efforts to ground this position in human experience, he began by admitting the incapacity of human reason to prove how this happened, even though reason could not deny that it did happen. Royce pointed to actual human beings, who responded to movements within them that came from a power greater than themselves, which enabled them to give themselves to the cause of a saving community. This real, but irrational condition, Royce called the "realm of grace" and he named the universal community in the realm of grace the "beloved community." Its members had responded to God's initiative and had given themselves freely to the love of the community and its individual members.

Royce insisted that if individuals only loved individuals, however ideal or devoted their love might be, both their morality and their religion would be limited. Divine grace alone awakened the individual to the love of a community and made the community itself lovable. "We cannot choose to fall thus in love," Royce claimed, "but once thus in love we choose to remain lovers" (129). This undeserved but practical gift of being able to make a total and concrete dedication of oneself to a genuine community served two practical needs for the human person. First, it helped the individual, as a divided self, to reconcile its own internal conflicts by showing it a higher value to which one could freely give oneself. Second, the genuine community was able to reconcile individual members with one another and with the whole body, bringing about a level of harmony that would not be possible without it. A community, composed of particular individual members, was genuine only if it opened itself to the universal community and actively dedicated itself to its realization.

This level of community, achievable only within the realm of grace, was made possible only by the "atoning deed." Atonement, or bringing the lost home into community, was so central to Royce's concept of the universal community that he was convinced that "if there were no Christians in the world someone would have to invent the idea of atonement" (165). In Royce's construction of the atoning deed, his goal was to root this Christian idea in human experience by showing that life revealed those suffering servants of the universal community who were willing to be wounded for its sake. Expressed in human terms, the human community depended on its human lovers; in terms of Christian faith, the power of such lovers came from the spirit of their crucified and risen Savior.

At the heart of Royce's philosophical project was his conviction of hope. Through the atoning deed, the world would triumph even from the worst of its tragedies. Royce suffered intensely throughout World War I from his experience of the fractured human community. The reality of the broken and sinful human condition disclosed to Royce the gravest of insights. The idea of a universal community required the corresponding idea of atonement. Every act of betrayal, every sin was a social act. It broke the bond of unity. As sin stood in the way of the human ideal, so must the human under the impulse of grace create the atoning deed and form communities that could arouse love, strong enough to join the world as one.

As Josiah Royce investigated the Christian idea for its doctrine of life, he determined that religious and ethical values were both distinguished and integrated. The religious idea brought the human person into graced union with the supreme value of life in the universal community. The ethical idea counseled the individual to each day's duty in the genuine community of its members. Royce interpreted Jesus' message about the kingdom to be essentially this:

> So act that the kingdom of heaven might come. So act, so as to help, however you can, towards making humankind one loving brotherhood . . . Use whatever human material you have for creating both the organization of communities and the love of them (199).

Grounded in the Christian understanding of life as Royce understood it, his practical notion of community yields three substantive criteria: 1) A community is genuine only if it is open to actively working for the unity of all persons; 2) In genuine communities, persons are committed in love to each member and devoted through loyalty to the cause of the community; 3) Because of the sinful human condition, a genuine community seeks to discern and accomplish the specific "atoning deeds" that alone will triumph over the tragedy of betrayal that has broken the community.

Royce saw two obstacles preventing the church from achieving genuine community. The first was the danger of sectarianism and the second was an official organization that promoted laws at the expense of the spirit. A church aspiring to be "true" must always be on guard against both dangers. Woven within Royce's thesis on the practical notion of community, love and loyalty, the individual and the community, and the human and the divine are inextricably bound. They have evidenced their effects in human history in the past. They offer guidance and practical content to shape the present. These "sacred pairs" continue to respond to our deepest ethical needs and our highest religious aspirations. But only within genuine communities can their meaning be intelligible and their distinction and unity realized.

Royce's Theoretical Analysis of Community

The further question that impelled Josiah Royce beyond a practical notion of community that responded to core human needs may need some revised articulation today. It concerned his desire to satisfy not only the human search for the good and the valuable but also for the true. And so he asked if the dynamic of community corresponded to any authentic pattern in the larger world. Royce believed that if the notion of community served more than basic human needs, it needed to point toward what was most lasting and largest in the universe. As an early twentieth-century philosopher, he was searching for a metaphysical basis for his central ideas. If the structure of community was true, it would prove to be a doctrine about the being, nature, and manifestations of God. Royce was seeking the clearest human-size view of the vastness of the universe and of the divine being.

By 1912, Royce discovered in a careful rereading of "the theory of signs," proposed by Charles Peirce, a foundation for his epistemology that now made it possible for him to probe the metaphysical character of community. Peirce contended that all comparisons required a "mediating representation" since the relationship between two terms could only be known through the introduction of a third that functioned as an interpreter.

Working from Peirce's theory and adapting it to the human situation, Royce masterfully conceived his theoretical understanding of community. From it, three salient elucidations will serve as generative principles to direct us in our work ahead. They are as follows:

1. his clarification of the problem of "the one and the many";

2. the relationship between the "community and the time process"; and

3. the synthesis provided by a "community of interpretation."

The One and the Many. Royce engaged the perennial philosophical problem of the one and the many head-on. For the purpose of our study, it will suffice to locate the core of this philosophical problem in the question of priority. Which entity, the one or the many, came first as the original design of the universe and as its goal? This question was argued in the philosophical schools of Plato where the One gained precedence and in Aristotelian thought where "the many" took priority over "the one." As Royce studied the dilemma, he concluded that simultaneity was a solution, and its paradigm was community. With a conclusion identical to John Zizioulas, but out of an entirely different frame of reference, Royce set out to establish community as the foundational category of all life and thought. Community presented itself in his theory precisely as "the one and the many." Unless it was, at the same time, both, it was not a community. Each dimension was distinct and could be looked at and valued separately but they could not be kept apart. The relationship that existed between the two was not dyadic or antithetical. To understand this, one needed to undergo a "paradigm shift." The move was from a one-level vision that saw individuals as the ultimate reality, to a new view with two levels of reality. With the two-level vision of reality, the individual and the community were mutually co-ultimate. The crux of Royce's teaching lay in one's grasp of this relational distinction. One could not understand what community was or meant if one took as a model the relationship between one individual and another. The individual and the community were related but distinct entities. The distinctiveness of each needed to be demonstrated.

Royce began with the individual and chose three common sense experiences to illustrate the individuality of the human self. In summary, his three examples are as follows:

1. The experience of human pain: One's pain was uniquely one's own. Try as another might to identify or feel the pain of another, it could not be fully known to anyone else.

2. The organized human idea: An idea belonged to its thinker. No one can read exactly the mind of another. One's thoughts remained one's unique secret, inaccessible by any direct intuition.

3. The deeds one does with one's life: One's doing of one's own deeds determines ultimately one's individuality. No other person can "do my deed for me"(238).

Royce was convinced that in his day the root of social sin lay in this third fact taken to the extreme. It led to the substitution of a partial truth about the human person for a fuller truth. It constituted, for Royce, the autonomous individual who lived by the maxim "I am responsible for myself" with no sense of the community from whom he had come or on whom he depended (240).

These common sense experiences of the human person point to the radical uniqueness of the individual self. They contain essential truths about the human condition. But these facts alone did not provide the whole truth about the human, Royce contested. Other facts suggest that these many separate selves were in some ways "one." He pointed out that a "larger self with a mind of its own must somehow come to be" since language, as an example, could not be attributed to any one mind. Yet, language was a mental product possessing intelligent unity. Individuals did not create language; a people did. Language, religion, and customs were demonstrations of a community self.

Royce next proposed three conditions that needed to be present in the life of an individual self to allow a community self to be compounded. He explained these:

1) An individual self must have the power to extend his life in an ideal fashion to include past and future events, which lie far away in time and which he does not personally remember.

2) There must exist in the social order a number of distinct selves capable of and engaged in social communication.

3) The ideally extended past and future selves of individuals must include at least some events that are for these selves, engaged in communication, identical.

Given these conditions, how then did many selves begin to understand themselves as a larger self? The full meaning of Royce's theory of community hinged on one's grasp of its crucial relationship with what he called "the time-process." This time-process provided the formal structures for the community self to develop (229–49).

The Community and the Time-Process. Genuine community was essentially a product of the time-process. This rule, that time was needed for the formation of a conscious community, found its validation in the formation of an individual human self. The self held only a fragment of its life in the present. The self came from its past. It both needed and was a history. Memory linked the self, its past to its present. For example, my idea of myself is an interpretation of my past, linked also with my interpreted hopes and intentions for the future. The self is in its essence an interpretation.

At the second level of human life, the idea of community presupposes that there are many selves who come together under these conditions:

> Let these many selves be able to look beyond their present chaos of fleeting ideas and warring desires far away into the distant past from which they came and into the future where their hopes lead them. Let each, on looking, enlarge his own individual life, extending himself into the past and future, so as to say of some far off event—I view that event as part of my own life, or for that coming event, I wait in hope for that as an event of my own future. Let these various extensions include one common event so that each self regards the same event as part of his own life and with that reference point those individual selves constitute a community (256).

A community of memory is thereby constituted by the fact that each of its members accepts as part of his individual life and self the same past events that each of his fellow members accepts. To accept the same future events as each of one's fellow members accepts is to be "a community of expectation." In the realm of grace, Royce called this "a community of hope" (252). This basic structure provided the abstract form into which life poured its rich contents and ideals. The richness of each community was determined by the vitality and significance, the breadth and depth of its shared memories and hopes. The actual life of a community in history shrank or expanded in virtue of its capacity to extend itself. Memories and hopes incited the human to the expansion of the self. In fact, the ideally extended self and not the momentary self constituted the self whose life was worth living, whose values lasted and whose destiny was worthy of the interests of beings who were above the level of mere individuals (252).

But for a community to be real, one more condition needed to be present. It was not sufficient that a community shared a common memory or hope since real community was a living being. It must attempt to accomplish something in time through the deeds of its members. These deeds belonged to the life that each member claimed as one's own present. In this way, the real and the ideal came together in a community of unique individuals. For a particular deed done by one of the members to be regarded as a "community deed" it must be fully embraced by each other member.

A community was real and concrete in history to the extent that it lived in relation to the whole time-process: past, future, and present. This integration enabled each member to say: "This is my community. Its past is my past and its future holds my hope. Its present deeds are my life writ large" (263).

Royce contended that no "real community" in human history realized more powerfully or effectively the presence of these conditions than the "idea" of the Christian community. In the "body of Christ" that the early church believed itself to be, what happened to one member of the community in the present was shared by all. In the ideal memory of Christ's death and resurrection, each Christian proclaimed "That event is my salvation and that triumph is my hope of future glory." The "Christ event" funded the community's hope and memory of a great common future.

This central Christian idea clarified the distinction and the connection between individual salvation and human solidarity. Both individual and community were bound together in the divine life of the Spirit. For Josiah Royce, this divine presence continues to find concrete expression "in the effectively united common life" (259). This spirit in the community makes possible a coherent plan of life that sustains a consciousness of unity amid the "monotony, friction and chaos" that would otherwise cause individuals to forget. Genuine communities have a common life, are aware of it, choose it, and understand themselves to be constituted by it.

The Meaning and Significance of Loyalty. As society became more and more complex and pluralistic, Royce envisioned that achieving this level of a community's self-awareness would become increasingly difficult. The greater the diversity of deeds done by individual members of the community, the harder it becomes for other members of the community to see and understand these deeds as constituting the very life they share as one. Royce maintained that the only solution to this greater complexity and obscurity was the gift of greater love. Royce agreed that this sounded "mystical but it was no mere emotion" (269). This conscious love for community and its individual members was an interpretation, a decision, which had for its object the common deeds of the community. Loyalty, as love for the unity of the community, did not melt away the many selves but effected the co-operative doing of deeds, which the spirit of loyalty both inspired and accomplished.

Royce insisted that this virtue was neither vague nor ambiguous, mere sentimentality nor an uncritical attitude. Loyalty was a thorough and passionate commitment to the cause of the universal community. One could evaluate all one's choices and actions by the criterion of whether or not they promoted the coming to be of the universal community. Any choice that fostered alienation, isolation, or disunity was disloyal. The cause of unity was served only by the individual, concrete commitments of the life of each loyal person. The kinship of loyal persons for each other bonded the loyal community and kept alive that great hope for the coming of the universal community.

A Community of Interpretation. With Royce's breakthrough insight of 1912 into Charles Peirce's theory of signs, Royce believed that he had found at last a framework on which to construct the category of community as the foundation of all reality. It is important to understand the terms used in Peirce's theory and Royce's application of them to the human situation so that we, in turn, will be able to make further applications to the needs of our day (273–95).

The life of a community depends on the way members interpret themselves to one another. Both the self and the community self are a life whose unity and connectedness depended upon some sort of interpretation of its plans, memories, hopes, and deeds. What then is interpretation? In Royce's application of Peirce, he determined that all interpretation involved:

1. A sign-sender—the object to be interpreted. It calls out "Interpret me."

2. A sign-receiver—the one addressed in the interpretation. It asks "What does this mean to me?"

3. A sign-interpreter—the one doing the interpretation. It says "Let me mediate between these two signs."

The introduction of this crucial "third term" changes the whole structure of human knowing. It creates the space where the genuine work of interpretation takes place. In every social experience, comparisons arise and one sets out to compare A and B. The comparison happens in a deeper sense when one asks "how" A is similar to or different from B. Likenesses or differences are simply signs that interpretation is needed but the signs cannot interpret themselves. They require introducing the mediating third term, the interpreter. This structural need for a mediating third term creates a "community of interpretation." So critical is this opening to a third term that it alone prevents these two distinct ideas from falling into decline, if left on their own, or melting into one another, if simply fused.

In the life of the human community, the free space for interpretation makes all the difference in the world. Within this world of interpretation, the everyday work of comparing and contrasting often means arbitrating conflicts, bringing into mutual understanding two "minds" in estrangement. A third "mind" distinct from the other two must be found, one who can introduce a "third idea," one that mediates between them and illuminates one to the other. In this triadic process, the interpreter remains always the most significant member. Her "will to interpret" focuses on the goal of achieving "final unity." The interpreter's role is first of all to be a servant, whose own ideas work only in self-surrender to the needs of the sign-sender and the sign-receiver. The interpreter desires to so conform to the mind of the sign-sender and to the comprehension of the sign-receiver that he can mediate the truth of the one to the other in such a way that it approaches the goal of unity (314–17).

Royce applied this theory of a "community of interpretation" inward to the work of self-interpretation and outward to social reality. Reflection, like all interpretation, is primarily a conversation. One needs to connect ideas of the self that come only in fragments. Interpretation aids a person to achieve new levels of self-possession, inner coherence, and unity. Its full significance is realized in its religious and ethical applications. Royce was convinced that "In our present day social groupings, common goals are seldom present to the minds of members. No one can love humankind in a worthier way than to express such love by increasing and expressing among us the 'will to interpret'" (318). In the full application of this theory of interpretation, Royce stretched it to conceive of God as a community of interpretation. Above all, he came to think of God in the form of the Interpreter who interpreted all to all and each individual to the world and the world of the spirit to each individual.

Royce concluded that all life existed in a "world of interpretation." The "real world," whether theoretical, religious, ethical, individual, or social was a situation of contrasts, where antitheses multiplied between the actual and the ideal, sin and grace, one's limits and one's hopes, good and evil. The "real world" was simply the response one gave to what this contrast was and meant. As Royce assessed a "true interpretation" in this, our problematic situation, he never suggested that one reached a definitive human interpretation. He insisted that the infinite nature of interpretation demanded that one be engaged in an infinite series of distinct interpretations. The adequacy of any single interpretation was conditioned by the willingness to engage the process of ongoing interpretation. A true interpretation was one that produced a community of deeds that have proven to be good (362).

The world of interpretation needs a community as its defining structure. Royce proposed it as the only "right attitude" with which to stand before the universe or to present oneself to the world. If one accepted such a view as God's design of a universal community, as the absolute, essential order of the universe and of social reality, how then should one face the problems of everyday life? Royce explained his conviction in terms of faith: "The believer, to whom every sign presented itself in need of interpretation, in whose belief, the world contained its own 'Interpreter'—such a believer both contemplates and shares in the world drama" (351).

This response of contemplation and action characterized the life of a believer and of a believing community. Such a faith stance before the world was ultimately, in Royce's opinion, an "attitude of the will" and one that was characterized neither by a desire to affirm oneself nor by a desire to deny oneself, but by a spirit of genuine loyalty. This attitude of the will fittingly accompanied Royce's idea of a universal community of interpretation. In this attitude of loyalty, the intimate connections between theory and practice were clearly pronounced. Loyalty was neither simply an affirmation of the self nor a denial of it. Loyalty was the disposition to imagine, and the practicality to acknowledge as real, the spiritual realm of a divine and universal community. In this world alone, the human person found salvation. Royce summed up his life's work with this thesis on community:

I cannot be saved alone. I cannot find or even define the truth of my individual experience without a community of interpretation. My knowledge of myself is based on knowledge derived from the community to which I belong. Community is real if anything at all is real. . . Whatever else the "Beloved Community" will be when it comes, it will be a community of interpretation (357).

A Roycean Interpretation of the Role of the Churches

Royce's understanding of the "Christian idea" teaches us the intensely practical lesson of seeing God in the form of community not as some distant scene. He saw Jesus' promise to be with us always as that spirit who interpreted the antitheses of the present. This antithesis makes available a reconciling mediator who sought the wider view. According to Royce, the victory that continually overcomes the world is the interpretation that reconciles. For the church to be faithful to its mission, it must become as genuinely catholic—that is, universal—as the spirit of loyalty requires. But Royce insisted that the church must also persevere in its interpretive work for the sake of the world, trusting in the ongoing presence of the Spirit-Interpreter at work in the community. This alone will permit the church to become inventive of new social arts, a need, in Royce's opinion, as great as those that have occasioned so many breakthroughs in the natural sciences. Josiah Royce affirmed the potential and responsibility of the churches to be about the "inventive social art" of designing concrete, genuine communities in the hope of the coming of the universal community. In light of his affirmation, we propose four challenges to the churches. Two of these challenges address the internal life of the churches and two apply to their mission in the world.

1. **We ask the churches to place a priority on the pastoral work of community formation.** Royce is clear that the church's end is community and its means are communities. Its goal, in and through the divine community, requires the church to be about the formation and development of concrete, historical communities that are genuinely and distinctively Christian in their practical demonstration of the good and their theoretical commitment to the true. Each community becomes, therefore, a concrete and particular embodiment of the three essential elements of the Christian idea. It demonstrates 1) loyalty to the universal community, 2) concern for the moral burden of the lost individual, and 3) commitment to the doing of the atoning deed.

In its commitment to community formation, the church can benefit from Royce's understanding of community's relationship to the time-process. Each concrete community needs to appreciate the significance of those defining moments in which shared memories of their past and hopes for their future are interpreted through the community's shared rituals and deeds in the present. In and through these shared rituals and deeds, the community is constituted. In its commitment to remembering, the community opens itself to self-critique in light of the Christian tradition. At the same time, it opens the tradition to ongoing critique in light of new questions that contemporary needs bring to it. In this mutual interaction, God's ongoing revelation to the community is manifested

2. **We ask the churches to grow as genuine "communities of interpretation."** The church's task of self-interpretation engages it in the ongoing work of comparing and evaluating ideas, roles, patterns of relating. Royce offers the church a method of interpretation that is triadic. All interpretations will require the careful determination of a mediating third term. This conscious awareness of a needed interpreter avoids divisive polarities and helps achieve the unity of the wider view.

Since no genuine interpretation can take place in a dyadic conception of reality, the church needs to consider how to interpret again and again, in light of a spirit-interpreter, relationships between the individual and the community, local church and church universal, women and men, working class and professionals, progressives and conservatives, blacks and whites, straight and gay, youth and their parents, the community and the institution, laity and clergy, worship and social justice.

What the church needs most in its work of interpretation in these increasingly complex and pluralistic times is more "genuine interpreters." Royce describes them as sincere and truth loving, led by the "will to interpret" with the single goal of unity as their objective. Every particular act of interpretation intends, but never fully achieves this goal of final unity. A commitment to find the larger whole that unites rather than divides, dismisses, or dissolves one partner in the relational life of the church is the ongoing challenge offered by Royce's theory of a community of interpretation.

Finally, each community must assume the task of interpreting individual members to each other, to the community itself and to other concrete communities in an ever-expanding vision of the universal community that is its goal. To take this process seriously, the church will need to facilitate the growth of communities where face to face encounters make genuine interpretation both possible and actual. Such specific tasks suggest that communities be understood by the church more as "corporate entities," with definable characteristics that distinguish them from any other group or social unit. With "a heart and mind of their own," communities remain inexhaustible mysteries, as incomprehensible as any human self, but nonetheless real and therefore demanding of ongoing interpretation in ever more authentic and coherent ways. Royce challenges the church to see the human constitution of concrete communities as the living embodiment of the divine community thus far achieved in history.

3. **We ask the churches to engage in genuine dialogue with a host of world partners** out of Royce's spirit of loyalty and the "will to interpret." Royce's understanding of the "community of interpretation" provides rich and fruitful insights as the church assumes its responsibility for ongoing dialogue with critical partners in the world today. The church needs to consider carefully how to present itself in dialogue with various and diverse cultures, with diverse faith communities, with the political systems that define our global reality in light of specific recommendations from Royce. As a mediating presence in the world, the church's commitment is to seek the truth with a vision that keeps ever before it the goal of unity and the coming to be of the universal community. This ideal of unity, as it is espoused by Royce does not imply easy solutions to irresolvable differences. His insistence on evaluating, weighing, pondering . . . aims at the most adequate interpretation possible at the time, seeking ever further achievement through the ongoing nature of the process of interpretation.

4. **We ask the churches to discern ministries of reconciliation and their commitment to "the atoning deed."** As churches assume greater responsibility for their role in promoting and nurturing genuine communities, Royce's understanding of communities of memory and hope will be enriched by those communities that commit themselves in the present to the doing of "atoning deeds." As particular deeds responding to specific wrongs, "atoning deeds" will need to be discerned by communities as their commitment to

overcome divisions and injustices, not with words or good intentions, but by those particular acts or changes that will mend the broken community, from the local to the universal level. In these communities, the church will come to realize its one universal mission through a plurality of expressions lived out in local churches.

Josiah Royce lived and served his community as a social philosopher. As he reiterated from time to time, he did not understand himself as a theologian, one professionally competent to say something about the divine or to pay attention to where the divine shows up in history. However, in his careful study of the human situation, he ended up with this to say: "If anything in the human situation is capable of manifesting the divine, it is genuine, visible communities and those who love them. The divine is seen here if the divine be seen anywhere at all" (98).

BERNARD LONERGAN'S DYNAMIC UNDERSTANDING OF COMMUNITY

Bernard Lonergan, a theologian as well as a philosopher, explicitly acknowledged, in direct contrast to Josiah Royce, that he would not be able to say anything about the human without simultaneously saying something about the divine. For Lonergan, the question of God "arises out of the very experience of the basic and primordial human drive toward truth, meaning and value" (1992, 2). God is at the source of the question that the human person is. For him, that primordial, inherent, human desire, impossible to deny, needs communities of meaning, truth, and value to accompany, direct, and respond to this fundamental human longing. It is to Bernard Lonergan's philosophical and theological contribution to our understanding of community over the course of his scholarly career that we turn now.

Born in Buckingham, Quebec, Canada, in 1904, Bernard Lonergan was ordained a Jesuit priest in 1936. Most of his research and teaching took place in Rome at the Gregorian University and in Canada, at Regis College in Toronto. He died in Pickering, Ontario, in 1984. Though Lonergan's two major works over his long career may seem few in number, they are massive. His first masterpiece, *Insight*, published in 1957, is a study in human understanding. His second, *Method in Theology*, is concerned, among other things, with theology's need to take history seriously.

As a methodologist, Lonergan was less interested in questions of "what humans know" and more with "how they know." Lonergan believed that human consciousness was structured by recurrent patterns. Amid the diversity and pluralism of contemporary thinking, these recurrent patterns provide a normative, transcultural framework for understanding human understanding. In Lonergan's unrelenting investigation of cognition, he asserted that all human knowing is a group enterprise. Very little of what humans know is self-generated. Knowledge comes from community and is destined to serve community.

In our efforts to clarify and distinguish community from other kinds of group arrangements, Lonergan offers a way and a caution. He helps us to conceive of community as a social process, an achievement toward which we aspire (a heuristic pattern) rather than a static concept that exists in time and space. Since his basic theory of community derives from his primary elaboration of the four levels of human consciousness, we will begin there. If one understands the concept of group consciousness in Royce's terms of the larger or expanded self, one is ready to appreciate Lonergan's process. Core dimensions of Lonergan's thought that we will develop for our study include:

1. A presentation of his process (heuristic structure) for achieving community;

2. His explanation of the "dialectics of community";

3. The differentiations of conversion critical to authentic life in community and for community's authentic life in the wider world;

4. Four kinds of "bias" that threaten communities;

5. The work of creativity and healing in human history.

The Process of Community

Bernard Lonergan reflected on the shift that occurred when a classicist culture, one that assumed that life was static and that there existed but one way to live authentically over time, gave way to a historical-mindedness. An historical-mindedness realizes that there are many ways of achieving human authenticity, depending on changing social and cultural influences across time. Such is the dramatic change that Lonergan uses to denote the rise of modernity. Though this might be taken for granted in a common sense way by most twentieth century societies, vestiges of classicism still persist. As Lonergan thought about human understanding, he concluded that the empirical data, accounting for *what* humankind makes of history, is always changing. But, Lonergan determined, there exists a recurring pattern within all human consciousness that provides a universal norm for *how* human persons make history and constitute themselves. Lonergan explained this pattern as a "transcendental method" that takes place at four levels of consciousness. These levels are "successive, related but qualitatively different" (1972, 9).

These four levels can be denoted with a primary operation that takes place in each: experiencing, understanding, judging, deciding. Whenever one is not sleepwalking, one is conscious—aware that these operations go on. The goal, however, is to become not only aware but to become more clearly and fully attentive to ourselves as the subjects intending the operations of experiencing, understanding, judging, and deciding. By attending to our experience, we see, feel, perceive, notice, and raise the relevant questions that propel us to want to understand. At the conscious level of understanding the subject must investigate, study, consult, and seek counsel. When no further questions of understanding remain to be resolved, one moves to the level of judging, where one weighs, considers, evaluates, and discerns once again until every relevant question has been satisfied. The issues at stake in this level of judgment concern truth and goodness. When one intentionally seeks the highest good and the truth, one opens to the divine. Once one reaches the clearest judgment one can make, one's knowing must take concrete form in one's actions. At the level of decision, one lives out the fruits of one's attentive experience, intelligent understanding, reasoned judgment, and responsible decision.

Bernard Lonergan is clear from the outset that no human self ever constitutes herself in a vacuum. There exists a "We" prior to any "I" and the process by which one constitutes an authentic self is one achieved only in a community of others. We move now specifically to the constitution of a community, having the tools of Lonergan's transcendental method of human consciousness as the operative framework.

A living community as a historical being, like the human individual, is never static or fully realized. It is dynamic, on the move and as such is a heuristic structure, in need of being discovered or achieved.[2] A community coheres or divides to the extent that common experience, common understanding, common judgments, commitments, and loves cohere or divide. For Lonergan, a community is an achievement of one mind and one heart, recognized as shared meaning. He insists:

A community is not just a number of persons within a geographical frontier. It is an achievement of common meaning and there are kinds and degrees of achievement. Common meaning is potential when there is a common field of experience, and to withdraw from that common field is to get out of touch. Common meaning is formal when there is common understanding, and one withdraws from that common understanding by misunderstanding, by incomprehension, by mutual incomprehension. Common meaning is actual in as much as there are common judgments, areas in which all affirm or deny in the same manner, and one withdraws from that common judgment when one disagrees, when one considers true what others hold false and false what they think true. Common meaning is realized by decisions and choices, especially by permanent dedication, in the love that makes families, in the loyalty that makes states, in the faith that makes religions (1972, 79).

The notion of community develops from Lonergan's logic of individual human consciousness. It is essential that a group not simply have common experiences but that they ask questions about them to seek further understanding, then discern the meanings and values that their common understanding of their common experiences yield. Only then can each person freely and wholeheartedly decide responsibly to embrace common decisions that the group reaches. In those common commitments, the community realizes itself and helps to constitute the world. History is no longer something that objectively happens to them but something that they play a part in making happen.

The Dialectic of Community

Because human persons are responsible for shaping human history, communities have a mission in the world. This outward drive into the world creates in the human and therefore in the societies constructed by them a certain dialectic. Lonergan names these two poles "spontaneous intersubjectivity" and the "good of order." The first pole is the result of the human need to love and be loved and the second comes from the natural intelligence of the human who discovers practical intelligence and a need to provide for the good of order. These poles produce an essential yet radical tension that Lonergan calls the "dialectic of community." He explains it thus: "There is then the radical tension of community. Intersubjective spontaneity and intelligently devised social order possess different properties and different tendencies. Yet to both by his very nature, the human is committed" (1957, 214–15).

When communities experience this tension between their internal group life and an external social task, it is easy to overlook the fact that this dialectic is healthy and the terms of both poles stand in need of negotiation. A Christian community, with a commitment to "the good of order," as a function of the group's practical intelligence, has a significant purpose to serve in human history and in the life of the church. However, the function of practical intelligence, in the life of a Christian community, in particular, is to order and facilitate the human good. Therefore, as Lonergan himself reflected on the distinct roles of both community poles, he gave a certain priority to the intersubjective dimension of human persons that is served in and by the love of a community. Lonergan explains this priority, in what he calls the gift of falling in love.

> For self-transcendence reaches its term not in righteousness but in love, and when we fall in love then life begins anew. A new principle takes over and as long as it lasts we are lifted above ourselves and carried along as parts within a more intimate yet ever more liberating dynamic whole (1985, 175).

This deeper and richer principle that comes to us "from above downward" conditions all we do to develop as human persons. It yields love in the family, loyalty in the community, and faith in God. As a gift, it is something that we cannot give ourselves. We cannot make ourselves fall in love. It is something that happens to us, but something for which, once it happens, we become responsible. This gift-character of loving stands to remind the developing human community of its dependence on God, when its own practical intelligence wants to take full credit for great advances in human progress. Lonergan realized first-hand that ongoing human progress tempts persons and communities "to cast off the shackles from above." But Lonergan would insist that the life of a community is dependent upon the God "whose spirit floods our hearts with love" (Rom. 5:5). He sums up the priority of the Spirit's gift carrying the community along in an essay entitled, "The Mediation of Christ in Prayer":

> Communities become themselves not just by experiences, insights, judgments, by choices and decisions, by conversion, not just freely and deliberately, not just deeply and strongly but as one who is carried along. One becomes oneself not alone but in reference to Christ. We are not our own; we do not belong to ourselves—This is the reality that we are—the higher part of the reality (1984, 16).

Falling in love with God, for Lonergan, is falling in love in an unrestricted fashion. The result of this open-ended loving transforms all understanding and transvalues all valuing, so that the very deeds done by communities for "the good of order" are empowered by a love greater than themselves. At times, this love simply carries them along, enabling communities to live and work for a cause and with a strength greater than the sum total of their individual members.

The Notion of Bias and its Effects on the Life of the Community

One of the reasons Lonergan gives for the frustration of the human project is the universal condition of human subjection to bias. He defines bias as a "block or distortion of intellectual development" that occurs in four principal manners (1972, 231). The first area is the neurotic bias of unconscious motivation that has been brought to light by depth psychology. Next, there is the bias of the individual egoist, whose choices are made for self-serving reasons. An even blinder bias, in Lonergan's opinion, is that of the group egoist, whose blindness for the group allows it to see nothing but the good of one's own exclusive circle as worthwhile. Finally, there is the general bias of common sense, which uses its practical intelligence in the area of the particular and the concrete but considers itself omnicompetent.

Each of these biases affects community. Biased communities persist but they remain inauthentic and imperfect. Though professional help may be needed to help overcome the psychic bias of the neurotic, the egoist goes blindly and unabashedly through her daily rounds, seeking loopholes in social arrangements and manipulating them for her personal advantage. Groups magnify their own importance and provide screens that justify their privileged ways before the judge of public opinion. The dominant cultural group might reasonably be expected to be the one most responsible for the healing and creating of persons and communities in the larger society. The fact that this is not the primary role undertaken by society's dominant group is testimony to the presence and activity of collective or group bias. History languishes under the effects of group biases that cause the rich to grow richer while the poor sink into misery and squalor. Finally, practical people are guided by common sense; everyday responses to the particular and the concrete. The difficulty arises in their being unable or unwilling to see the value of larger movements, the bigger picture, long-term trends. The bias of common sense is unready to sacrifice immediate advantage for the enormously greater good of society in two or three decades. All bias blocks the unfolding of personal and social growth, prevents creativity and social transformation.

The Role of Conversion in and for Community

With recurring echoes of Josiah Royce, Bernard Lonergan notes that "if human progress is not to be ever distorted and destroyed by the inattention, oversight, irrationality and irresponsibility of decline, people have to be reminded of their sinfulness. They have to acknowledge their guilt and . . . learn with humility that the task of repentance and conversion is lifelong" (1972, 117–18). Lonergan does not, however, simply speak about conversion in general terms. He differentiates three particular kinds of conversion—religious, moral, and intellectual—all of which are necessary for human progress.

The healing of human society is dependent upon a healing at the existential level of the human person if social decline is to be interrupted and reversed. Such an interruption requires a radical transformation in the will of the human subject, moving it from an unwillingness to respond to the exigencies of self-transcendence toward a breakthrough that opens the human person to Ultimate Value. This transformation of willingness corresponds to Lonergan's understanding of religious conversion. In Lonergan's own explanation of the role of religious love in bringing about social transformation, religious conversion is a springboard for moral and intellectual conversion to follow.

Religious conversion is the result of "being grasped by ultimate concern." It is falling in love in an unrestricted fashion. It is a permanent and total self-surrender without condition, qualification, reservation. It is revealed in retrospect as an undertow of existential consciousness, as a fated acceptance of a vocation to holiness, bounding in truth and moral goodness but going beyond them with distinct dimensions of its own. "It is other-worldly fulfillment, joy, peace, bliss. In Christian experience, these are the fruits of being in love with a mysterious, uncomprehended God" (1972, 242). Religious conversion, or falling in love in an unrestricted fashion, transforms human consciousness and reorients one toward the entire cosmos. As Lonergan describes it:

> Where hatred reinforces bias, love reveals values, where hatred reinforces bias, love dissolves it, whether it be the bias of unconscious motivation, the bias of individual or group egoism, or the bias of omnicompetent, short-sighted common sense. Where hatred plods around in ever-nar-

row vicious circles, love breaks the bonds of psychological and social determinism with the conviction of faith and the power of hope (Gregson, 56).

Moral conversion changes the criterion of one's decisions and choices from satisfaction to values. It is the result of coming to choose in freedom one's own authenticity in the realization that one's choices affect the self as much as the chosen or rejected object. Moral conversion takes place when a person realizes that it is up to her to decide for herself what she is to make of herself. It consists of opting for the truly good, even for value over personal satisfaction when value and satisfaction conflict. Lonergan reminds us nonetheless that moral conversion falls short of moral perfection. It is one thing to choose the good, it is quite another to do it. It is the doing of it consistently over a lifetime that constitutes the authentically good person.

Intellectual conversion is a radical clarification and consequently the elimination of the myth that human knowing is something like "taking a look." It is more than the sense experience of an individual, what one sees, feels, hears in the world of immediacy. Genuine knowing is not the reality looked at; it is the fruit of faithful commitment to the transcendental process of experiencing, understanding, judging, and deciding. To be liberated from the blunder of believing that one knows what one gleans solely from the realm of experience is to discover the transcendence proper to the human person. It is to become responsible for the making of oneself that takes place when one knows precisely what one is doing when one is knowing. Intellectual conversion for an individual and for a community means sustained reflection on one's experience, a commitment to the arduous task of seeking further understanding, more reasoned judgments, and more responsible commitments. It opens the way for further illumination and transformation.

A fourth kind of conversion, which appears in Lonergan's works only after 1975, is named affective conversion. This "change of heart" or "principle of self-transcendence reaches its term not in righteousness but in love . . . where a new principle takes over carrying persons along in an ever more liberating dynamic whole." Only by growing keener in the awareness and distinctions of one's feelings is one free to deliberate at the level of judgment on what is good, not just for me but what is good for us. Affective conversion sets the stage for the moral rectitude that discerns the truly worthwhile from the merely self-gratifying. This conversion is demonstrated by a commitment to love in the home, loyalty in the community, and faith in human destiny (1985, 1979).[3] The interplay of each of these kinds of conversion in the ongoing process of becoming authentic persons and communities grows ever more intimate and integrated in the concrete drama of human history. Conversion overcomes each of the biases and provides the conditions for the possibility of genuine human and world progress.

Today's crises in personal and social development focus our attention on the need for liberating power. Such liberation is possible within the philosophical system of Bernard Lonergan if and to the extent that every person and community opens itself to life-long conversion. Each crisis will determine the kind of conversion demanded. But genuine religious conversion of the kind that Lonergan describes will always be paramount in a world where hatred looms large and divisions threaten the unity of families, neighborhoods, tribes, and nations. For religious conversion that "promotes self-transcendence to the point, not merely of justice but of self-sacrificing love, will always play a redemptive role in human society in as much as love can undo the mischief of decline and restore the cumulative process of progress" (1972, 55).

COMMUNITIES OF CREATING AND HEALING HUMAN HISTORY

In this book we are not able to deal extensively with the ways communities help society itself emerge as a healing dynamic in human history. We have posited: 1) that community is a basic building block in human wholeness; 2) that community building is a spiritual and theological task as well as a social one; and 3) that America—particularly through its individualist culture—has neglected the central task of community building and maintenance. Our focus must remain on the importance of community, lest this book also fall into the American trap of thinking either too individually or too grandiosely. Chapter 7, however, does deal directly with the intersection of communal and societal issues, demonstrating that the two, though distinct, can never be completely separated.

In treating Lonergan's thought, we must pause briefly to do justice to the connections he makes between community and society. For Lonergan, just as community is fundamental to the emergence of the individual, so are communities the foundation of society. Society today is suffering a crisis of meaning and purpose. The contribution of Bernard Lonergan to the contemporary crisis extends back to his assessment of the social condition of North America more than a quarter of a century ago. Lonergan expressed his conviction that the principles needed to direct our society, which was more and more being run by the decisions of multinational corporations, were totally inadequate. "They suffer," he claimed, "from radical oversights. Their rigorous application on a global scale heads us for disaster" (1975, 103). But the new system needed for our survival does not exist and when survival requires something that does not yet exist, then the need for creating it is necessary.

The creative task is to find the answers to the life-size questions that this generation asks for the sake of our world. The creative process is an accumulation of insights coalescing in ways that complement and correct one another. They seek the good, which is never an abstraction but always concrete. "The whole point of the process of cumulative insight is that each insight regards the concrete while the cumulative process heads toward an ever fuller and more adequate view" (104). The cumulative process culminates in a system but the system is always changing. When fresh insights dry up, new challenges come, but the responses fail to emerge.

Why does creative activity meet frustration and begin to reverse itself in decline? Though every particular answer addresses a specific question, one underlying answer concerns the intrinsic limits of insight itself. Insights can never flow in closed or biased minds. To receive insight, persons and communities must be open to the new. Bias blinds the neurotic, who evades the insights his analyst knows he needs. Bias blinds the individual and group egoists, who see only those insights that will benefit their own petty or narrow situations. Bias blinds the "good" people of common sense, who cherish their single talent, their one way, their omnicompetent view, long after it has ceased to work. "Common sense" people are left insisting that there is nothing left to be done but to muddle through. Insights dry up in once creative communities that have become self-centered and shortsighted.

For society to flourish, it requires not only the creative work of converted communities. It must begin with the healing activity that, Lonergan insists, comes with being-in-love. It is made concrete in the love that makes families, the loyalty that bonds communities, the faith that informs religion. It is love alone that reveals values, touching hearts, and enlightening minds. Christians describe it in terms of God's grace, but its healing rays are known by many names. Such healing power needs to converge with the creative insights of open and inclusive communities to provide the way forward in the societal mission of creating and healing human history.

CONCLUSION

The methodological contributions of Bernard Lonergan provide a framework for understanding communities as dynamic achievements built up in human history by concrete groups of persons, who have commonly held meanings and values that are lived out in corporate commitments. By relying on the precise elements of shared experiences, understanding, judgments, and decisions, Lonergan helps distinguish communities from mere collectives of individuals, even those who come together for a designated time period to accomplish some good work. As a companion to Royce's theoretic specifications, Lonergan's dynamic structure of community as achievement provides strategic processes and evaluative criteria for moving isolated individuals to more communal patterns of life together. Such a shared life is constituted by commitments to each person and commitments by the community to social entities beyond it. By such responsible and committed actions, communities help build up their own life and help construct the world.

Lonergan's precise specifications offer interpretive criteria for understanding the pitfalls that groups encounter on their way to more meaningful communal life. He does so by pointing out the biases of the neurotic, the individual, and the group and the bias of common sense as destructive impulses working at every level of human consciousness to thwart human growth toward communion. As remedy for these destructive forces, Lonergan challenges individuals and groups to ongoing conversion, not just as some abstract "change of heart," a lofty spiritual goal, but as a concrete, practical response to particular real life invitations at the intellectual, moral, affective, and religious levels of human development. To this human endeavor, Lonergan adds the inbreak of God's love, coming always as gift to override, undergird, and direct all human activity toward its ultimate goal in "an ever more intimate yet ever more liberating dynamic whole" (1985, 175).

As we continue to make our case for the building of communities by North American churches, we will rely on Lonergan more and more. We are confident that his dynamic and emergent patterns of communal self-realization can be fleshed out in infinitely diverse ways by specific groups, willing to invest in the creative and healing work of becoming community.

Chapter Seven

Communion and Liberation:
The Contribution of Liberation and
Feminist Theologians to Understanding
Communion

P art 2 of this book presents twentieth century contributions to the understanding of communion and to the achievement of community, made available to us through theological and sociophilosophical scholars. Each scholar presented held both Christianity and community as central concerns. This chapter continues that conversation and offers helpful critique of some interpretations of communion/community from the perspective of liberation and feminist theologies. Here, we will argue from the underside of human history and insist that there can be no communion without liberation, no communion without mutuality; no communion where there is willful exclusion.

A penchant for the particular and the practical, a critical consciousness of the many forms of human domination, with a clear bias for the oppressed and excluded, and a commitment to the embodied and historical character of theology unify the various methods employed by liberation theologians. Their model is the life and ministry of Jesus of Nazareth for whom faith and action were radically inseparable and in whose person, communion took shape in concrete and demanding ways.

Though the origins of a movement are not easy to pin down, most researchers of liberation theology trace its beginnings to the Second Conference of Latin American Bishops (CELAM) who met in Medellin, Colombia, in August of 1968. Their goal was to discern how they could make visible in the social realities of their countries the communion character of the church defined at Vatican II.

The theology born at Medellin itself emerged from a spirit of communion as each bishop, representing a particular local church, entered into mutual dialogue with the pressing needs and concerns of that place. Those needs, though still muffled in the hearts of a vast majority of silent and oppressed people, were rooted in material poverty. As a result of this conference and its sequel at Puebla, Mexico (1979), Latin American theology returned to its roots in the life of actual communities. Bishops and theologians articulated a "preferential option for the poor" as they pledged themselves to respond to the pressing questions and urgent needs of their people. This critical correlation between faith and history required an expanded definition of theology. No longer could theology understand its goal simply as "faith seeking understanding," as Anselm had defined it in the eleventh century. In historical situations of grave injustice and massive human need, liberation theologians came to articulate their vocation more precisely as "faith seeking transformation."

Grounded in these liberative dimensions of theology, feminist theologians understand their own work as a further commitment to a particular form of liberation. Their focus is women as an oppressed group in need of liberation for the sake of genuine communion. The root oppression for feminist theologians is not primarily material poverty, with its dehumanizing effects and grave injustices, but patriarchy. This millennia-old social construction of the male sex as superior to the female has secured in place insidious structures of male domination, which have for so long subordinated, oppressed, and excluded women from a full life in the human community.

From this historical point of departure, this chapter will introduce certain theological presuppositions and principles, coming from theologians writing not to or about communities in general, but for and about particular communities or groups of oppressed persons. Their primary insight is that there can be no communion without liberation. Freedom is inherent in the theological meaning of communion as Maximus the Confessor, John Zizioulas, and Karl Rahner so pointedly insisted.

For the purposes of this study, we will limit ourselves to those resources that can speak most directly to the oppressive situations confronting our North American reality today. Among the constellation of principles used constructively by liberation and feminist theologians, we will highlight the following four: *to see and understand our reality*

1. a process of awakening or conscientization (Latin American term);

   beyond individual

2. a social and structural understanding of sin, grace, and conversion;

   create a space for difference to grow

3. a respect for "difference" as requisite for genuine communion;

   model of the Trinity — interpenetration

4. a reliance on creative imagination and multidisciplines to reconstruct the broken communion.

Vision to see another way; alternative way

THE PROCESS OF AWAKENING OR CONSCIENTIZATION

Gustavo Gutierrez, "the father of liberation theology," explains that the
Medellin Conference enunciated the twofold character of liberation theology, consisting of the concrete, historical situation and the perspective of
faith with which to interpret that situation. Gutierrez has said that the
fundamental question emerging from this twofold character concerns what
we need to awake from and denounce in order to live more genuinely a life
in communion.

Theology seeks to provide a language for speaking about God. Liberation theology deals with a faith that is inseparable from the concrete
conditions in which the vast majority of the inhabitants of Latin America
live. For such theology the central question is "How is it possible to tell the
poor, who are forced to live in conditions that embody a denial of love,
that God loves them? . . . Every theology is a question and a challenge for
believers living other human situations" (xxiv).

Gutierrez claims theology needs to acknowledge the contrast or gap
between one's faith vision and the reality of one's historical situation. In
conditions that deny love, do not speak about God as love. In situations of
oppression and domination, do not speak about "God as communion," or
of the church "as a sign and instrument of this communion with God and
all persons" (LG, 4) In a world where people are systematically excluded
from basic human rights, and/or denied food, housing, education, and
access to land and the means of production, one starts to do theology by
"waking up" and asking challenging questions to the present situation in
the light of one's faith. One cannot speak of a God of life and relationship
in the midst of death and alienation without asking if this depraved situation is God's will for these people. For the Latin American people, as
Gutierrez explains, the resounding "no" that ushered forth from asking
this question provided the starting point for the long process of
conscientization. This was an awakening from the silent stupor that had
kept the poor subjected to their oppressed state for so long. In light of this
emerging sense of God's will to release the poor, theologians—grounded
in base communities of poor people—began to speak about salvation as
liberation. This is God's desire not just as the final destiny of God's beloved children, but as the goal toward which the human family presses
together in history.

Gustavo Gutierrez clearly identifies concrete communities of poor people as "the historical womb from which liberation theology has emerged." No theologian sitting alone in his study thought up liberation theology. It was birthed and continues to develop from "the life of the poor, and in particular, of the Christian communities that have arisen within the bosom of the present-day Latin American Church" (xxxiii). There, theology becomes critical reflection on praxis (action done reflectively), the complex praxis of freeing a particular group of poor people from all that prevents them from growing toward fullness of life and communion with self, others, God, all creation. This continual waking up is done in the light of the church's faith, which "rouses Christians to commitments to God's will and also provides criteria for judging them in the light of God's Word." The three-fold task of each community's process of doing theology is simply to see, to judge, and to act in this gospel light.

The liberation we seek is "God's gift of definitive life to God's children, given in a history in which we must build communion," Gutierrez asserts (xxxix). Only by holding together the dual character of communion as grace and task can we avoid reducing communion to some vertical, disembodied spiritual union with God or to merely small group ties, or to one form or another of social, economic, or political horizontalism, he insists. In other words, for people of faith, the building of communion is simultaneously a social and a theological commitment.

The reduction of communion to some disembodied, spiritual, or abstract concept is rejected by feminists as well in their clarion call to women to wake up from the numbing effects of patriarchy. The awakening entails questioning the social construction of reality in which the primary mode of all relating is various patterns of domination/subordination. "Somebody has to be on top" is the way Dorothee Soelle, a German feminist theologian, has summed up patriarchal thinking. Only by paying attention and challenging all such patterns of thinking and acting (i.e., mind over matter, the individual over the community, rich over poor, intellect over affect, white over black, teacher over learner, clergy over lay, speech over silence), do feminists hope to overcome the lack of mutuality inherent in our patriarchal consciousness and social structures.

Catholic theologian Rosemary Radford Ruether describes what occurs for women once a process of awakening begins. The initial response is one of "cognitive dissonance," she says. "What is, is not what ought to be" (1993, xviii). An Asian-American feminist theologian, Rita Nakashima Brock illustrates the experience of awakening as "women's awareness of a mismatch between our lives and the social, cultural and religious expectations, stereotypes and attitudes imposed on us" (1995, 6).

The metaphor of "awakening" to describe this change in consciousness provides a means of explaining how the same patterns and structures,
traditions and rituals, attitudes and behaviors that women once accepted
unquestioningly can now be named oppressive. Vatican II proclaimed
unabashedly in *The Church in the Modern World* that "every type of discrimination, whether social or cultural, whether based on sex, race, color,
social condition, language or religion is to be overcome and eradicated as
contrary to God's intent" (GS, 29). This awakening to sexual discrimination has been metaphorically described by two Roman Catholic feminists as the "melting of the sexist Ice age" and as "another Copernican
revolution."[1]

Christian feminists unite to offer an insistent "no" to sexual discrimination as contrary to God's desire for the human family. This clear rejection
has provoked a twentieth-century awakening of women's consciousness
to the oppression of patriarchy, as a male-privileged, social construction
that has fostered both in church and society the social sins of sexism, clericalism, and misogyny.

This core principle of "conscientization" may have more to say for
our particular North American quest for community. There is an awakening occurring among many North Americans that we must confront those
cultural conditions and social behaviors that foster isolation and alienation, competition and total self-reliance as contrary to God's design for
the flourishing of life in the human family and the cosmic community.
The cultural values of unrestrained profit, rampant consumerism, immediate gratification, and presumptive privacy numb us to the pervasive
conditions of our isolating individualism. These dominant American values often shape our social behavior rather than those that promote
responsibility for life-together in community. The length of time these
conditions have been in place here in the U.S. serves as little excuse for our
cultural blindness when considered in light of the age-old structures of
patriarchy and the grave conditions of class and economic inequity being
challenged by liberation and feminist theologians today. From their critical lenses, we learn to see communion as a demanding task of theology as
well as a privileged and fundamental category.

SIN, GRACE, AND CONVERSION AS SOCIAL AND STRUCTURAL

The second principle shared by liberation and feminist theologians is an
understanding of sin and grace as social and structural as well as personal
and interior. Again we turn to Gustavo Gutierrez for clarity of insight.

But in the liberation approach, sin is not considered as an individual, private or merely interior reality—asserted just enough to necessitate "spiritual" redemption which does not challenge the order in which we live. Sin is regarded as a social, historical fact, the absence of fellowship (*koinonia*) and love in relationships among persons, the breach of friendship with God and with other persons, and, therefore, an interior, personal fracture. When it is considered this way, the collective dimensions of sin are rediscovered (1970, 103).

With its penchant for the particular, liberation theologians insist that sin cannot be encountered in itself but only in concrete instances, in particular alienations. "Sin is evident," Gutierrez explains, "in oppressive structures, in the exploitation of humans by humans, in the domination and slavery of peoples, races and social classes. Sin appears as the fundamental alienation, the root of a situation of injustice and exploitation" (103).

At both Medellin and Puebla, the Latin American bishops spoke of oppressive structures and social injustice as the ways in which "sins of unsolidarity," of disconnection, are crystallized. Puebla taught that sin is a "rupturing force" that prevents human growth in communion. "Sin is not just something done by each individual but is also committed in these sinful structures, which are created by human beings" (281). The bishops' teaching on sin has been summarized: "When human beings sin, they create structures of sin, which, in their turn, make human beings sin" (1996, 198).

If sin is this fundamental rupture, the root of all injustice, grace serves as its counterpart. Thus, radical liberation from this fundamental alienation is the gift Christ offers us. The Christian life, in fact all human life, is, for Gutierrez, a passover. The human journey is an ongoing transition from sin to grace, from death to life, from injustice to justice, from the subhuman to the human. Christ introduces us by the gift of the Spirit into communion with God and with all human beings. More precisely, it is because Christ introduces us into this communion, into a continuous search for its fullness, that he conquers sin, which is the negation of love—and all its consequences.

Gutierrez makes clear connections between the concrete, social dimensions of grace as the "coming of the reign of God" and at the same time, "as the ultimate precondition for a just society and a new humanity" (103).

Though God's reign comes in Christ as the acceptance of a free gift, surpassing all human expectation, nonetheless, it comes to humankind in history. The history of salvation and human history are fundamentally one, if one believes that God is present and active in our lives and world.

Therefore, all struggles against exploitation and exclusion are attempts against selfishness. They are works of communion, bringing forth God's reign. Every effort to build a just society is a liberating act, a work of saving grace. Liberation theologians recognize grace in concrete human acts, social structures, and communal commitments, which, despite all the ambiguities inherent in the human condition do not weaken the basic orientation or objective results of grace. In the "continuous search for communion's fullness," grace is the energy that seeks to build genuine communities for a just society.

The movement from sin as alienation and selfishness to grace as communion and self-gift takes place as a conversion, or change of heart, which has both personal and social dimensions. The bishops of Lima, Peru, made this clear in a pastoral letter. They explained that although conversion "affects the deepest regions of the human person, it is not limited to the interior life but must also be translated into attitudes and commitments that regard changes in reality as a requirement of Christian love." Countless examples of a Latin American spirituality that understands "conversion as social" abound. Archbishop Oscar Romero exemplified such a conviction by his life as well as his words.

"Nowadays, an authentic Christian conversion must lead to an unmasking of the social mechanisms that turn the worker and the peasant into marginalized persons. Why do the rural poor become part of society only in the coffee and cotton-picking season?" (1979, 1).

Rooted in liberation theology, Pedro Arrupe, S.J., Superior General of the Society of Jesus from 1965–81, emphasized the same meaning of conversion. "It has been said that interior conversion does not suffice . . . Today, we must be aware that what we must reform is our entire world. In other words, personal conversion and structural reform cannot be separated" (1975, 178).

The will to conversion leads to this kind of concrete social analysis and transformation. It recognizes exclusion as contrary to God's design and understands the change needed as more than heartfelt. Conversion rends unjust social structures as well as human hearts. The call to conversion sounds again from liberation perspectives, this time challenging churches in North America to include a critique of social structures in their examination of conscience, prayer of repentance, and commitment to change.

Theologians writing from a feminist perspective of liberation likewise view sin as primarily structural, impacting the social situations in which women are excluded from full participation in church and society. In a theological elaboration of sin as structural, Elisabeth Schüssler Fiorenza rejects the individualistic interpretation linking sin with Eve and opts for a collective understanding of sin as original, an inherited condition. As such, sin produces a "consciousness that is self-alienated and collaborates in its own and others dehumanization and oppression" (1998, 1). As institutionalized injustice, structural sin produces collective discrimination (e.g., against women) that does not recognize its own culpability, because such situations are justified by the religio-cultural symbols, value systems, and discourses constructed and reinforced by the sinful systems themselves.

Feminist theologians have similarly rejected the privatization of sin that has occurred because of a one-sided emphasis on sexual morality, locating sin in the home and neglecting the wider society. Susan Ross emphasizes the social link. "Human sexuality and social practices are intrinsically linked; 'the personal is the political' is one of the key statements of the women's movement" (1993, 201). Once again, human sinfulness is rooted in conditions and choices of selfishness and exclusion. It impacts personal, interpersonal, societal, and cosmic relationships.

In her examination of the text of Genesis 3, Mary Aquin O'Neill interprets "the subordination of women to men to be the result of sin and not part of the created order portrayed prior to what has come to be known as the Fall. It is difficult to overestimate the significance of this insight for an anthropology that begins with a vision of human beings called to be the image of God together," she claims (1993, 142). In summing up the effects of sin that makes it "possible to hate the very process that continues life, the very earth that sustains life, the very other whose presence made life less lonely," O'Neill concludes that:

> It is possible for that hatred to be institutionalized in patterns of attitude and behavior that precede and shape subsequent generations before they come to consciousness, before they are capable of what the Christian community considers to be personal sin. In this way, the sacred text suggests what contemporary feminist thinkers are coming to articulate with increasing clarity and passion: negative attitudes toward the earth, toward the body and toward women are of a piece. The social sin of sexism cannot be separated from the other social sins that do not yet have such a commonly accepted name, but that entail a disregard for the limitations placed on human power by the earth that is our mother and by the human body that is our most intimate connection to her and through her to the whole cosmos (143).

In her concluding insights about sexism and other forms of social sin, Mary Aquin O'Neill does not put the sole blame on men. She considers women and men both implicated in a history of distorted relationships, of testing limits, of "a human history that is in exile" (143). Further implications of social sin as a "disregard for the limitations placed on human power by our Earth and by the corporate Human Body" remain to be explored. We will tap into this and other resources of feminist theological principles for our North American cultural critique.

The story of human history in exile is not the end of the story that Christian feminist theologians tell. The account of human sinfulness has its counterpart in a story of grace as well, a grace made available in Christ through the Spirit. Many feminist theologians concur with other liberation thinkers that Jesus of Nazareth embodied in his person a social grace with radical implications. In him, the personal was clearly the political. By living out the "will to communion," Jesus confronted the prevailing social structures, a confrontation that led ultimately to his death at the hands of the dominant power brokers of his day.

Feminist theologians affirm the life of grace made visible in Jesus but expand the understanding of life "in Christ" as a graced existence, that is pre-eminently social and not limited by gender restrictions. Elizabeth Johnson, for example, insists that Jesus' relationship to divine saving grace, "points the way to a reconciliation of opposites (the female and the male) and their transformation from enemies into a liberating, unified diversity" (1993, 128). Furthermore, according to Johnson, faith in the resurrection of Jesus affirms that he now lives a new life, hidden in the glory of God, by the power of the Spirit. Johnson describes the implications of this Christian faith.

> While Jesus' life is now hidden in God, his presence is known on earth where two or three gather, bread is broken, the hungry fed. But this indicates a transformation of his humanity so profound that it escapes our imagination. . . . After his death and resurrection the focus of the ongoing story of Jesus shifts from his concrete historical life to the community of sisters and brothers imbued with the Spirit. From the beginning, this community is marked by the confession that Jesus is the Christ, the anointed, the blessed one. Intrinsic to this confession is the insight that the beloved community shares in this Christhood . . . Biblical metaphors such as the Body of Christ (1 Cor. 12:12–27) and the branches abiding in the vine (Jn. 15:1–11) expand the reality of Christ to include potentially all of redeemed humanity, sisters and brothers still on the way. Amid the sufferings and conflicts of history, members of the community of disciples are *en christo,* and their own lives assume a christic pattern (129).

The mystery of the grace of Christ, for feminist theologians, is a creative outpouring of the Spirit "who is not limited by whether one is Jew or

Greek, slave or free, male or female" (130). The Spirit makes the body of the risen Christ the body of the community. This theological truth undergirds the affirmation that women participate fully in the life of Christ, sharing the gift and responsibility of grace. Grace in the body of Christ is the social force (the Spirit's lure toward communion) binding us together in a community of equal disciples.

In addressing the need for a societal conversion to liberate us from the patriarchal oppression of women, feminist theologian Rosemary Radford Ruether "calls the Church to become an agent and support system for the process of conversion from patriarchy. Such a conversion requires community. It cannot be done alone" (183). Conversion for the Christian feminist theologian is an ongoing call to the church as well as by the church. As Anne Carr insists, conversion of the church calls for a change in its thinking, its judgments, its decision-making structures. Because the church has been entrusted with the prophetic and liberating word of the Gospels, some feminist theologians, women and men, are asking the church to think and act in new ways, to choose imagination over the authoritarian structures of power, prestige, and caste. They ask the church, its all-male hierarchy, and its male-dominated structures not just to permit thinking in new ways but to lead in this thought, to demonstrate that the power of the gospel is strong enough to reverse the patterns of history where "no oppressor ever willingly handed over what he thinks is power" (1988, 35).

Feminist theologians consider the ongoing need of personal conversion for the sake of the community and society even as they call social bodies, like the church, to a radical change of mind and heart. Rosemary Radford Ruether has offered an important reminder to women and men, concerned about conversion as a shared human response to grace.

> Women need to acknowledge that they have the same drives and temptations to sin as males have—not just sins of dependency but also the sins of dominance, of which they may have been less guilty not for want of capacity but for want of opportunity . . . If we are really to effect change, we must take the responsibility for the capacities for both good and evil in all people (1980, 847).

A REGARD FOR "DIFFERENCE" AS REQUISITE FOR COMMUNION

The theological concept of communion has struggled throughout history to find its social embodiment in human communities that neither sacrifice "difference" for the sake of unity, nor promote differences to the neglect of achieving shared meanings and values. Communion, as a particular relational bond, is constituted by a unity-in-diversity, or a unity that inherently differentiates. In other words, there can be no communion without honoring and safeguarding "difference." Within the framework of liberation and feminist theologies, this regard for "the other" takes the particular form of "a preferential option for the poor" and a commitment to the "full flourishing of women's lives." Over the decades, this focused "regard" has deepened as the poor and women have taken on the faces of greater and greater uniqueness and diversity, inviting further recognition and reverence of differences. In Latin America, liberation theologians admit an initial blindness to the particular plight of persons of color, indigenous peoples, women, and children among the poor. Feminist theologians, white, middle-class, and Euro-Americans, have confronted their own failure to reverence the diversity in women's struggle for liberation as women of color, poor women, and Hispanic and Asian women.

In the U.S. cultural context where concern for the individual is so highly revered, it may be crucial to our developing ethics of community to pay attention to this principle about the concrete "other" that has emerged in liberation theologies. At the heart of this principle is the conviction that every human person deserves to be recognized as a subject, rather than an object, of history. Each is a moral agent, capable of seeing, judging, and acting for herself or himself within the web of relationship that is her community and larger social network.

For both liberation theology and its feminist practitioners, a renewed interpretation of God as Trinity, God's three-fold oneness, has provided critical insights into and new potential constructions of a social reality rooted in relationships of mutuality rather than domination. Writing as a liberation theologian, Leonardo Boff has found that "consideration of the three distinct persons in the Unity of the Trinity produces a critical attitude toward personhood, community, society and the church" (1988, 304). In his subsequent critique, he challenges the two dominant forms of society, embodied in socialism and capitalism, as aberrations of God's design for human life together. He views the liberal-capitalist social system as "responsible for the greatest divisions in human history between the rich and the poor, between the races and the sexes; a system that today operates on a world-wide scale" (304). Shored up by the individualistic profit-interests of the elites who hold power, "capitalism . . . promotes domination based on the One; one all-embracing capital, one market, one world of consumers, one legitimate view of the world, one way of relating to nature, one way of meeting the Absolute. Differences are regarded as pathological and deviations from the norm: they are either eradicated or at best barely tolerated" (305).

The opposite failure characterizes the way socialism has functioned in modern society. Without engaging a critical process whereby differences are accepted and valued between persons and communities, socialism imposes a social schema from above. There is no realization of the social dimension starting from the base, with personal relationships, building networks of communities, which in turn become the basis for the organization of civil society. Boff explains:

> Bureaucratic imposition of the social dimension does not produce a society of equality . . . but one of collectivization. . . . The type of community that emerges from socialist practice seems to annul individuals, not recognizing them as different-in-relationship, which would safeguard differences, but subsuming them into a homogenizing, egalitarian whole (305).

As Boff decries society's failure to regard the other respectfully, not giving voice to those excluded from the centers of power, nor allowing space for diversity to flourish, he sees in the Christian understanding of trinitarian communion a source of inspiration and Christian commitment to social change. This vision of tri-unity beckons to Christians as their "permanent utopia." This life in communion perdures as the horizon toward which Christians press historically and are drawn mystically. Boff elaborates something of how this vision might look.

> The Three "Differents" uphold their difference one from another, by upholding the other and giving themselves totally to the other, they become "differents" in communion. In the Trinity there is no domination by one side, but convergence of the three in mutual acceptance and giving. They are different but none is greater or lesser, before or after. Therefore, a society that takes its inspiration from trinitarian communion cannot tolerate class differences, domination based on power (economic, sexual or ideological) which subjects those who are different to those who exercise that power and marginalizes the former from the latter (307).

Speaking from a feminist perspective, Elizabeth Johnson understands the symbol of the Trinity, as it has been creatively retrieved and interpreted in the late twentieth century, as speaking directly to the human community's intuitive and heartfelt sense of it "highest good, its most profound truth, its most appealing beauty" (1997, 300). As a symbol of humankind's highest good, the image of God as "incomprehensible three-fold koinonia" is not literally about numbers. "The intent is much more subtle," Johnson explains. "To say that God is one is to negate division, thus affirming the unity of the Divine being. To say that God is three is to negate solitariness, thus affirming relationality at the heart of God" (305). Without preserving otherness, the capacity for relationship—the heart of life—collapses. The mystery of God's three-in-oneness is about salvation, "about the Trinitarian mystery of God, actually empowering relationships of mutuality, equality and inclusiveness among persons and between human beings and the earth" (300).

This core symbol of God decries all human forms of exclusion, of disregard for any other living being. Johnson explains how the trinitarian symbol of God works both positively and negatively. The symbol works positively "by inspiring efforts to create a community of sisters and brothers, interwoven with the whole web of earth's life according to the ideal that the Trinity models." It functions negatively "by prophetically challenging social and ecological injustices that subvert a community built on relationships of participation." The goal of all creation is to participate in the trinitarian mystery of love, the preservation of infinite diversity in infinite unity. Trinitarian communion is effective "wherever (a single) human heart is healed, justice is done, peace holds sway, liberation breaks through, the earth flourishes—wherever sin abounding is embraced by grace superabounding" (301).

Using the Trinity as model once again, Catherine Mowry-LaCugna asserts that by radical faith in a trinitarian God who is for us, with us and in us, "we do not know a shadow-image of God but the real living God of Jesus Christ in their Spirit. The God who saves—this is God" (1985, 13). LaCugna articulates a feminist interpretation of the Trinity that sees Jesus Christ as the embodiment of trinitarian communion, a man with total regard for every other, a person of the Spirit, feeding on God's will. Dwelling in Christ through baptism, women can speak the truth to power and secure a voice for the other, the excluded or marginalized, for the sake of furthering this trinitarian life in communion here and now. She insists that "the life of Jesus Christ is at odds with the sexist theology of complementarity, the racist theology of white superiority, the clerical theology of cultic privilege, the political theology of exploitation and economic injustice, and the patriarchal theology of dominance and control" (1993, 99). Catherine LaCugna calls the Christian community to its responsibility to "be an icon of God's triune life" and admonishes the church for its participation with society in "shoring up the sexist arrangement in which men dominate and eclipse women."

Such eclipsing and disregard for the other that liberation and feminist theologians abhor drives their commitment to promote the kinds of life together where "the other" takes her place at the inclusive table of participation, dialogue, and mutual regard. The image of coming to the conversation table has become significant for feminists as they strive to empower women to become visible and to find their voice.

Elizabeth Johnson uses the fifteenth-century icon of the Holy Trinity written by the Russian monk, Andrei Rublev to unpack the symbol of the table, depicted there, as an image of shared hospitality and inclusive love. The icon recounts the story of Genesis 18, where three heavenly messengers visit the home of Sarah and Abraham and encounter at table a satisfying meal from their hosts' gratuity. In turn, the three strangers extend to them the divine pledge of a child. The scene depicts genuine openness to "the other" and in the embrace, the mystery of divine/human communion is revealed. This biblical story of divine/human communion is used by Rublev to image the triune God "in a circle inclining toward one another, but the circle is not closed" (1997, 299). What the image suggests, Johnson explains, is a God in communion, each turned lovingly toward the other, yet "lovingly open to the world, seeking to nourish it" (1997, 299). A circle that will not close, a table that is open to all epitomizes the feminists' insistence on making room for the other at the table of conversation, the table of life. The theological category of communion symbolizes the ultimate exclusion of all exclusion in a commitment to live as God would have us live.

Feminist theologians propose equal participation in a genuine conversation as a primary method for growing in communion. Here, difference is recognized and valued in a dialogical relationship of give and take. Here, one recognizes the other as other and yet similar to one's self. This dialogical space allows for a respectful distance, without which there is no genuine meeting between persons. Such a relational understanding of distance is important for feminists, concerned about a certain tendency among women to lose themselves in relationship. The metaphor is helpful for North Americans, as well, who seek to preserve and promote both healthy individuals and healthy communities. In this "good distance," similarity and difference are both preserved and mediated. This spatial image of "good distance" resembles closely the image of holy space created by the Spirit of communion, present where two or three come together. Herein, Christians encounter the Bond of unity who differentiates and the Giver of diversity who unifies.

Genuine regard for difference as requisite for a life in communion seems a goal, elusively beyond our human grasp. For Christians committed to social change, it remains the paradigmatic design of God that we have traditionally called "the reign of God." As such, it breaks into human history when persons cooperate in grace to build a more just society. In a world that systematically excludes two-thirds of the world's people from access to the world's goods, the liberating vision of an inclusive community table needs to be conjured up and proposed. This alternative design contrasts with emerging forms of exclusive living, secured in gated communities and lifestyle enclaves, where those excluded can be neither seen nor heard. Within the contemporary situation of such global disparity, we face new questions about the intersection of faith and history. A radical challenge to see, judge, and act at this our moment in U.S history confronts us. We now look at what is needed for us to take the gospel of community seriously in our day.

CREATIVE IMAGINATION AND MULTIDISCIPLINES: HEALING THE BROKEN COMMUNION

A serious and critical appraisal and deconstruction of unjust social structures has been an indispensable contribution to theology coming from the liberationist perspective. Of equal importance and an even more daunting task is the corresponding work of reconstructing the broken communion that the oppression of the poor and of women so poignantly demonstrates. A first step in this long-term process of reconstruction, of building communion, is the capacity to imagine an alternative social order, one different from what the dominant powers tell us is the only way it can be. To this task of conjuring up and proposing alternatives to the existing oppressive structures, liberation and feminist theologians have given themselves over the past two decades. Some of their discoveries have much to say to the work we are recommending in this book.

Their first proposal is the need for a creative imagination. This is critical, since as human persons, we are so culturally conditioned to life as we know it, that it is difficult to recognize the role we play in the social construction of our own reality. Ever since the Enlightenment, the power of human imagination has been downplayed. Despite Albert Einstein's insistence that he treasured this gift of imagination far more than his scientific reasoning, the power of rational thinking has triumphed to the neglect of other ways of knowing. The twentieth-century social philosopher Max Weber has imaged the modern imbalance as a situation of "living in an iron cage of reason." An iron cage suggests the need for a freeing space, a "good distance" where other human gifts can be nourished.

Liberation theologians have found such a space in the coming together of small communities. Here, the good distance becomes also a critical distance, where the reigning forces of society can be called into question. Here other meanings and values can be sought together in a space that supports and encourages mutual conversation and conversion, empowering the creative imagination.

Such creative environments have provided for both feminists and even more powerfully and spontaneously for the poor of Latin America the birthing place for an alternative consciousness, a radically Christian consciousness. From them, a new social reconstruction is being proposed, embodied, ritualized, and presented to the larger society of which these small communities are dynamic cells or living building blocks. It is not happening without resistance and struggle, but their efforts and their commitment testify to the power of their communal imagination. For the Christian communities in Latin America and for Christian feminist communities throughout the world, that imagination is funded by their image of God in communion with us and of God's design for our world as a furthering of that communion among our sisters and brothers and with all creation.

The small or base community movement in Latin America over the last thirty years presupposes a shared vision of the "reign of God." This biblical image provides the guiding light in which each small community gathers to reflect, judge, and act to bring about that new future where persons will be liberated from all forms of bondage that keep them from fullness of life. Though the fullness of this future rests in God, nonetheless, it is built everyday by the historical acts of human beings cooperating with God in realizing this divine intention. Of necessity, small community reflection and action have a political cast.

After prayer and reflection on their historical circumstances in light of the gospel, communities assess what needs to be done. As Oscar Romero asked in addressing the faith communities of San Salvador: "Why do the rural poor become part of society only in the coffee and cotton-picking season?" (1979, 1). At this point, social analyses, particularly of the political and economic factors that prevent the realization of the community's vision, need to take place, critical theories understood, and appropriate solutions determined. As an outstanding spokesperson for the base community work in his own country of Peru, Gustavo Gutierrez acknowledges that the political order is the primary place where action for liberation takes place. Only "in the political fabric" does a person develop as "a free and responsible being, as a person in relationship with other people, as someone who takes on a historical task. Personal relationships themselves acquire an ever-increasing political dimension" (47).

Leonardo Boff, writing on the base community movement, challenges the church to provide a much-needed alternative to the "wild atomization of existence and a general anonymity of persons lost in the cogs of the mechanisms of macro-organizations and bureaucracies" (1986, 1). This challenge resembles closely the one we are reissuing in the North American context today. Boff characterizes the alternative life, emerging in these basic church communities by "the absence of alienating structures, . . . rigid rules and hierarchies, by direct relationships, by reciprocity, by a deep communion, by mutual assistance, by communality of gospel ideals, by equality among members . . . and by an enthusiasm generated by a community life of interpersonal ties" (4).

It is unrealistic to think that communities can ever realize the goal of full communion as long as the dimensions of sin and selfishness, identified earlier, prevail in the human condition. Nonetheless, it is reasonable to conjure up alternatives that approximate more closely the final end toward which history under grace presses. Boff has this realistic expectation of communities. Here is where members struggle for a type of sociability in which love will be less difficult, and where power and participation will have better distribution. Communion must be understood as a spirit to be created, as an inspiration to bend one's constant efforts to overcome barriers between persons and to generate a relationship of solidarity and reciprocity.

Life in community provides the basic place for imagining and practicing the kind of just relationships that have implications for the structures needed in a more just society. The multiplication of such social structures makes it less difficult to envision a more just society where members and communities themselves interact in their larger social and political settings. Communities can point the way toward alternative patterns of relating that societies themselves could never be able to imagine.

The Second Vatican Council's dynamic and historical understanding of the church as "the community of God's people journeying in history toward ultimate fulfillment in the realm of God" caught and freed the imagination of many in the 1960s. At the same time, feminism was entering a new phase, offering alternative images of women's roles in work, family, and society. The convergence led many Christian feminists to propose new ways for women and for lay Christians, in general to see themselves and to act out the conviction "we are the church."

Grass-roots movements began to spring up as creative space where women could reflect on their experiences, ponder scripture, and imagine a new reality for becoming "signs and instruments of communion" in the world. For some women, this creative space called into question many of the existing social structures that had for so long excluded them from full and equal participation in the life of the church. In coming together to share scripture and their lives in mutually accountable ways, women and men began to envision "a massive transformation of the church's structures." They sought "to free them of the patriarchal, hierarchical and clerical assumptions that prevent the church from becoming a prophetic community of equal disciples committed to the task of liberation for all people" (1993, 164).

Rosemary Radford Ruether contends that communities are critical to this transformative task (both for the church and society), since such a massive shift is not likely to take place from the top down. Rather, she envisions feminist base communities reconstructing the church from the margins inward or from the bottom up. From 1985 forward, Ruether uses the term "Women-Church" to describe this creative space for women to re-imagine and reconstruct the ecclesial, social order. She predicts the need for such communities to exist on the margins of the institution as long as patriarchy continues to dominate the way persons relate to one another. "Women-Church is a feminist counter-culture to the ecclesia of patriarchy that must continue for the foreseeable future as an exodus both within and on the edges of existing church institutions" (1985, 62).

In a 1992 work, *A Democratic Church*, edited with Eugene Bianchi, Ruether recommends five principles needed in the construction of a new social order within the Catholic Church. These principles, she contends, were generated by actual communities of Women-Church, living into a new reality. Here, women relate to each other in new patterns of mutuality and find energy to address the reform needed in the larger institution. From these communities' reflections in light of the church's long tradition (and other feminist sources missing from the patriarchal tradition), new ways of shaping "life in communion" have presented themselves. The emergent principles for fostering communion together include participation, conciliarity (networking with larger groupings of communities to discern the good of the whole), pluralism, accountability, and dialogue. To these principles, Ruether adds concrete strategies for effecting this needed change, such as nonviolent resistance to oppressive uses of authority and to those acts that impede the church's mission in the world, educational programs, and the support of alternative ministries that foster these principles in the church.

Elisabeth Schüssler-Fiorenza, a biblical feminist scholar, has reflected on the present situation in light of the church's past, searching for hints of an alternative consciousness operative there. In her creative reconstruction of the Jesus Movement and early Christianity, she finds a challenge to the prevailing patriarchy in an egalitarian gathering of female and male disciples around Jesus. She claims that the church later capitulated to the patriarchal order of society. But we are left, nonetheless, with a "dangerous memory" that today summons the church to recapture its egalitarian vision from its past for the sake of the future.

For Schüssler-Fiorenza, the gathering of Women-Church is the space needed for creative revisioning to happen. She calls these nurturing communities the "ecclesia of women":

> We have begun to gather as the ecclesia of women, as the people of God, to claim our own religious powers, to participate fully in the decision-making process of the church, and to nurture each other as women Christians. Baptism is the sacrament that calls us into the discipleship of equals. No special vocation is given. No more perfect Christian lifestyle is possible (1983, 344).

CONCLUSION

Both liberation and feminist theologies propose a principle of retrieving a critical and creative imagination for the work of healing the broken communion of human history. For both, community serves the efforts of liberation by paying attention to and nurturing an alternative consciousness without which the capacity to transform the present social structures cannot develop. Communities of critical reflection, informed judgment, and prophetic action become not only agents to "reinvent the Church" (Boff) but to transform the social and "political fabric" of which they are a part (Gutierrez).

The practical demands of making communion visible in a human situation of contrasts or "broken communion" require the use of multidisciplines along with theology. Economics, political philosophy, social analysis, ritual studies, historical criticism, even poetics are placed at the service of liberation by theologians who understand their task of making a practical theology of communion the central project of human history and our cosmic responsibility.

The principle of employing the imagination and multidisciplines, along with the other principles used constructively by liberation theologies, provide valuable resources for the work that needs to be done in our own North American context. We are indebted to liberation and feminist theologians for keeping the theological category of communion close to the ground; refusing to let it drift into irrelevant abstractions. Their work is demanding and prophetic. They challenge us to remember that there can be no communion without liberation; no communion without mutuality; no communion where there is exclusion because of race, gender, class, religion, or sexual preference.

The critical dialogue needed between a people of faith and its concrete historical context sets the stage for the drama we hope to see enacted more passionately here in the U.S. The actors include contemporary churches entrusted with a gospel of community and this present social situation, now seriously threatened by community's demise.

PART THREE

THE CONTEMPORARY NORTH AMERICAN SOCIAL SITUATION AS CRISIS OF COMMUNITY

INTRODUCTION

Sometime in the twentieth century it became clear that the American dream had soured. One can cite any number of turning points in this realization. The great depression, the holocaust, the flight to the suburbs in the 1950s and 1960s, the bombing of Hiroshima and Nagasaki, the Vietnam War, the "me" generations of the 1950s and 1980s. We will not sort out this complex historical causality here. Instead, we will note it on a more general level, in specific relationship to our theme of community.

One of the paradigms of American consciousness has been that of the pioneer. This myth is based in seventeenth and eighteenth century history, but has subsequently shaped the way we see ourselves in so many different arenas. The story goes something as follows.

There was a European who was persecuted by society. This single individual managed to spring clear of oppression in America. There she/he set out to make a life for her/himself. This required launching out into the lonely wilderness and facing the untamed rigor of nature. This individual persisted and made a home in the middle of the wilderness for her/himself. The heart of America consists of the bravery and endurance of these rugged individuals.

When this story stayed within the American psyche after the western frontier was settled, it reappeared in a series of perverted twentieth century forms. Instead of becoming pioneers in the western wilderness, twentieth century Americans saw themselves as professional pioneers. They launched themselves into the breach of American capitalism and competed fiercely against other people, rather than the landscape. Since there were no more homesteads to settle in the wilds, the twentieth-century American launched the innovation of the suburb. These rugged individuals founded a myriad of places to live, most appropriately named "bedroom communities," where you did not have to develop relationships with any-one. Each of these forms made the chance for American communities to develop more and more unlikely.

Part 3 takes up these themes that were originally invoked in the in-troduction. In two sections it looks at the ways American society is in crisis because of its lack of ability to develop community.

Chapter Eight

THE AMERICAN DISASTER

Jennifer[1] lives alone in a gated community outside St. Louis, Missouri. Twenty-seven years old, she is single and enjoys her apartment and job. She works from 8 A.M to 6 P.M. in health care administration, a position she took four years ago after graduation from college in Minnesota. Her family lives in a working-class suburb on the east coast. She has made some acquaintances at work and keeps in regular telephone contact with college friends and family. She works out three times a week at a health club, and goes to church about once a month. She has had one serious sexual relationship while in Missouri, but is currently unattached. Her car, which is essential to her life, is eighteen months old.

The rhythm of her life is relatively stable. Her work and exercise routine take up most of her time during the week. She usually gets home between 7 and 9 P.M.—depending on her exercise schedule—grabs something to eat in front of the TV, and goes to bed. On weekends she does some exercise, watches some more TV, does some shopping, and sees a friend or goes to church. She likes to travel for vacation, and also will occasionally visit her family or college friends on a long weekend.

On the one hand, Jennifer's life is right out of a flashy commercial for a new car. She has almost everything Americans want. Freedom to lead her own life, money to treat herself regularly, and good looks are in ample supply. As her likeness to the commercial indicates, she is not far from the American ideal. On the other hand, there is a haunting quality to Jennifer's lifestyle. What she lacks is community. The way her life represents both a cultural ideal and an almost complete lack of in-depth connections to any group illustrates what this chapter understands as "the American disaster."

With some variation Jennifer's life is like many Americans overall and very similar to what many others would like their life to be. It may not be that everyone can afford membership in a health club, but the growth of that industry indicates that there is still a growing market for it. The amount of TV Jennifer watches actually may be less than most Americans, but her gravitation toward it in nonworking moments is almost archetypal to the contemporary American psyche. The priority she gives to a good-paying job and the consequent geographic distance of her friends and family is not exceptional. Her nonmarried status now represents the majority of Americans. Although most Americans do not live alone, more and more do, and the number of persons in living units steadily declines. That Jennifer goes shopping more often than to church or any social or cultural club is typical.

Whether the many Americans whose lifestyles resemble Jennifer are "happy" is not easy to answer. The direct correlation between the rise in alcoholism, drug addiction, and depression and the emergence of this lifestyle cannot be the sole indicator in responding to such a question, but certainly heightens the question itself. The increase in violence and anti-social behavior in America might be related to this increased lack of community. Provisionally, one can at least note some obvious personal down sides to this lifestyle without necessarily identifying the exact causal relationships. As mentioned in the introduction, Robert Putnam does believe there is a connection between the lack of community and these signs of "unhappiness."

A recent interview with retired baseball superstar Mike Schmidt illustrates the malaise beneath the surface of American affluence and individualism. About a visit back to the major league dugout, Schmidt says, "When I walked into the coaches' room, they looked at me as enjoying a life they'd probably rather have, given the choice. Financially, I don't have to keep a steady job. But I'm looking at them thinking, 'What a great life you've got' . . . I'm not sure what I'm going to do in the morning when I wake up. Sometimes I'm bored or stressed out from just talking on the phone, not sure what I'm going to do. I get migraines . . . I don't feel a lot of substance in my life. It's like I'm living my life just for me."[2]

What catapults this community-less lifestyle into the category of an "American disaster" are not just its complex connections to personal "unhappiness" but its social, economic, cultural, and ecological consequences. The relative "unhappiness" of such community-less persons is one thing. The effect of this lifestyle on the society, millions of people around the world, and earth itself makes up the heart of the disaster.

The mobile American individualist is a cornerstone for the huge discrepancies in income levels among Americans. The tendency of so many of us to live like Jennifer decreases understanding in American society by isolating us from one another. The huge dependency on oil, cheap labor around the world, and a national servant class—all produced by our mobility and isolated living units—are intimately and complexly related to growing social strains and violence. The devastating consumption of natural resources from both our country and around the globe by Americans—whether they be affluent corporate executives or addicted Walmart shoppers—has already changed the climate of earth itself and has resulted in the largest extermination of species in the history of the planet.

Adding to the disastrous character of this lifestyle is the completely paradoxical public image it has. As noted earlier, this life—so devoid of community, so conducive to depression and addiction, and so destructive of social connectedness and environmental wellness—is held up as the ideal for which Americans should strive.

Perhaps most curiously, none of these observations about the disastrous consequences of our lack of community in America is new. Many of these American anticommunitarian character traits were noticed almost two hundred years ago by the visiting French writer, Alexis de Tocqueville. More recently, in the past fifteen years, a number of American historians and sociologists have described in great detail both the major causes and consequences of the American lack of community. The works of Robert N. Bellah, Robert Wuthnow, and Robert D. Putnam form the centerpiece of this new attention to America's lack of community. This chapter summarizes the work of three social historians in order to help sharpen our focus on the need for community in our country. In addition, we recommend their full works to our readers. We acknowledge our indebtedness to these astute social analysts, our shared concern to wrestle with similar questions, and our focus on some of the same, urgent needs facing North Americans today. This summary concentrates on their understanding of the lack of community in America.

ROBERT BELLAH

The publication of *Habits of the Heart: Individualism and Commitment in American Life* by Robert N. Bellah and four other academic colleagues[3] in 1985 was the clarion wake-up call concerning the deep loss of community in America. "It seems to us," Bellah *et al.* write, "that it is individualism . . . that has marched inexorably through our history. We are concerned that this individualism may have grown cancerous . . . .that it may be threatening the survival of freedom itself" (vii).

In a rich tapestry of vivid American stories and incisive social science, *Habits of the Heart* weaves a portrait of American collective consciousness in rapid decline, due to the triumph of American individualism. Although occasionally making sharp judgments about what it observes, the book is not overly moralistic, pursuing the authors' desire "to know what individualism in American looks and feels like, and how the world appears in its light" (vii). Hundreds of real American lives are described with compassion and interest.

The issue of community is important to Bellah and colleagues, but in the end is a subset of their moral goal of "public involvement" (163). Their basic analysis describes the American disaster most directly in terms of the loss of commitment to "the public good" (252–70). It goes like this: "Individualism of this sort often implies a negative view of public life . . . .One cannot live a rich private life in a state of siege, mistrusting all strangers and turning one's home into an armed camp" (163).

Community is nevertheless near the heart of this major work's critique of contemporary American society. Individualism's devastating effect on the possibility of people living and working together is illustrated in what they call the managerial and therapeutic cultures as well as in the American icons of the "Lone Ranger" (145). Even when "a few examples of those who have attempted to articulate a socially responsible individualism within the context of communities . . ." are cited, the authors "see that this is no easy task in a society in which the first language of modern individualism, fusing utilitarian and expressive components, and the practices of separation that go with it, are so dominant that alternatives are hard to understand" (155).

The lack of community is central to America's disintegration, according to *Habits of the Heart*. Similarly the possibility of developing community is basic to any redemptive vision of the country's future. America then must choose between an individualism[4] gone awry and "a renewal of commitment and community, if they are not to end in self-destruction" (277).

In the process of laying out this American disaster, Bellah *et al.* work hard to articulate what the hope of community really looks like. This hope is based both within concrete signs of some actual community and a keen definition of community itself. That definition of community proposed in *Habits of the Heart* combines many of the concrete and dynamic elements developed by Josiah Royce and Bernard Lonergan (chapter 6) to suggest that

> Community is a term used very loosely by Americans today. We use it in a strong sense: a *community* is a group of people who are socially interdependent, who participate together in discussion and decision making,

and who share certain *practices* (which see) that both define the community and are nurtured by it. Such a community is not quickly formed. It almost always has a history and so is also a *community of memory*, define in part by its past and its memory of its past (333).

Bellah's strong sense of community leads him and his colleagues to pay attention to its absence by and large in our contemporary situation. Conditions of social interdependence, shared practices, and shared histories have become less and less the experience of life in America. *Habits of the Heart's* pivotal analysis of the loss of American community, written in the 1980s, did not base its case, however, just on what had happened in the social upheavals of the 1960s and 1970s and the reactionary trends of the 1980s. This book's understanding of the inherent dangers of American individualism depends largely on the analysis of American culture done by the nineteenth century French observer Alexis de Tocqueville. It is from Tocqueville that the title *Habits of the Heart* comes.

Bellah's analysis is based in part on Tocqueville noticing that even nineteenth-century Americans "form the habit of thinking of themselves in isolation and imagine that their whole destiny is in their hands" (37). Bellah knows that alarm about the lack of community in America in not new, since Tocqueville also said, "There is danger that he [the American man-*sic*] may be shut up in the solitude of his own heart" (37).

The roots of American rejection of community are tellingly recorded by Tocqueville. Bellah *et al.* note:

> Tocqueville's argument was that in older societies, one knew where one stood relative to others because of the existence of a network of established statuses and roles, each of which implied an appropriate form of attachment. In the mobile and egalitarian society of the United States, people could meet more easily and their intercourse was more open, but the ties between them were more likely to be casual and transient. A further reason for the casualness and transience had to do with what Tocqueville calls the American's "restlessness in the midst of prosperity." . . . This restlessness and sadness in pursuit of the good life is intensified, says Tocqueville, by the "competition of all," which in the United States replaces the aristocratic privilege of some (117).

In a haunting recall of Jennifer's life described at the beginning of this chapter, Bellah follows Tocqueville further: "So the efforts and enjoyments of Americans are livelier than in traditional societies, but the disappointments of their hopes and desires are keener, and their 'minds are more anxious and on edge.' How could such restless, competitive, and anxious people sustain enduring relationships, when 'they clutch every-thing and hold nothing fast'" (117).

Noticing the way America then has enculturated such anticommunity behavior began with Tocqueville and is closely followed by Bellah: "As Tocqueville observed, when one can no longer rely on tradition and au-thority, one inevitably looks to others for confirmation of one's judgments. Refusal to accept established opinion and anxious conformity to the opin-ions of one's peers turn out to be two sides of the same coin. There has been a long-standing anxiety that the American individualist, who flees from home and family, leaving the values of community and tradition behind, is secretly a conformist" (148). Where American lifestyles resemble Jennifer's more closely, serious questions about the norms of social confor-mity need to be faced.

But Tocqueville and Bellah are not just cynical observers of the lack of American community. As Bellah notes, Tocqueville "singled out family life, our religious traditions, and our participation in local politics as help-ing to create the kind of person who could sustain a connection to a wider political community" (vii). Bellah and his colleagues also end ambitiously with a chapter about "Transforming American Culture."

> It would be well for us to rejoin the human race, to accept our essential poverty as a gift, and to share our material wealth with those in need . . . . Such a vision arises not only from the theories of intellectuals, but from the practices of life that Americans are already engaged in. Such a vision seeks to combine social concern with ultimate concern in a way that slights the claims of neither (296).

In our book both Bellah's analysis and vision are crucial. The gospel of community is evoked by both a critique of American individualism and a vision of a renewed religious tradition; a tradition that does not slight either social or ultimate concern.

ROBERT WUTHNOW

The work of Robert Wuthnow, professor of sociology and director of the Center for the Study of Religion at Princeton University, complements the analysis of Bellah *et al.*, while advancing another way of describing the current upheaval. In his recent book, *Loose Connections: Joining Together in America's Fragmented Communities,* Wuthnow acknowledges and charts how "some evidence suggests that a growing number of people regard their neighbors as inherently untrustworthy (especially if they are a different race or nationality) and as alien to their idea of a like-minded community. It is easy to infer from such evidence that many Americans are turning their backs on the general welfare and pursuing their own interests as single-mindedly as possible. Given such inferences, it is hardly surprising that the passivity and narcissism of contemporary Americans are recurrent themes in thoughtful social analysis" (3).

Wuthnow posits—twelve years later and in some contrast to Bellah—that new, but somewhat distinct, efforts toward community formation are now underway.

> As Americans sense the fragmentation of their communities, many are now talking seriously about making connections with other people. They talk of coming together for the good of their communities, either in informal personal networks or through larger and more formal organizational partnerships. But these connections are often looser than was true in the past. Instead of cultivating lifelong ties with their neighbors, or joining organizations that reward faithful long-term service, people come together around specific needs and to work on projects that have definite objectives. These loose connections apparently suit many Americans today because of the permeable institutions in which we live (7, 8).

Where people do find themselves in community settings, Wuthnow charts how many of them "do not come right out and say so, but their own commitment to their communities is beginning to wear thin" (28). Instead of long-term commitment, as charted in Bellah's definition of community, Wuthnow finds a new set of arrangements, which are serious but more limited in terms of their length of time and scope of interest. New volunteerism in the suburbs "permits many suburban residents to focus on their own interests, without having to confront the serious problems that are prevalent in many other communities" (109). Working together in the inner cities is "against the odds" (110–34). In small towns, "the looser, more diverse, long-distance relationships that characterize their civic activities are helping them meet" challenges that "threaten their familiar way of life" (156). All this points toward a new paradigm of self-understanding, Wuthnow suggests. Herein, the "good citizen" is "learning to work with others, gaining self-knowledge, developing patience, and grappling with the reality of human suffering." This model is meant to produce "a person of character," not a commitment to community (178).

It is difficult to dispute Wuthnow's observations. And, while his encouragement at the nation-wide trend of establishing loose connections is heartening, comparisons with Tocqueville and Bellah *et al.* provoke further questions about how these bonds support life together. These loose connections seem hardly distinguishable from the casual and transient relations Tocqueville noticed and worried about in nineteenth century Americans. Similarly Bellah's portrait of the twentieth-century individualist with all the incumbent dangers is strikingly reminiscent of Wuthnow's good citizen, who is primarily a person of character and less a participant in community. Wuthnow, Bellah, and Tocqueville then seem to agree on these patterns of behavior, but disagree on their implications, Wuthnow being far more positive than the others.

Another significant agreement among all of these observers cuts to the core of this book's interest. It is clear that Wuthnow's good citizen is not interested in community as Bellah defines it, "a group of people who are socially interdependent, who participate together in discussion and decision making, and who share certain *practices* that both define the community and are nurtured by it." Wuthnow's seems to agree that the new "good citizen" is more interested in a looser "civic participation" than in a "community of memory." To pursue the fact that Wuthnow is heartened and Bellah worried about the trend away from community would divert us from our present purpose. That both agree that community is on the wane reinforces this chapter's case about the state of American culture.

Without wanting to discourage the virtues of Wuthnow's good citizen, *Re-Imagining Life Together in America* is interested in the development of a "strong sense" of community as Bellah *et al.* have defined it. It is the particular community commitment offered within the framework of Christian church that we find promising. This is not because we reject good citizenship or because we think Christianity is inherently better. It is because the possibility of the real practice of community in relationship to a longer tradition of belonging is most available for many Americans in Christian churches.

ROBERT PUTNAM

While integrating much of Tocqueville, Bellah, and Wuthnow, the recent major work of Robert D. Putnam, *Bowling Alone: The Collapse and Revival of American Community*, looks at the problems Americans have in living together with additional subtlety and activism. Like Bellah, Putnam takes both an anecdotal and empirical approach in analyzing the long-term issues of an American sense of civic engagement and belonging. Like Wuthnow, Putnam sees the last several decades as different in important ways from the longer view of America's struggle for community. In some distinction from Wuthnow and Bellah, *Bowling Alone* takes seriously the task of proposing solutions to the current decline in American community. Putnam's picture of the current situation is both nuanced and direct:

> During the first two-thirds of the century Americans took a more and more active role in the social and political life of their communities—in church and union halls, in bowling alleys and clubrooms, around committee tables and card tables and dinner tables. Year by year we gave more generously to charity, we pitched in more often on community projects, and (insofar as we can still find reliable evidence) we behaved in an increasingly trustworthy way toward one another. Then, mysteriously and more or less simultaneously, we began to do all those things less often (183).

The major question for Putnam then is "Why, beginning in the 1960s and 1970s and accelerating in the 1980s and 1990s, did the fabric of American community life begin to unravel?" (184)

The emerging phenomenon of the book's title—the growing tendency of Americans to bowl alone—illustrates perfectly what Putnam is describing. It turns out that although "sports participation is modestly but unambiguously down over the last decade or so" (109), bowling is one of the few sports that has grown in recent years. The crucial aspect of this trend, however, is that "league bowling has plummeted in the last ten to fifteen years," Putnam notes. This change away from bowling in organized groups is so drastic that "if the steady decline in league bowling were to continue at the pace of the last fifteen years, league bowling would vanish entirely within the first decade of the new century" (112).

Putnam wants to make sure that we not think his bowling example eccentric. "Lest bowling be thought a wholly trivial example, I should note that, according to the American Bowling Congress, ninety-one million Americans bowled at some point during 1996, *more than 25 per cent more than voted in the 1998 congressional elections*" (113). He insists on his conclusion: "Whether or not bowling beats balloting in the eyes of most Americans, bowling teams illustrate yet another vanishing form of social capital" (113).

The poignancy of this image of loss of American community comes alive in one of Putnam's examples:

> Before October 29, 1997, John Lambert and Andy Boschma knew each other only through their local bowling league at the Ypsi-Arbor Lanes in Ypsilanti, Michigan. Lambert, a sixty-four-year-old retired employee of

the University of Michigan hospital, had been on a kidney transplant waiting list for three years when Boschma, a thirty-three-year-old accountant, learned casually of Lambert's need and unexpectedly approached him to offer to donate one of his own kidneys. "Andy saw something in me that others didn't," said Lambert. "When we were in the hospital Andy said to me, 'John, I really like you and have a lot of respect for you. I wouldn't hesitate to do this all over again.' I got choked up." Boschma returned the feeling: "I obviously feel a kinship (with Lambert). I cared about him before, but now I'm really rooting for him." This moving story speaks for itself, but the photograph that accompanied this report in the *Ann Arbor News* reveals that in addition to their differences in profession and generation, Boschma is white and Lambert is African American. That they bowled together made all the difference (28).

As evocative as Putnam's bowling examples are, his book covers a vast range of stories and—more tellingly—keen sociological analysis. He examines political participation, civic involvement, religious belonging, connections in the workplace, and informal social connections. Beyond this analysis of social engagement, Putnam draws on studies of attitudes about community participation. He looks at altruism, volunteerism, philanthropy, reciprocity, honesty, and trust, inasmuch as they can be measured over the past thirty years. Nor does he miss emerging trends. Like Wuthnow he is interested in current interest in small groups and particular social movements. Putnam even examines with care the trends toward and away from community on the internet.

The evaluative tone of *Bowling Alone* does not overstate. Putnam cautions: "It is emphatically not my view that community bonds in America have weakened steadily throughout our history—or even through the last hundred years. On the contrary, American history carefully examined is a story of ups and downs in civic engagement, not just downs—a story of collapse and of renewal" (25).

Putnam does have a definite opinion about reasons for the decline of community in America. He states that: "Much of the decline . . . during the last third of the twentieth century is attributable to the replacement of an unusually civic generation by several generations (their children and grand-children) that are less embedded in community life" (275). Nevertheless, Putnam delineates the vestiges of community loyalties that still do persist in contemporary America. He reports that in response to a Yankelovich Partners survey of "what are the ways in which you get a real sense of belonging or a sense of community?" family and friends are "most commonly cited, followed by co-workers" (274). Even though these ties still abide, all the categories of community, from political and civic, through religious and work-related, are currently in decline, Putnam concludes.

Perhaps one of the most unique parts of *Bowling Alone* is its activist dimension. Noting that "it is within our power to reverse the decline of the last several decades" (25), Putnam devotes nearly one-fourth of the book to "What Is to Be Done?" (365). He develops seven major proposals for the reinvigoration of American community, all of which are meant to be accomplished by the year 2010.

These seven goals are to act to ensure that

1. "the level of civic engagement among Americans" coming of age in 2010 "will match that of their grandparents when they were the same age."

2. "America's workplace will be substantially more family-friendly and community-congenial, so that American workers will be enabled to replenish our stocks of social capital both within and outside the workplace."

3. "Americans will spend less time traveling and more time connecting with our neighbors than we do today, that we will live in more integrated and pedestrian friendly areas, and that the design of our communities and the availability of public space will encourage more casual socializing with friends and neighbors."

4. Americans "spur a new, pluralistic, socially responsible 'great awakening,' so that Americans will be more deeply engaged than we are today in one or another spiritual community of meaning, while at the same time becoming more tolerant of the faiths and practices of other Americans."

5. "Americans will spend less leisure time sitting passively alone in front of glowing screens and more time in active connection with our fellow citizens," and "foster new forms of electronic entertainment and communication that reinforce community engagement rather than forestalling it."

6. "significantly more Americans will participate in cultural activities from group dancing to songfests to community theater to rap festivals," and "discover new ways to use the arts as a vehicle for convening diverse groups of fellow citizens."

7. "many more Americans will participate in the public life of our communities—running for office, attending public meetings, serving on committees, campaigning in elections."

The seven point "agenda" Putnam sets for Americans in one sense can be understood as much larger than the focus of this book on the "gospel of community," in that Putnam addresses a variety of arenas besides the religious life about which we are thinking. From this point of view, our book is primarily focused on Putnam's proposal 4, the need for a "great awakening" and the development of spiritual communities of meaning.

On the other hand, we want to suggest that involvement in communities of faith encourage participation in all of the other arenas of Putnam's proposals. Just as Lonergan insisted that community is the foundation of society, so from this perspective, does a community of faith provide an orientation to life that enables and compels people of faith into all the other dimensions of Putnam's community.

CONCLUSION

Together Bellah, Wuthnow, and Putnam provide an analysis of what we have called "the American disaster." The haunting and surreptitiously destructive life Jennifer leads in the name of the American dream can be understood in historical and cultural perspective through the works of these recent authors. Although the analysis of each author is somewhat different, they together represent a major diagnosis of what has happened in the triumph of American individualism over community. In striking complementarity, these three observers of contemporary American society also identify what is at stake in this decline of community.

This book proposes that participation in local church communities promises a way out of this disaster, both for individuals and major sectors of the public at large. We suggest that the combination of deep traditions of belonging within Christian tradition, the prevailing dominant location of churches in America, emerging social understandings of God, and more refined and precise sociological theories and prophetic insights gleaned from liberation and feminist movements can help many Americans rediscover the power of community.

However, as the contribution of a liberation perspective on community reminds us, this proposal cannot be pursued naively. The American churches, it turns out, are not outside the influence of American individualism. There are ways in which substantial segments of American church life have been co-opted from community and toward a religious individualism. In this regard, American churches are not resources for community, but rather complicit in the destruction of community life. Our next chapter examines the ironies of American church life, which simultaneously inhibits and enables new forms of community. It is only after addressing this substantial irony that we can press our case for churches as a pivotal resource in the recovery of American community.

Chapter Nine

THE CRISIS OF COMMUNITY IN THE CHRISTIAN CHURCHES OF AMERICA

There is a deep irony in this book's major proposal that local church life in America can help Americans out of their excessive individualism and into more substantial community. The task of this chapter is to address that irony.

The irony is this: many American churches themselves exhibit and promote some of the worst expressions of anticommunitarianism. In other words, even though we are proposing that church life can help re-imagine life together in North America, the reality is that much church life in America works against a sense of community.

We still hold to our thesis, and part 4 of the book will press our case. But this proposal can only be taken seriously after we have looked directly at some characteristics of American churches that militate against community. Three destructive characteristics of American church life need to be recognized: clericalism, formalism, and a particular religious expression of individualism.

CLERICALISM

Clericalism wears many faces in our American churches; some "kindly" and others "abusive," but all are disempowering and anticommunitarian. The abusive clergyperson has become part of the national fingerprint. Even though recent headlines have emphasized certain kinds of felonies committed by the ordained, clerical abuse takes additional forms beyond the present scandal of sexual misconduct. Movies have often portrayed such characters with devastating clarity and a surprising amount of sympathy. The recent film *The Apostle* shows a charismatic preacher whose genuine gifts of compassion and inspiration are in the end overshadowed by his egocentrism and cruelty to those closest to him. In many ways, *The Apostle* only serves as an update of the 1950s classic film, *Elmer Gantry*, in which a deeply gifted preacher slowly falls victim to his own megalomania.

The pentecostal type preacher in these films is not the only kind of abusive clergyperson. Both mainstream Protestantism and Roman Catholicism have produced thousands of clergy, who combined insecurity, selfishness, ambition, and role-inflation in ways that undercut Christian community living.

One way that many American clergy have undermined community is through their accruing of power and attention to themselves. It is as if the sole focus on clergy in liturgy is intensely and complexly related to some clergy's power-hungry leadership styles. In Roman Catholicism the governance of parishes explicitly and formally emphasizes priestly pre-rogatives. Rooted in a larger hierarchical tradition of papal and episcopal governance, some local pastors unilaterally control finances, educational programs, and liturgical life—often without any other collaborative bodies. Where there are operative lay committees or structures, they are only consultative to clerical authority. As our examples of emerging new communities in chapter 11 indicate, some Roman Catholic communities are working on new, more collaborative models. Nevertheless centers of power in parish life have remained strongly clerical with laity having little voice.[1]

Many evangelical churches—although not related to the authority traditions of pope and bishop—have similar governance structures in which the pastors reign nearly supreme. In these evangelical pieties, the inspired character of the preachers themselves are the basis for their having nearly complete control over the laypeople.

The damage done to community by mainline Protestant clericalism is perhaps a bit more subtle. Democratic structures predominate in the ways these communities govern themselves. Typical Presbyterian, Lutheran, and Methodist congregations require a variety of church councils and committees to decide on church programs in contrast to the pastor-centered governance of most Roman Catholic and many evangelical churches. Nevertheless, the experience of clergy domination in Protestantism is often at least as intense as that of the more hierarchically governed denominations.

It is possible that the undermining of community by mainline Protestant pastors has to do with the ways these pastors' words are central to Protestant worship. In the vast majority of Protestant worship services the pastor's speaking completely dominates all other activity. Not only do few, if any, other people speak during the worship, but the act of worship itself focuses on the words of the pastor. The "Word of God" is associated with the sermon, and such Protestant worship often does not include communion. This focus on the pastor's words in worship carries over into the relational dynamics of congregational life. Since the pastor's words carry so much weight in worship, they often overcome the democratic governance structures of the church itself. The pastor's words, opinions, and feelings are made sacred in ways that result in their governing the community rather than the structures and experiences of the entire community. This focus on clerical wisdom for the Christian community is then often rationalized by appealing to legendary heroes of the past. By appealing to heroic piety and theologies based on individual leadership patterns of the past, the pastor becomes Moses, David, Paul, or even Jesus in the minds of the congregation. The pastor's own psyche becomes the Word to be followed. The iconic symbol-value of "priest" and "pastor" becomes reified in this particular person, collapsing the all-important distance between symbol and symbolized.

So in all sectors of American church life, the dangers of clericalism persist. As a distortion of genuine relationship, clericalism refers to that cultural condition of clergy domination that is created and sustained by clergy and/or the congregation. Clericalism disrupts community decision making by imposing the clerical will on the body. The life-giving interaction and ever-deepening exchanges inherent in a community thinking through its shared experiences are short-circuited by arbitrary clerical prerogatives. The way that caring for one another enriches relationships and deepens understanding is interrupted by clerical perceptions or clergy insistence that care dynamics and the power to speak always pass through the pastoral and priestly offices. The notion of the body of Christ as Spirit moving in the dynamic of Christian community is distorted and replaced by arbitrary clerical privilege.

How clericalism came to be such a powerful disruption of community-building needs to be studied thoroughly. But before one can understand a cultural condition, one must first become aware of it. Just as a process of awakening serves as a first step out of patriarchy's tight grip, so church people must wake up to the fact that both congregations and clergy have been complicit in greater or lesser degrees in perpetuating a culture of clericalism.

Just such a wake-up call has sounded in the Roman Catholic Church in 2002 with the alarming news of sexual misconduct, abuse, and criminal acts by clergy against vulnerable youth and children that has gone on for years. We do not in any way want to overlook the church community's primary responsibility to care for the victims/survivors of this horrific abuse.

But in light of our topic, it would be irresponsible of us not to underscore the fact that this shocking revelation painfully discloses a pervasive sickness endemic to a clerical culture. This sickness has less to do with sex and more to do with secrecy, in a culture that is skilled in cover-up, accountable to no one outside the clerical circle and accustomed to privilege. Clericalism's elite and closed system destroys community at every level. It fosters instead an exclusive club, whose members often misuse power and may even mistakenly perceive themselves above the law. The crisis in the Catholic Church at present is a crisis not of ordained priesthood but of this clerical culture. It is clericalism that must die so that genuine communities of clergy and lay can emerge with new life.

It is not our intent to analyze the root causes or historical conditions that have fostered clericalism, or to impugn guilt on any persons or groups for its relational distortions, but we can briefly identify several factors in its development that are disruptive of Christian community. We cite two major factors: the overlapping of ritual and governance functions in the office of the clergy and the intense connection between ordination and patriarchy.

The first factor is relatively unique to Christianity as religious expression. Unlike many other religions, Christianity developed a structure of leadership in which those in charge of the ritual were often also those at the head of the community. This merging of ritual and social leadership is evident even in the verbal confusion in Christianity between "pastor" and "priest." Although the pastoral role of caring for the community is easily differentiated from the priestly role of ritual and prayer leader, it is the same person who does both in most Christian communities. This has not been the case for many religions of the past, nor is it the dominant pattern in many contemporary non-Christian religions. The built-in tension in the ancient near east between the king and the high priest allowed for a system of checks and balances in governance, which is not possible in a church where clergy perform both roles. In none of the major Eastern religions do the ritual leaders have central roles in determining the relational dynamics or governance of life together for the ordinary practitioner.

The second factor in clericalism's disruption of Christian community, the linkage between patriarchy and clergy, stands at the center of major debate and discovery in the American church today. The emerging presence of women clergy in America in the last fifty years is not only changing the character of Christian community in some cases, but is raising questions about the gendered nature of clergy power in others.

Before returning to the new possibilities and problems posed by women clergy today, it is important first to describe how male privilege and clergy have been intimately linked for most Americans experiencing Christian community up to now. That until recently all pastoral/priestly power was male has seriously harmed the growth of community. This male dominance has first of all excluded women from direct participation in a variety of leadership roles, and therefore deprived communities of the insights and skills of half of the human race. Similarly, that virtually all clerics have been male has resulted in many Christian communities ignoring women's arenas of life. The silence of Christian community in terms of domestic abuse serves as one example of how devastating and pervasive relational dynamics have gone unexamined by Christian communities.

Examining how patriarchal privilege and male clericalism wed likewise reveals much about the arbitrary exercise of power in Christian communities. The ways that male pastors and priests impose their will on Christian community can often be traced to insecurities within the clergy themselves. These insecurities—often intimately related to ambiguities inherent in being male—are not processed directly by the pastors as a part of normal growing into adult men. Rather the ambiguities are denied by the pastors in asserting social dominance and privilege within the Christian community. This can perhaps best be seen in many clergy's rejection of women's participation and leadership in church settings. At least one reason for this non-negotiable refusal of women's participation may be the pastor's own personal, unprocessed insecurities in relationship to women. In this way, male privilege and clericalism bond together in a tight mutual reinforcement.

As mentioned throughout this book, there are some major signs of hope in the past fifty years that this complicity between patriarchy and clericalism can be broken. The women's movement of the later twentieth century has challenged clergy's destructive effect on Christian community in several ways, but perhaps most directly in the emergence of women clergy. In several denominations women's clerical leadership is now entering its third generation, and patterns of difference between male clergy leadership and that of women are becoming apparent. That women clergy are more consultative and process-oriented in the ways they relate to their congregations can now be seriously entertained as an overarching hypothesis. The lack of arbitrary clergy privilege in many women's pastorates exhibits promise that cooperation in Christian community can be enhanced through increased women's presence in leadership. While affirming this hope, we are aware of two other, more complex dynamics in the ways women's leadership is impacting Christian community:

1) Some women clergy have, like their male counterparts, exhibited the same arbitrary clerical privilege as they enter the priestly and pastoral offices.

2) Similar, hopeful contributions to a new kind of pastoral leader are being made by lay and religious women in many American Christian communities, thus challenging the very notion of a clerical caste.

Despite these rays of hope shining through the entrenched barriers of clericalism, the arbitrary and debilitating influences of priests and pastors on the formation and maintenance of local Christian communities remain imposing. If churches are to show Americans some ways out of individualism and toward community, clericalism must be challenged directly on many fronts.

FORMALISM

Distinct from—but not totally unrelated to—clericalism is another major anticommunitarian trend in American church life. This is the deeply embedded tendency of Americans to experience religious life as a submission to a certain kind of mindless formality. Perhaps the most common expression of this is habitual and unthinking church attendance. "Going through the motions" has perhaps no better example than the image of the American churchgoer mindlessly following the worship routine. Attention to this dimension of American religious life came into focus in the 1950s and 1960s with a series of studies on what was called "the comfortable pew." In these analyses church attendance became a formality linked both to codes of cultural acceptability and to American habits of consumption.

It is the destructive impact this formalism has on Christian community that needs to be emphasized here. When Americans just "go through the church motions," they generally avoid the human interaction necessary for the creation and support of meaningful community. In contrast to the ways most Africans go to church to enjoy and interact with one another, many Americans simply make an appearance in a church building, often without ever offering more than a perfunctory greeting at the door. This tendency comes to light regularly in the experiences of persons seeking new church homes. The classic complaint of such seekers is that they attended an entire worship service without having any human contact at all.

This tendency away from human community within the American worship experience is most evident in Roman Catholic and mainline Protestant churches. Many a Roman Catholic parishioner will confess to attending Sunday Mass without directly speaking to a sister or brother worshipper at mass. Despite clear, liturgical reform that focuses on the significance of the gathered assembly, parishes continue to exist where a priest simply "says Mass" with the minimal expectation that individuals repeat certain memorized words, kneel at the appropriate time, and take the elements of communion. In these settings, actual human exchange is both rare and difficult. The role of substantial human interaction to build up the social (and mystical) body is hardly factored in for many of these worshippers. To make matters worse, where such church attendance is both mandatory and habitual, the worshippers themselves build up a resistance to community-related interactions. Although these liturgies purport to focus on the body of Christ, the social alienation of formalism often turns the eucharist into a caricature of itself.

Many mainline Protestant services have equally destructive—if somewhat different—antisocial patterns of behavior. Here the power of rote body movement is somewhat less entrancing and alienating, simply because there is less of it. A Protestant worshipper can often worship for an hour or longer and move more than an inch only two or three times. The worship consists almost entirely of sitting and listening to someone up front. There is little or no chance for these Protestant worshippers to respond physically or verbally. If there is any response to the worship leader(s), it is usually a response that is printed in the worship bulletin and read in a unison monotone. Since the focus of Protestant worship is predominantly "the Word" and since that "Word" is proclaimed from the pulpit, the community members themselves remain lame.

Evangelical churches provide distinctly more community-building interaction in worship than many Roman Catholic and mainline Protestant churches. In these worship services hearty and personal words of welcome, deep and often spontaneous, personal expressions of prayer occur, and even physical embrace of one another is not uncommon. Later in this chapter we will return to ways that evangelical Christian communities disempower community. But in terms of the ways American formalism undermines Christian community, evangelical Christianity is less affected.

The underpinnings of this anticommunitarian formalism in American Christianity lie perhaps in deeper currents of Christian theology and piety. Often in the history of the churches, the value of worship, doctrine, and Scripture have been affirmed independent of their social reality. In fact, these dimensions of church life have been described as independent of and unsusceptible to the contingencies of life together as human beings. In this rationale, we human beings exhibit our flawed human characters when we interact. But sacred worship, infallible doctrine, and inerrant Scripture all rise above the ordinariness of actual human community interaction. As we have seen, especially in our theological study of communion in chapter 4, such an abstracted and a-social way of looking at Christian life contradicts some of the deep and long-held affirmations of worship, doctrine, and Scripture themselves. Nevertheless, this abstract and otherworldly interpretation of Christian life has been influential, and is linked to the ways formalism undermines Christian community in America.

INDIVIDUALISM AND AMERICAN CHRISTIANITY

Perhaps the most obvious irony of our proposal that churches can help Americans become less individualist and more community-minded is that major parts of American Christianity support and enhance an individualist approach to life. One might even say that substantial parts of American Christianity form some of the foundations of American individualism.

In a 1999 article in the Roman Catholic journal *America* entitled "Religion and the Shape of National Culture," Robert Bellah has suggested that "the dominance of Protestantism" in America "is responsible for many of our present difficulties" (9, 10) related to the lack of community in America. Although acknowledging that "this is not entirely fair, as it overlooks the community-forming capacity of Protestantism so evident earlier in our history" (10), Bellah traces tellingly in both sociological and historical terms the ways American Protestantism undergirds the larger national tendency toward the rugged individual.

Early American Protestants—especially the Baptists and Quakers—focused on the "absolute centrality of religious freedom, of the sacredness of individual consciousness in matters of religious belief," Bellah notes. This has resulted, according to Seymour Martin Lipset, in the United States differing from all our European and North American neighbors in that we alone have a predominant religious tradition which is "sectarian rather than an established church" (10). While all the other societies have national churches, the United States has an indecipherable array of separatist churches. Bellah recounts the beginnings of this Protestant individualism:

> Roger Williams was a moral genius, but he was a sociological catastrophe. After he founded the First Baptist Church, he left it for a smaller and

purer one. That, too, he found inadequate, so that he founded a church that consisted only of himself, his wife, and one other person. One wonders how he stood even those two. Since Williams ignored secular society, money took over Rhode Island in a way that would not be true in Massachusetts or Connecticut for a long time. Rhode Island under Williams gives us an early and local example of what happens when the sacredness of the individual is not balanced by any sense of the whole or concern for the common good (11).

Bellah suggests two dimensions of Protestantism that have been formative of Williams-like individualism in our day, one whose current effects are mainly historical and ideological, the other "very much alive and well today."

The first and more historical influence comes from the early Protestant reaction against Catholic notions of "the sacred in the world" (11). The early Protestants linked this idea of the sacred in the world to the major political and religious corruptions within Roman Catholic dominance in the secular world of the sixteenth and seventeenth centuries. Since the same people were devastatingly corrupt in the way they dominated and at the same time associated their own domination with the presence of God in the world, Protestants understandably "pushed God out of the world into radical transcendence." This helped separate God from much Roman Catholic corruption of that day. However, it also set up new conditions that propelled America toward isolating individualism. It discouraged Protestants from thinking involvement in human community was linked to God, since God was perceived as radically transcendent. "Even more ominously," Bellah adds, "into the empty space left by the absence of God (in the world) came an understanding of the self as absolutely autonomous" (11). This absolutized individual self could decide whatever she/he wanted, only in consultation with the radically transcendent God and in separation from human community. This leads directly to the second Protestant influence Bellah identifies.

"This is the near exclusive focus on the relation between Jesus and the individual, where accepting Jesus Christ as one's personal lord and savior becomes the whole of piety." Bellah elaborates, "If I may trace the downward spiral of this particular Protestant distortion, let me that it begins with the statement, 'If I'm all right with Jesus, then I don't need the church . . . '" Bellah's critique of Protestantism turns out to concentrate on a particular kind of contemporary Protestantism, the very one which has, by and large, escaped destructive anticommunity formalism, but unfortunately has fallen into equally devastating religious individualism. "The general tendency of American Evangelicalism toward a private piety pulls everyone influenced by it very much in this direction (of individualism). Some may think that Jesus-and-me piety is quite different from the individual as the preeminent being in the universe, but I am suggesting that they are only a hair apart," Bellah says (12).

This linkage of Protestant evangelicalism with devaluing of community is confirmed in the recent studies of Robert Putnam and Robert Wuthnow. Wuthnow asserts "Mainline Protestant churches encourage civic engagement in the wider community, whereas evangelical churches apparently do not . . . "(in Putnam, 78). Putnam adds, "The same contrast appears at the congregational level: self-described conservative congregations are less likely than liberal or moderate congregations to offer social outreach services or programs, with the notable exception of right-to-life activities" (78). Clearly rooted in the early Protestant idea of God transcending the world, "among evangelicals, church attendance is not correlated with membership in community organizations" (77, 78).

This embedded tendency does not seem to be just about contemporary religious moods, but are lodged in a larger and specific Protestant root. Wuthnow summarizes: "Whereas the mainline churches participated in progressive social betterment programs during the first half of the twentieth century, evangelical churches focused more on individual piety" ("Mobilizing Civic Engagement," 6 in Putnam, 77).

Bellah's linkage of Protestantism and individualism identifies more than just a Protestant danger. Since American culture has been dominated by Protestants, there is a way in which American Catholics, Jews, and Muslims have also inculcated this religious base for the individual who does not need community. Combined with the anticommunity tendencies of clericalism and fundamentalism, this religious form of individualism presents an ironic and articulate objection to our thesis that churches can point Americans back toward healthy community involvement.

CONCLUSION

How, then, shall we integrate this important, but negative, data into our larger proposal linking churches and community? We propose two strategies.

First, these ways that Christianity undercuts community must serve as constant warnings to all who seek Christian community. It is vital that those in Christian community stay awake and keep vigilant against clericalism, formalism, and religiously expressed individualism. Clergy must be acutely self-critical as well as called to accountability as a community member, given the harmful legacy of clerical domination of community. Abstractions and formalities cannot be portrayed as once and for all divinely ordained realities. These formalities can only be granted provisional status in Christian community, needing to be reclaimed again and again, while relational dynamics and connectedness among actual people need to be privileged. Spiritual assertions of uniquely individualist relationships to Jesus and/or God also need to be held in suspicion. The presence of God in the world—no matter how corrupt particular human communities become—must always be affirmed. Communities and individuals need to remain attentive to and suspicious of both mindless formalisms that eliminate human interaction and forms of intense personal piety that separate individuals from groups.

The second strategy for integrating this negative data is not to allow it to obscure the deeper traditions and possibilities of Christian community. Bellah, himself a Protestant, as we have already noted in the introduction to this book, claims a larger community-affirming "Catholic imagination"—a phrase he borrows from Andrew Greeley's *The Catholic Myth* (1991) and *The Catholic Imagination* (2001)—as countervailing resource to the individualist tendencies within Protestantism. Similarly, again as cited in our introduction, Bellah insists that involvement in local churches is key to America developing deeper community. It is, of course, this second strategy of situating the anticommunity tendencies of American strategy within the deeper and broader flow of churches' community-enhancing resources that we have outlined in parts 1 and 2 and to which we now turn in part 4.

PART FOUR

A GOSPEL OF COMMUNITY FOR THE TWENTY-FIRST CENTURY

INTRODUCTION

For isolated and detached Americans there is good news. The good news comes from a wide range of new church experiments in our day that have reclaimed the deepest traditions of Christian community. In this final section of the book we now explore in depth this gospel of community for our day.

Through personal stories of ordinary people, encountering and forming Christian community, chapter 10 takes us inside a new spirit of church community. It maps a social and spiritual strategy for those who seek depth, connectedness, and a sense of belonging. Chapter 11 enfleshes this strategy with sketches of five actual church communities. Paralleling the five early Christian communities of chapter 2, these five contemporary communities illustrate the power, breadth, and promise of a new gospel of community in the present. Chapter 12 concludes by placing these specific examples and strategies in terms of what we see God doing in the divine building up of earth itself. Situating our hopes for togetherness and belonging in ultimate perspective, this final chapter reaches for vocabulary about the relationship between God and our American search for community.

Part 4's direct address to the good news of community needs a sociological preamble. This is because it is not at all the case that churches across the board provide hopeful signs of community for Americans. There are specific streams of the gospel of community in current-day North America. And there are huge backwaters of ecclesial life that still stifle hope and belonging. Where then is this stream of hopeful church community in American society?

Much of this new community impulse is happening in relatively unlikely settings. For Roman Catholics, these new communities—as the examples in chapter 11 will illustrate—are often in parishes outside the diocesan mainstream, particularly in urban areas, in new efforts at restructuring traditional parishes, in subunits of parish life, in nontraditional, extra parochial parish settings; such as intentional eucharistic communities and university campuses, in men's and women's vowed congregations, in social justice ministries, and in communities of exile. For Protestants and Anabaptists, the strongest trend toward new community is in small, mostly urban, congregations. Mainline denominational models have generally remained stagnant, while new communities flourish at the margins. Where large Protestant churches do nurture a new community vitality, they—like their Roman Catholic counterparts—involve a special programmatic emphasis on creating subgroups. Beyond Protestantism and Catholicism, a new brand of postdenominational cell groups and churches are springing up with surprising vitality.

There are some patterns emerging within most of these swirls of new community. They tend to be smaller than much of the rest of American church life. Most of the renewed Protestant and postdenominational congregations have fewer than two hundred people. Where larger Roman Catholic or Protestant churches exhibit new community, almost always there are substantial subgroups of ten to thirty people per group that carry much of the new impulse.

Worship in these new communities shows much more flexibility and creativity than conventional church liturgy. Interpersonal sharing, innovative music, ritual and movement, a renewed claim of contemplative and prophetic traditions, deep symbols and unconventional settings regularly make up this new liturgical spirit in community. Informality, a broader spectrum of participation and leadership, and artistic expression occur much more often than in the older models of American church.

Governance in these new communities—which will be described in more detail in chapter 10—is much less authoritarian and hierarchical. The communities seem to improvise their structures of life together more freely. A larger variety of people take responsibility for determining what the community's commitments and character are.

The specifics of this new wave of church community in America vary. The spirit within these new groups invites a closer look.

Chapter Ten

THE EMERGENCE OF CHRISTIAN
COMMUNITY IN CONTEMPORARY AMERICA

What we have seen and heard we proclaim to you as well, so that you yourselves may have community with us. This community of ours is with God and God's son Jesus Christ (1 John 1:3).

T he reader may recognize this selection from 1 John as the opening text of this book's introduction. There we observed that gospel communities emerged "in the fragmented society of the hellenistic Mediterranean, where people had lost a sense of who they were." The "good news" that 1 John announced was community itself. We're a long way from the hellenistic Mediterranean here in the twenty-first century, multicultured United States. But a feeling of "lostness" (still) permeates many people's sense of who they are.

Chapters 8 and 9 looked at the contemporary situation in our North American context and focused on some of the anticommunity forces at work in our societal and church cultures, not unlike the situations described in chapter 1. Chapters 10 and 11 will seek to counteract those tugs against community by "proclaiming to you what we ourselves have seen and heard," an eruption of new communities in the fragmented societies of North America. Established local churches have both stunted and fostered this development. Nonetheless, we sense that new stirrings are being evoked from the inherent faith of the people, from the churches' deep memory of community life; its strong roots, its many ruptures, and its relentless return. It may be the case, after all, that human persons, created in the image of God, are coded for community in their very genetic make-up. For many spiritual seekers today, the way of community demands to be taken seriously as central to the Christian project in the world.

Several times throughout our writing, we have quoted someone's use of "Copernican Revolution" to describe the impact of a certain event on the people who experienced it. This time, we choose to use the expression ourselves. We believe that something of the magnitude of a "Copernican Revolution" is underway in North American churches. The movement to which we devote this chapter and apply this analogy is this emergence of "small Christian communities" here in the United States. This development is taking place in the midst of, despite, and to a large extent in response to, the contrast situations present in the larger society.

As co-authors, our personal experiences of pastoral ministry vary, accounting for some differences in the range of groupings we might at first so name "small Christian communities." But after many clarifying conversations and sharing of experiences, we discovered that the components we include in so defining a group are shared by both of us. The purpose of this chapter is to sketch a limited panoramic view, from our perspective at least, of some community renewal efforts underway. We believe that this movement seeds new hope for the future, making possible more authentic forms of life together, both in the public square and in the gatherings of church. This chapter will begin, by way of story, to assemble a constellation of terms characteristic of today's resurgence of community in American church culture. Next, the chapter will consider some patterns of behavior we notice communities practicing as they grow from groups of rather diverse individuals to differentiated but more cohesive communities. The chapter will conclude by positing some "lessons to be learned" from the churches and by the churches about promoting community life in the harsh environment that is our individualistic North American reality.

COMMUNITY: THE TIE THAT BINDS

Quiet and pensive, Mark looked back at you and out at the world with eyes that searched for reasons and probed deeply for meaning. It was not surprising to learn that Mark was a first-year medical student, the serious type, who had come to church for the first time with another young medical student, a native of the area whom he had just begun to date. Mark was "unchurched," even though both his parents had some early church affiliation, long abandoned. Despite his shy and retiring manner in a setting that encouraged embracing and outreach, Mark kept coming back. As Diana and Mark fell in love over the next three years, Diana's strong faith and supportive faith community beckoned Mark still further. What was the source of this community's joy and passion, especially the passion for justice and social transformation that permeated their worship and flowed into their community commitments? When Mark became a member of the parish's "community of inquirers," he found the space to ask questions that had surfaced for him over his three years of being welcomed weekly in this Sunday assembly. After a year of journeying in this community toward baptism, Mark was received into the Catholic Church at the Easter Vigil 2001 and two weeks later, he and Diana married in the same parish church. As Mark invited the parish community to gather for their wedding liturgy, one sensed the same placid personality, but he was now more confident and hope-filled, grounded, and directed at the same time. Mark expressed his own grateful sentiments for "finding a home where he and Diana could become their best selves." They could not imagine, he mused, pledging their lives to each other without being bound in turn to a community that nurtured, challenged, and connected them with a larger world to love.

Community: Source of Healing and Accountability

Anne Marie, a shy, quiet woman from County Mayo, Ireland, shared with her small community one Tuesday evening a nudge she was experiencing during the community's prayer and conversation together. The group had talked about the meaning of forgiveness in their own lives and in the Gospels. Several noted the gap they felt between Jesus' readiness to forgive unconditionally and their own tendencies to hold onto hurts. As the conversation moved from shared experiences to action steps, Anne Marie stammered out her resolve to write a letter to her brother back home in Ireland, with whom she had not spoken in years. A rather inconsequential squabble over the family farm had torn their relationship apart. No one offered a response to Anne Marie or followed up with any personal resolution.

Driving home that night, Anne Marie questioned herself about such an intimate personal disclosure. She felt dissatisfied, exposed, and foolish. Throughout the week, she said to herself repeatedly, "I'll write that letter tomorrow," but she never did.

The following Tuesday, when the community gathered, Anne Marie was amazed to hear three people from the group recount their personal moves toward reconciliation during the week, all inspired by Anne Marie's courageous outpouring. Anne Marie was humbled and aware that it was God's Spirit working through her. She confessed her own failure to carry out her proposed action, but with new conviction, she reiterated her resolve. The community agreed that God's nudging presence was once again made real for them through one another. God had spoken in the hesitant, Irish brogue of Anne Marie.

COMMUNITY FOR LIBERATION

Chrissie reluctantly agreed to go with her husband Paul when friends invited them to join a small faith community that met in their home every other Monday. For months Chrissie remained quiet while the group read, prayed over, and helped each other connect their lives with the scripture readings for the next Sunday; then prayed aloud for one another and for happenings in their neighborhood and world. Suddenly one Monday evening, Chrissie came to voice. The group had been sharing experiences from their childhood that flowed from the gospel text of Jesus inviting the "little children to come to him." Chrissie began to describe her experiences of growing up in a single-parent family with her father and three sisters. Her father, a Vietnam veteran, loved his daughters but raised them by means of a strict regiment of daily duties and exacting measures of accountability. She shared her vivid memories of lining up to respond to his questions: "Whom do you love?" and "Who takes care of you?" to which she and each of her sisters dutifully responded, "You, Dad."

At twenty-eight, Chrissie confessed that deep down she understands that her father did the best he could. But at the same time, she is beginning to realize that she and her sisters are so conditioned by fear and punishment, that they find it difficult to trust themselves or others. When someone asked if her father believed in God, she answered quickly that she only heard God referred to in her house as "the man in charge up there." Lights suddenly went on for Chrissie as she began to see how her image of God resembled more closely that "man in charge up there" than it did a God who hugged little, insignificant people, close to the heart.

That evening's sharing provided a breakthrough experience for Chrissie and her community. As they reflected further on how much our images of God are shaped by key persons and relationships in our lives, they began to see their responsibility to help free others as well as God from the constricting images that enslave them. Along with several members of the community, Chrissie now volunteers at least five hours a week at St. Anne's Home where young babies with HIV and/or alcohol syndrome need to be held and rocked.

Community in an Age of Social Mobility

For almost ten years, Jim and his wife, Helen, met weekly to share faith and life with their small community in Cranford, New Jersey. Two years after Helen's death, Jim's feeble health required his going to a nursing home, where he has lived for the past six years. Jim can no longer move freely, think clearly, or meet weekly with his faith community. In fact, Jim cannot even feed himself.

Jim and Helen never had children of their own and they had left the few relatives they did have back in Chicago, when they moved East sometime after World War II. In many ways, Jim might be considered family-less. Why then did his situation initially present such a quandary to those who observed his daily life in the nursing home?

Each day at about 5:30 P.M., residents and staff noticed a very caring visitor arrive to sit with, feed, and be present to Jim. "Are you his brother," the questioner began, "a son, cousin or nephew?" The next day, the question might change slightly, "Are you Jim's daughter? niece? sister?" Each day for the first few weeks, the answer would be the same until eventually everyone in the nursing home began to understand. Josie, Frank, Ellen, Fran, Tom, Barbara, Jerry, and Alice were members of Jim's community. Yes, Jim did belong to them; yes, he was a part of their family. Of course, they would continue to be there each day to feed and express their care for Jim. Their lives had long ago been woven together. Why should anyone be surprised?

Community and Social Transformation

The following account retells in a much too abbreviated form a tragic event that helped transform St. Nicholas parish in Evanston, Illinois.[1] The powerful drama seeks to explore concretely the question "Where can we find the church giving birth to genuine communities of transformation today?" One Sunday morning in July 1996, Father Oldershaw, pastor of the 1300 family, multicultural parish community, preached a life-changing homily in which he simply said, "a terrible thing has happened, two families have been touched by tragedy. How do we respond?" The terrible thing to which Oldershaw referred was the murder of seventeen-year-old Andrew Young, one of four children of Stephen and Maurine Young, members of the Evanston Bible Fellowship Church, by seventeen-year-old Mario Ramos, one of six children of Manuel and Maria Ramos, Mexican immigrants and members of St. Nicholas parish since 1990. That single question "How do

171

we respond?" posed within the context of faith to this eucharistic assembly, set in motion an intense, community-wide process of healing and reconciliation that may be best described in Josiah Royce's words as "the atoning deed."[2]

Tedious community meetings began by exposing the multiple barriers that divided the Hispanic members of the parish community from their Anglo counterparts, and then, they initiated the hard work of dismantling these barriers. Outreach efforts began to the grief-stricken Youngs, the family of the victim, to the confused and later repentant Ramos in prison and to his overwhelmingly shamed parents. These three sources of pain and brokenness became the focus of various communities' commitments and resulted in profound conversions and personal healings for those who sought to help as well as for those who received their care. More dramatic moments of the story include a letter asking for forgiveness, which Mario Ramos wrote to Andrew Young's parents, while he awaited trial for the murder of their son. Ironically, the letter was composed while Maurine Young, mother of the slain Andrew, was typing one of her own to Mario. In it she told of her prayers for Mario and her own search for meaning in life. She concluded with "I don't know if you'll ever feel up to asking my forgiveness for killing my son, so I'll go first, I FORGIVE YOU."

As outsiders were themselves drawn into the awesome power of reconciliation at work, more and more felt the effects of grace healing this broken community. The chaplain of Cook County jail summed up his experience. "You know," he said, "if every parish did what St. Nicholas did, we might be shutting down this whole place some day."

EMERGING ELEMENTS AND PATTERNS FOR BUILDING COMMUNITY

In overlapping ways in the stories recounted here and thousands not recorded, elements emerge to suggest that community, as an intentional design for life together, not only enhances the lives of its members but the social fabric of neighborhoods and society as well. We will trace five of these life-enhancing elements: 1) a sense of belonging, 2) a chance to forgive and be forgiven, 3) a space for quiet and reflection, 4) a genuine care for one another, and 5) a commitment to build a more just society.

At a time when feelings of lostness prevail and relationships are threatened, people are trying out new "social experiments" on the hunch that there is more to life than its commodification. With the vast proliferation of systems of communication, many people question why they often feel so little heard, known, or understood.

The search for alternatives to a culture of expediency and competition is but one impulse for the emergence of new forms of community life in our social context. For the young medical student, Mark, a desire for belonging as well as shared beliefs led him to embrace the justice-minded, liturgical community that is now home for him and Diana. This "sense of belonging" cannot be overlooked in describing needs to be met by community today. Though the number of maximum community members may vary with the corresponding structuring of the community's life, nonetheless, community requires a space where each member is known by name, missed when absent, and given an opportunity to participate actively in the life of the group. Without such an environment, belonging needs remain unsatisfied.

The core virtue of hospitality might be linked with this nascent human need to find a home where it is possible to become our best selves. How inclusive this spirit of hospitality becomes in practice distinguishes genuine communities from their more common counterfeit versions, lifestyle enclaves (Bellah), where exclusivity and homogeneity are safeguarded by alternative, cultural norms.

A second element of community emerges not only in Anne Marie's confessed alienation from her brother but in every human person's need to forgive and be forgiven as an integral part of life together. Community provides a fertile context in which forgiveness becomes both necessary and possible. Without community, little need exists to forgive or be forgiven, since little opportunity exists to come close to others, let alone love them. Jean-Marie Tillard, O.P., a Canadian theologian, has called forgiveness the knot in the thread of communion that links us to God and one another. The gift of practicing this virtue is no small contribution that community extends to otherwise isolated individuals in the U.S today. The practice of forgiveness as a way of life together demonstrates community's capacity to call its members to significant levels of accountability for how they desire to live. This gift of finding other persons with whom one is willing to be accountable for the shaping of one's life as well as one's world is accompanied by the demanding work of holding each other responsible in agreed-upon ways to live out these espoused values.

Newly developing communities here in the U.S. provide space for people of faith to share, revise, and appropriate meaning and values in their lives. By providing an environment for prayer and quiet reflection, Bible-reading, life-sharing, and committed action, communities make a serious countercultural contribution to the nonreflective, control-dominated, consumeristic values espoused as conventional wisdom. This third, contemplative element of quiet and prayerful reflection responds to a growing hunger among restless, American seekers for deeper meaning and spiritual values in their lives.

A fourth characteristic of community is its care for each individual member, the nurturing of the community's inner life. The story of Jim, a longtime community member now unable to feed himself, reflects this commitment of community members for the well-being of one another. Each becomes genuinely part of one another as they are, quite literally, knitted together into one body in community. This kind of agapic love reveals itself in good times for sure, but it is undeniably evident in hard times, showing up in nursing homes and hospices, in prisons, and soup kitchens. This genuine care and self-giving love for the community and each member is the great gift and deep responsibility of authentic life together. As did the staff at Jim's nursing home, we witness, in faltering or heroic ways, love's self-gift in concrete communities around us today.

Fifth, communities matter because they exist not for themselves alone, regardless of the benefits derived from such social inventions. Communities have an outer life toward which their energies are directed, as well as an inner life. Perhaps, it is this dimension of a community's role in social transformation that offers the best hope and greatest challenge to those concerned about both community and social change today. The danger is real for us in the U.S., conditioned as we are by a culture of insistent individualism, to take care of ourselves alone, whether that self is an isolated individual self or the still isolated, corporate-self of a closed community. The interconnectedness that makes us a part of all life, radically constituted in a web of relationships, is a hard truth to penetrate the seemingly self-sufficient North American ego. But when this scientific proclamation resonates with the enduring message of the Christian Scriptures that "we are all one body," a new insistence sounds in a world, fragmented and torn apart by divisions and competition.

Signs of hope loom large where communities dare to take a stand against injustice in their neighborhoods and churches, in political arenas on the state, national, and global level. The parish of St. Nicholas in Evanston, Illinois, witnesses convincingly to the power of gospel-inspired communities to help tear down the walls that divide Hispanics from Anglos, blacks from whites, Muslims from Jews and Christians, in so many of our cities. As the warden reflected, we would have need of fewer prisons if every church responded to the violence and tragedies around them as St. Nicholas parish did.

The gaping disparity between the hungry and the sated here in our own country is a pressing indictment of community's breakdown in a country where over-consumption and malnutrition live side by side. The story of Ann's community in Western New York, recounted in this book's introduction, demonstrates that "social transformation" is often an emergent process of one good deed after another.

Skills of social analysis need to combine with prayerful reflection on the contemporary social situation to help communities understand that the dynamic of Christian living is as much about disturbing the comfortable as it is about comforting the disturbed. Authentic communities stir one another with the prophetic awareness that until all are loved and welcomed, no community can rest complacent. Here, North American communities can benefit from the experience of the base communities in Latin America, where social analysis functions hand-in-hand with biblical reflection to shed light on a community's decisions and actions.

Though communities of social transformation are surfacing on the horizon of the new community movement in North America, the jury is still out on whether or not many nascent communities will expand their group consciousness beyond self-nurturance. Can new communities emerging in our North American church context move to a genuine concern for others outside their group, especially the stranger and the marginalized?[3] Upon such socially committed, inclusive communities, the future of our churches, society, and planet may well depend.

COMMUNITY-ENHANCING ELEMENTS: CONCLUSION

These community-building elements of belonging and accountability, reflection and caring, as well as commitment to social change are showing up in varying degrees and in various constellations in emerging communities today. Their effects are being felt by the individuals and communities who strive to practice them. But also, in rippling and inter-connected ways, they are informing the larger social fabric of our life together. It is our conviction that such communion virtues have the potential to become some of the emerging habits of a new North American heart to inspire more genuine forms of life together in the next generation.

SOCIAL PATTERNS OF BEHAVING

Beyond these community-building elements, it is important to pay attention to behavior patterns emerging in group-life today. We have lessons to learn from how groups understand themselves, shape their lives together, and interact with other levels of community, church, and society. As participant observers in community formation over the past thirty years, we have noticed some common patterns helping to constitute these new forms of life together. We will reflect on several that we find critical in fostering authentic community and study them under the headings of 1) time needs, 2) sharing needs, 3) identity needs, and 4) power relations.

TIME NEEDS: COMMUNITY AND THE TIME PROCESS

In an age of instant gratification, it is clear to social analysts (e.g., Royce and Bellah) and persevering practitioners that community does not just happen overnight. Among many converging factors, community is always the fruit of a time process. Groups may come together in the hope of growing into a community and that intentionality is helpful. But time is essential. This is true for individuals seeking to become members of an established community as well as for individuals coming together to form a community for the first time. Here, we differ somewhat from Robert Wuthnow's positive assessment of emerging, relational patterns and feel that too many patterns of "loose connections" are just not good enough.

The need for time together was evident in the journey of Mark, who entered into a three-year process of learning about a community's memories and sharing their hopes and visions of God's future before committing himself to a meaningful life with them in the present. For Chrissie, it took months of meeting with a group before she could share memories of her past experiences of her father. Once received, they became a part of the community's memory, able to influence their future hopes as well as their present decisions.

As Josiah Royce explained early in the twentieth century, communities come to be out of shared memories and shared hopes that help define their life together in the present. These dimensions of a past held in common and a future awaited together provide the character of a community's present commitments. The capacity to extend oneself into a common past and future help constitute the Community Self, just as these tri-fold time - frames inform the individual self. Often groups use the label of community without paying attention to the demands of the time process involved in its processual and sustained development.

Sharing Needs: Toward the Achieving of Shared Meanings and Values

In related but distinct ways, the insights of Bernard Lonergan explored in chapter 6, provide tools for assessing patterns in authentic community living, which can distinguish them from behaviors typical of group conformity or random collectives. Over the past twenty-five years, an awakening to the incredible diversity characteristic of all life provides a healthy suspicion of all imposed uniformity, posing as genuine unity. Sameness, therefore, is a guise for death rather than a characteristic of community life. How then may a group of persons achieve community? To recognize community as a process to be achieved over time sets the stage for some patterns of behavior to develop that make community possible or inhibit its growth. Lonergan insists that community coheres to the extent that shared meanings and values result in shared decisions and commitments. These meanings and values are the fruit of shared experiences and common understandings.

As we have observed and been a part of community formation efforts over the years, it has been extremely helpful to illumine our experiences through the lens of Lonergan's grid. Unless a space for quiet and reflective sharing is made possible for persons today, other cultural conditions make it unlikely that people will share significant experiences together, let alone try to understand them more fully or derive deeper meanings and values to assess them or make decisions out of the questions and choices they pose.[4] Yet it is this process that constitutes persons as well as communities and consequently the meanings and values of society itself.

This pattern of behavior, in fluid and messy forms, recurs over and over again in communities that cohere and make a difference in our world over time. Notice them in the Renew Group in Buffalo, New York. The shared experience of a gospel text led this community to seek further understanding in light of a contemporary situation, followed by the uncovering of gospel values and the decision to act on those values by establishing the Food Shuttle of Western New York. Similar patterns of behavior may be traced in the community's commitment to feeding Jim in the nursing home. Likewise, as this pattern of sharing experiences, understandings, meanings/values, and commitments wanes in the life of a group, community itself begins to diminish.

IDENTITY NEEDS AND THEIR NEGOTIATION

One of the gains that modern, western culture has contributed to contemporary society is a keen awareness of the dignity of each individual person. With this gain has come the impetus for overcoming the many injustices suffered by individuals and groups, such as women and blacks, whose individual rights had not been fully recognized or valued. But with this benefit, the insistence given to the rights of the individual in western culture has become so excessive that attention to the common good or needs of the community is now being threatened. The time has come to name the dangers inherent in the insistent individualism bred in our western consciousness. We must now re-imagine and reconstruct a social order, where community is understood as the primary locus for self-emergence in a cosmos of interdependent relationships.

In order to do this serious work of social reconstruction, we have significant learnings to incorporate from our past as well as present that put the rights of individuals and community in dialogue rather than in opposition. Our past is a mixed record of the priority given to community. Order and unity were too often prized by the powerful in both church and society to the neglect of alternative voices coming from outside the centers of powers. The rights of the individual were too often disregarded where the dominant power spoke for all. In a postmodern society, where a significant number of people are suspicious of one-way, universal proclamations, the work of enlarging community boundaries must pay attention to the rights of individuals and of individual communities.

Robert Wuthnow's description of contemporary communities having porous boundaries may be apt and potentially helpful. Negotiations need to be ongoing and in this sense, the boundaries porous, between a community's inner life, where attention is given to personal needs of each member and needs of the group as a whole, and its outer life, where a community needs to be open to and responsible for and to the larger church and society of which it is an interconnected part. The dialectic of community, as Bernard Lonergan described it, helps keep communities aware of this healthy tension between intersubjective needs and the good of the social order.

Such negotiations can be detected in the example of Chrissie's community, whose members' communal response to Chrissie's experience of childhood deprivation was to reach out to other children needing nurturance today. Where a community never moves beyond itself to concern for the larger community, chances are that another form of cultural individualism is simply replicating itself. Various forms of pseudo-community are springing up all around us and, as substitutes for authentic community, pose serious problems rather than solutions to our cultural malaise.

Those "porous boundaries and loose connections" get tested within the group itself as members negotiate individual needs with the needs of the community. This may take the shape of calling an individual member to some agreed-upon measure of accountability for the life of the group. What is the level of connection necessary for community to cohere? When are connections simply too loose for community to flourish; the boundaries too porous for any community self to emerge and grow? In different but related ways, questions must be asked about how a particular community is linked to other communities in an open and interdependent system. What structures make it possible to challenge a community to greater accountability for the common good beyond its members?

Conversations about the expectations and assumptions members bring to the group are critical in these negotiations. Honesty in sharing one's experience of the group and of one's place within the community provides a sure footing for further understanding of how to provide for the psychic and physical space needed for healthy individual and community growth. Working out "identity needs" provides ample reminder of the many levels of conversion needed by individuals and communities, if they are to overcome the biases that prevent the achievement of more authentic community.

Within this arena of self-disclosure, discovery, and discerning of needs, occasions for misunderstanding and misjudging abound. Listening, process, communication, and conflict mediation skills become integral components of striving for more genuine versions of life together. Here, too, the invitation to forgive and be forgiven becomes a lifeline, offered to make possible the values of authentic community-living for the sake of the world.

Power Relations: Understanding Power in Relational Modes

Community, as a corporate body of interconnected persons, provides a human laboratory where both personal and social power are recognized, claimed, validated, and placed at the service of a common good. Within community, uses of power can be studied, critiqued, and revised to meet new needs and changing relational patterns. The intimate connections between personal power and social power reveal themselves in the communal setting. Community is where individuals become aware of their personal strengths and weaknesses, learn which strengths are needed and valued by the group, and how to be in relationship with the group and its members by means of them.

To speak about human interactions as "power issues" often carries with it a highly emotional charge. Power, at best, has an ambiguous meaning; we both need it and are unnerved by it. Spiritually, we are aware of power as both divine and demonic, creating and healing, corrupting and destroying. In human history and in personal experience, we have witnessed "power" as both a way to care and a way to crush.

If we are to explore community life in terms of power, we will need to correct misconceptions that may still distort our thinking. First, power is not a static category, an entity that someone possesses or gains. Power is a relational term, a process or way of interacting with others.[5] Power has to do with strength, an energy to influence and make a difference. It has both a personal and a social face. Personal power was evident in the role assumed by Father Oldershaw, the pastor of St. Nicholas parish, who stood before his community and summoned from them a response to tragedy by his question "How are we to respond?"

Evelyn and James Whitehead have explored the faces of power in five dimensions: "power on," "power over," "power for," "power against," and "power with." As the most straightforward face of power, "power on" is simply one's capacity to influence and make something happen. It is seen as initiative and competence. "Power over" organizes and controls, coordinates and leads. "Power for" advocates and represents, nurtures and reveals itself as "strength for others" (1986, 160). It walks a thin line between care and constraint, between the goal of mutuality and the promotion of domination (strong over weak). When we recognize "power against" we know it as confrontation, experience it in conflict or in competition. It is an important face of adult maturing, dangerous as it can be.

Growing numbers of communities seek to enhance the personal face of "power with" by focusing on the conviction that "we are strong together." This face of power emerges when persons recognize their own strengths and are not diminished by the strengths of others. This personal claim to strength makes room for an awareness of one's weakness as well. Because one's strengths are visible, one does not need to expend one's energy in hiding one's limitations from the rest; personal strength is not devoted to self-defense. Perhaps, a growing sense of "power with" led Ann Marie to share her experience of alienation with her brother, or led Chrissie to reveal the constraints of her childhood.

At a social level, this face of "power with" commits itself to greater levels of mutuality, collaboration, and shared decision making. This face of power is never finally achieved, nor is it possible in every social situation. Communities grow into it by persevering through the developmental phases of time together. Personal and social power as communal strength is always in ongoing negotiation, becoming more fully actualized. For the sake of a more global solidarity, communities, committed to investigating and improving the power of human relationships, strikes us as imperative.

From an exploration of power in community, the question of authority springs up relatively early. Authority is a group's interpretation of power. No group comes to understand itself as sharing a common identity and purpose without acting out of or asking explicitly about its understandings of authority. Who gets to say what happens next for this group? Whose "voice" counts anyway and why? "It is what we make of power among us that determines the shape of authority" (1986, 167) in a community or any social organization. Members of a community do not just learn the patterns of authority that govern them. They help create them. We may passively accept or resist the patterns of authority at work in our life together or we may actively partner in the social process of determining the interplay of power between us and what faces of power are authentic in the life of the community.

Given our dominant culture where "rugged individualism," self-reliance, and competition are so highly valued, and where bureaucratic leadership styles characterize our social structures so pervasively, coming to re-imagine appropriate faces of authority in community is no easy feat. Authority springs from a community's judgment of how power flows best among them; obedience is the response the community gives to this decision. Where community espouses a growing sense of "power with" as its dominant face, new conceptions of authority are emerging. Authority is being claimed as a relational category, a reciprocal and dynamic pattern of relating in which energy flows from a group to a leader and from a leader to the group in an exchange that is mutually self-authenticating. Governance itself is understood as a relational concept that has to do with our way of being together.

Community, as a social structure distinct from conformity or collectivity, is a possibility to the extent that we come to understand authority as a relational term. No one can claim legitimate authority for oneself. It is a gift and responsibility entrusted to someone from others. Authority and obedience, both mutually constitutive and relational, exist hand in hand. In our autonomous and individualistic culture, obedience and authority are both suspect and are perceived far too often as conditions of subservience and domination. They connote little mutuality or the interplay of mature, adult relationships.

Communities today face the awesome task of re-imaging the vital interconnectedness of healthy patterns of authority and obedience as responsibilities we share with and for one another. Authority emerges from the community and remains always accountable to it. Its role is to foster the love and collaboration of community members for the sake of one another and the common good. Obedience too is a relational response; it requires putting one's life freely in the hands of the community at the service of a higher good, a good that one perceives beyond oneself. In the process of self-giving, both in the roles of authority and obedience, the self is not diminished but expanded. To be in the position of authority or obedience is to be in a mutually accountable relationship of equals, seeking together more authentic patterns of life together as an ever-emergent common good.

Aspects of obedience and authority as relational roles governed the communal work of St. Nicholas parish in Evanston, Illinois, as it discerned through leadership and membership how it would respond to the great tragedy that had befallen its neighborhood. A focused study of all the interactions that took place within and among the communities of St. Nicholas over a two-year period would be needed to say more about the dynamics of leadership/obedience at work. We do know that by a faithful commitment to seek the common good, a community was healed and the social situation was transformed.

CONCLUSION

This chapter has attempted to keep its community building elements close to the ground, emerging from stories of concrete, contemporary communities. A commitment to begin with and return to the practical and the particular has guided *Re-Imagining Life Together in America* throughout. As a result of this starting point, generative elements of community have surfaced and patterns of social behavior have recurred in instructive ways. These elements and patterns suggest ways of being together that advance community rather than thwart its development. Some of these elements include a spirit of hospitality, expansive enough to create a place of belonging for lost individuals searching for a "saving community," not very different from the American situation analyzed by Josiah Royce at the dawn of the twentieth century. Within this constructed, hospitable space, occupied by graced yet flawed human beings, we named the need to forgive and be forgiven as a personal and communal practice essential to community survival and growth. Newly emerging communities serve as a powerful antidote in a cultural climate of noisy agitation by providing a human space for quiet and reflection. This supportive aspect of group life offers an alternative value to individuals and communities in danger of losing their spiritual moorings. Likewise, new communities are developing genuine bonds of mutual care for their members and for the life of the group in contrast to the conditions of isolation and anonymity bred by a highly mobile North American ethos. In addition to bonds of mutual care being promoted by these more genuine forms of life together, communities provide the space where values that promote the common good, especially the good of those who are most at risk in the larger society, can be espoused and lived out in mutually accountable ways. We are convinced that this element of responsibility to help make the world a better place has more potential for growth in an environment of community than in isolation.

In addition to these community-building elements, this chapter reflected on social behaviors that are helping to nurture life together in our contemporary situation. We looked at the need for time in the formation of a community life and the importance of shared participation in the achievement of common values and meanings to define the character of a community. Next, we explored the negotiation of identity needs; those of individuals in relationship to other group members, of individual member in relation to the community as a whole, and of a community in relationship to those beyond it. Finally, this section opened up the question of power relations in group life, advocating for an emerging face of power, recognized as "power with," a power found with others in relational patterns that value mutuality and equality.

Consistent with our method of starting with and returning to the practical and concrete in developing our thesis of a new gospel of community, chapter 11 provides a way of grounding some of these principles in the concrete life of five new communities.

Chapter Eleven

ENCOUNTERING DIVERSE "FORMS" OF CONTEMPORARY CHRISTIAN COMMUNITIES

Anew gospel of community is making itself heard in cities, suburbs, and rural areas throughout North America today. This chapter will introduce and distinguish five of these communities as articulations of this community story emerging in contemporary American churches. As an American people we have recently undergone a massive national tragedy and incredible, personal suffering. In the wake of September 11, 2001, our very understanding of contemporary America has suddenly and radically shifted, our deepest sense of self, our security and our relationships with others have been called into question.

We present these diverse communities as "seeds of hope" for a world in the throes of anguish. In these new communities and in many other concrete ways, we have witnessed the transformative words of Mohatma Gandhi: "We must be the change we wish to see in the world." This imperative seems to us alive and embodied in the personal and communal experience of many communities of faith across our country today.

While we have chosen only five samples for our study here, we hope to recommend many others as models of and for a new gospel of community. In addition to our personal familiarity, our single criterion for choosing these particular versions of community is the diversity that the five represent. We begin with a large-scale, diocesan-wide effort, now national/international, to revision communities in Catholic parish life. We next move to an extraparochial, nonterritorial, eucharistic community in Northern Virginia; a Midwestern liberal, Protestant congregation; a rural, Mennonite fellowship; and finally to an East Coast urban Catholic parish. Our presentation of each of these five communities will highlight intentional responses to some of the crises of community happening in our social, political, and ecclesial institutions at present. We see these responses calling into question the very stuff of our social mores, the "habits of the American heart."

RENEW AS A PROCESS FOR COMMUNITY FORMATION: ITS VISION AND IMPACT

Father Walter Plominski has served as pastor of four Roman Catholic parishes in the Rochester, New York, diocese over the past fifteen years. Each parish setting, which differed in size and somewhat in geography, was made up of various social classes, races, and ethnic backgrounds, but all four shared this in common: each participated in a three-year renewal program, initiated by Walt, called Renew, and each parish was significantly changed as a result. Beyond a doubt, in Father Walt's estimation, the most dramatic change resulted from the formation of small groups over the three-year period of Renew. Many of these groups remain in place in all four parishes, others have begun since Renew ended. The groups enable a new way of being church to spring up within the parish setting. Though not every small group participant has continued as a small community member, the opportunity is made available to everyone. The seeds of a new community movement have been planted. If emerging church communities are "seeds of hope" for a revitalization of community life in North America, then the Renew process may aptly be called a tiller of the soil.

This is not the first time we used "Renew" as a proper noun in our narrative about small communities. But here, we will focus on it specifically as a program designed to encourage and promote small community development, not on the fringes of church life but at the very heart of it. As a community renewal movement, Renew originated as "an idea, dream, hope" of one, local church in the broader context of the Roman Catholic Church. Its architects, Reverend Thomas Ivory and Reverend Thomas Kleissler wanted to implement in practical ways the vision and pastoral direction of Vatican Council II. Such was the mandate they had received from their bishop, Peter L. Gerety, Archbishop of Newark, N.J., in 1976. Since Vatican II had called for the full, active, and conscious participation of the whole People of God in the life of the parish community (SC, 14), both priests agreed on the need for a concrete, long-term plan if this was to happen. They described their goal and purpose as "a massive effort of spiritual renewal and formation for parishes if they were to be vibrant faith communities where Christian values were nurtured" (3).

The designers of Renew were aware that just as the Roman Catholic Church repositioned itself to embrace the modern world, that same "modern world" began to lose its moorings. The staples of strong family ties and ethnic neighborhoods were no longer in place to assure the passing on of faith and values. The support systems of the past needed to be intentionally revisioned for a changing social situation. People had to find ways to come together.

Renew provided a process to do this—to bring people together over a period of two and one-half years, six weeks at a time for five "seasons," in people's homes, using carefully designed resources. This new, social arrangement brought many Catholics together for the first time with neighbors and other parishioners in an experience of

1. praying with the scriptures,

2. making connections between faith and everyday life,

3. developing bonds of mutual support,

4. awakening to a need for ongoing learning and,

5. working together to make the world a better place.

These common elements of the small group experience flow from Renew's clearly discerned and articulated program design, where its purpose and objectives are stated: "(Renew's) primary purpose is the spiritual growth of the People of God as a vibrant faith community." From this purpose flow three concrete goals:

1. to teach and witness to the Word of God

2. to develop and build small faith-sharing communities

3. to establish justice formation and action. (6)

Such a three-fold commitment to share God's Word, build community, and act for justice continues to motivate many communities formed by this three-year formation process. In reflecting on the contribution of Renew, Tom Kleissler does not hesitate to say that Renew's small groups are an initiation phase, a getting one's feet wet in the waters of community life, which ultimately invite participants to come in deeper.

As Renew spread throughout Catholic dioceses around the country in the 1980s, it became clear that Renew groups were making a difference not only to group members but also in the larger community.[1] The initial experience of an "alternative culture" where people came together "up-close" in mutually supportive and potentially empowering and accountable ways disturbed the *status quo* of the parish and neighborhoods, of which they were a part. Parish life seemed to become messier and more engaging. People began seeking more biblical and theological education, more access to and networking of social justice resources, more active participation in liturgical and pastoral ministries. For some parishes and dioceses, Renew's spiritual and community formation process provided a wake-up call, enabling both lay and clergy to imagine and begin to plan for more communal, participative models of life together. The vision of a parish as a "community of communities" began to take shape.[2]

By the year 2000, Renew had been implemented in over 150 U.S. Catholic dioceses (75 percent), over 13,000 parishes, and in the lives of more than 15 million people in the U.S. It has likewise served more than 120 dioceses in more than 20 countries in the world. The numbers are stunning and impressive, but deeper reasons on why Renew stands out for us, as a major player in the new community movement among North American churches, may emerge from some reflections on one pastor's experience and on one parish's evolution.

A New Vision of Parish Leadership

Father Walt's decision to initiate Renew as pastor in four different parishes is compelling. It's no easy task to undertake new programs, let alone one that requires the careful coordination and planning over a three-year period that Renew does. The thoughts of overseeing this program for twelve years could be staggering, but Father Walt's decision was made after comparing, weighing, and judging alternative ways of leadership. The time investment was more than worth it, he explains emphatically.

> Pastoral ministry requires hard work and commitment. I've experienced myself and countless others put in 100 urns of energy and produce but 20 urns of fairly meager results. In putting in place the committee structures needed for Renew to happen, the same 100 urns of personal energy are needed but the energy flow multiplies a thousand-fold. Something is set in motion by the small group component that makes things happen. That something is grace. I've literally seen people set on fire.[3]

It's not hard to hear overtones of John Zizioulas' sense of the community as saving grace for the early church. Drawn together by Spirit in Christ, we are saved by one another.

In the process of forming communities, Renew changes the culture of a parish. Walt describes that change in culture in ways suggestive of an attitude adjustment—from a clerical mindset to a community-centered one. In chapter 8, we spent some time uncovering three anticommunitarian forces at work in North American churches and sketched clericalism as first among them. Held securely in the grip of patriarchy's patterns of male privilege and its taken for granted hierarchy of power, clericalism breeds a culture of domination and control by the clergy over the laity. Genuine community becomes unlikely, if not impossible. Walt's experience offers hope that Renew acts as an effective antidote in overcoming the relational distortions of clericalism.

> Renew puts people in living rooms, around kitchen tables in such a way that God can find them directly. I'm no longer the sole mediator of God's love and presence. People experience God in their lives through one another, as they share their stories in dialogue with the scriptures. I see the faith life of people become more and more self-actualized. I no longer spend time asking for volunteers to help with parish needs or "corporal works of mercy." The small communities help people deepen their personal faith and the response of deepened faith is mission. What is God asking of us? What is God inviting us to do with the gifts that are ours? These are the questions I am asked over and over.

As Father Walt continues to share his experience of Renew from his position as parish leader, it becomes clear that something has happened to him as a person as well as a priest pastor. Community, as opposed to clericalism, draws people together. "This coming Sunday," Walt exclaims, "I'm going to a baby shower for one of the couples in my small community. You see, even the exclusion associated with traditional baby showers has been broken down in this inclusive culture of Renew." Father Walt has seen so many new couples welcomed into community by way of the small groups that he can't imagine how large parishes manage without them. So many young adults need to relocate. They leave friends and family behind and settle far from their family of origins. "Here in Caldonia," Father Walt announces proudly, "these young people know firsthand that their small faith community will be there for them, another kind of family."

Renew has provided another level of belonging through its small group component that is proving healing as well as welcoming. Small groups, in

Walt's description, offer a "doorway" for people who have been estranged from institutional church life for years.

> I've seen it happen over and over. Sometimes, it's the spouse of a person hosting a small group session. Other times it's a neighbor or friend invited to stop by. Repeatedly it's the experience of hospitality found in this environment of mutual care and trust that beckons people back.

Speaking personally once again, Father Walt confesses that he has become so much more attentive and observant as a person. "I have become accustomed and eager to listen for and to people's stories of life and grace in pain and struggle, growth and change." Walt's experiences of community are both personal and ministerial and one informs the other. He speaks again as pastor.

> My own role is becoming one of pointing out, reflecting on and celebrating "grace at work." Each week our parish bulletin carries personal stories sent in from our small communities testifying to their encounters with the living God. We call the column "Listening to Grace." What a prelude it has become for us as we gather for Sunday eucharist—where we celebrate and commit ourselves once again to become what we eat—the Body of Christ for one another and for the life of the world.

CONCLUSIONS

Father Walt is a barrel of stamina and enthusiasm. We learn from him about a new focus for his energies. He made a decision to invest his time and talents in implementing Renew with its intentional planting of small community seeds. One major result we have traced in his story is a new level of mutuality and inclusion that is growing between lay and clergy, male and female. How Renew has succeeded in a more systemic way to dislodge the dominant culture of clericalism is a question that deserves fuller attention. But this one priest's account certainly seems to indicate a shaking of the foundations. Community, at last, has a chance to rise from the ashes. Stories of community building inspired by the Renew process could fill several books, and we hope they will be written. Stories of support and sharing, of commitment and conversion, of faith deepened and hope restored, of new beginnings and meaningful partings are all a part of these emerging communities' shared memories around the country. Father Walt's "stories of grace" repeat themselves in ever diverse and similar fashion. The stories need to be told from many perspectives as folks recount their personal experiences of growing into community together.

Some Aspects of the Evolution of One Renew Parish

This next story recounts a bit of the evolution of a parish with Renew as a critical impulse. When Pat called the Parish Center at the Church of the Presentation, in Upper Saddle River, New Jersey, one wintry Tuesday morning, she was panic stricken. She needed a priest to come to the hospital immediately. Pat had been driving on snow covered and icy roads, taking her young daughter and her daughter's friend to school when the accident happened. Pat was not injured but the two children were unconscious and in critical, emergency care.

Although there is a pastor and one associate at the parish, no priest was there to respond to Pat's pastoral need. But a quick phone call to Pat's small community facilitator set in motion a whole dynamic of caring responses. Within twenty minutes, members of Pat's community began to gather in the hospital emergency room to wait and pray, comfort and support her as the crises of the accident played themselves out. With extensive time and loving support, both children eventually recovered fully.

As a single parent in an affluent town, Pat could have easily felt isolated. Upper Saddle River has its fair share of busy, upwardly-mobile people, respectfully minding their own business as neighbors and colleagues pass them by, mostly behaving in similar fashion.

People in Search of Spiritual Depth and Community Life

But the social milieu at the Church of the Presentation encourages another way of relating, a way that made all the difference in the world in Pat's life that snowy Tuesday morning. It continues to make a difference in the lives of many who find their way to this parish today.

Located in northern Bergen County, the Church of the Presentation in Upper Saddle River records in its parish registry seventy-seven different postal zones. Parish members come from many towns of northern New Jersey and southern New York. The parish understands itself today as a magnet parish, attracting persons from far and wide who are seeking spiritual depth and community life. This was not always the case, however.

In 1976, Reverend Jack McDermott arrived as pastor with a vision of parish that he had tested over his preceding nineteen years of priestly ministry. Jack was convinced that the hierarchical structures of parish leadership with its image of the pastor on top, prevented the church from being identified with the whole people of God. From day one, Jack's leadership engendered a spirit of togetherness. Over a two-year period, Father McDermott visited every household within the parish's territorial limits, introducing himself as "Jack" and simply expressing his desire to get to know neighbors and parishioners. Everyone recognized the goodwill gesture, and some, who had long ago distanced themselves from the Catholic Church, found in Jack a listening ear and caring presence. Many later came back to help create the kind of community they heard Jack describe.

So, some community-building efforts were already underway at Presentation when the diocesan Renew Program began in 1978. Still, the parish embraced it wholeheartedly. And in the twenty years since Renew ended in 1980, the parish commitment to building community has not waned but sustained, even transformed, an initially disconnected group of very mobile, highly educated, economically privileged parishioners.

GETTING PEOPLE TOGETHER

As a structured process, Renew provided a way for parishioners to take part in the same "get people together" desire that motivated Jack McDermott. They found that they too could reach out to neighbors and parishioners, welcoming each other into one another's homes. People admit that this sounds easier than it really was. The desire for openness and hospitality was great, but the social obstacles were formidable. The greatest barrier to community formation, in this local situation, proved to be the social pressures of economic status, with its demons of competition and rivalry. Many community members laugh honestly at themselves today, when they recall going to a small group meeting in someone's home for the first time. The temptation to compare the size or grandeur of one's living room or kitchen, the amount of land or quality of china was often overwhelming. The slow movement from self-consciousness and critique to genuine care and concern for others has been named by many as grace, that praying together and honest sharing stirred up over time, gently or not.

This culturally specific barrier of economic status, which breeds isolation in much of suburbia, needed to be broken down before other elements of community could emerge. One community member described how her own cold wall of fear began slowly to melt, as group members began to share honestly "the stuff" of their lives rather than their possessions in the light of scripture. Suddenly, differences that seemed to keep people at arms-length gave way to feelings of connection, as memories and hopes, hurts and struggles, concerns and longings found their way into one another's keeping. Little by little, people were discovering meanings and values they had in common. Some of those values seemed to expand their worlds beyond their small group, as needs of the larger church and world, political and business concerns came to be addressed in the light of the community's faith.

SHARED, PARISH LEADERSHIP

The small group component of the Renew process emerged as a significant change agent in how the parish now understands itself. With many gifted, professional members of the parish community connected with each other by means of small group interaction and outreach after a three-year period, a stronger, clearer vision of a shared, parish leadership emerged. Until his retirement in 1998, Jack McDermott served the parish in many ways as its spirit-interpreter, a function Josiah Royce named as most essential to the life of the community. Here is a person whose love for the unity of the community impels him to interpret one group to another in such a disinterested way, that each can understand and claim the other as part of one's self. In the process, gifts as well as wounds, shared by community members, are integrated into a larger community self. Without referring to Royce in any conscious way, community members of Presentation repeatedly speak of Father Jack as this unifying lover of the community and each of its members. Jack came to see his own pastoral role as the coordinator of the community's many gifts and resources in ever more responsible and effective ways.

Those many gifts and resources of the Church of the Presentation keep burgeoning. The parish booklet, introducing the parish and its ministries to newcomers today, lists over forty ministerial groups, organized into areas of evangelization, catechesis, worship, spiritual renewal, and ministerial formation. All ministries aim to encourage the full, conscious, and active participation of all members in the life of the whole community. This committed life of service flows from a deep sense of belonging to and being responsible for community. As such, community is never a taken-for-granted acquisition of which the parish can boast. It continues to be the result of the Spirit's gift and the people's response over time.

THE INTERPLAY OF CHURCH AND WORLD

In reading Presentation's small Christian community newsletter, entitled "Where Two or Three Are Gathered," one notices the impact that the larger world has on small communities and the impact they in turn have on the world. One story (September 2001) recalls a young man's experience of his small community's participation in Presentation's Wednesday Evening Homeless Shelter. The parish serves as an overflow center, providing dinner, cots for sleeping, and breakfast for ten to twelve homeless men. Two community members spend the night in order to provide support and presence. This particular evening, the young man and his wife volunteered to stay over. Throughout the evening they listened to some of the men's stories. "All had sorrow and pain. They also had hope and all seemed to have some kind of personal resurrection story." By the time the overnight guests had gathered their belongings into black plastic bags and boarded the van taking them into Paterson, New Jersey, the next rainy morning, the young man had gathered his thoughts on his experience of spending a night in the shelter. He concluded: "I was touched by the difference between their lives and mine. I couldn't help but think of my earlier lack of compassion for homeless people. Now, I was steeped in reflection on the complexity of life. Perhaps, some felt that our small community was Jesus to these men, but I know these homeless men were Jesus to me."

The story of Pat's community standing by her side at the hospital, with which this section opened, described the internal life of one community responding to the personal needs of an individual member. In addition to attending to these intersubjective needs of community members, the Church of the Presentation has nurtured other qualities of community that tend to promote "the good of order" (Lonergan's category), as well. In fact, there are far too many examples of "community virtues" being practiced for us to recount here. Many are having a significant impact on the larger church and world of which this parish community, with its many small communities, is a part. Because of the social location of this particular parish, one significant quality deserves to be highlighted. Through ongoing theological, liturgical, and biblical education at the parish level, some communities are coming to see that the church and world live in them, as much as they live in the church and world. As this awareness becomes more intentional and recognized, the community begins to hold itself accountable to its consequences. One way in which this accountability has been claimed is among some business executives at the parish, who have met together weekly in order to discern connections between their faith life and their business decisions. Becoming active members of a group committed to "Socially Responsible Investments," they have called themselves to deeper responsibility for their resources. Such intentional community commitments have great potential for promoting social change. These communities hold promise of growing stronger as mediating structures between otherwise isolated business executives and the society shaped by their critical decisions.

Conclusion

Renew has put people together in living rooms, spacious or small, lavish or limited. It has moved some people out of those living rooms and into their corporation's boardrooms with new communal awareness of their responsibility in shaping economic, global policies. Renew has also enabled people to find their way into settings, like homeless shelters and soup kitchens, that disturb and subvert formal ways of seeing the world or other people. In the process, new realizations of belonging to one another have happened. Because of Renew's amazing outreach to so many diverse settings of Roman Catholic people, as well as it practical hands-on approach to community nurturance, we present it to our readers as a major player in the work of community formation, taking place at this time in our churches. We realize that no program in and of itself can substitute for the work of building community entrusted to a particular group of people, one by one. Renew is but a tiller of the soil, but breaking up a clod of earth is a noble and laudable task. We see hope in building upon this foundational work.

THE NOVA COMMUNITY

The years following the Second Vatican Council gave birth to many creative initiatives, as Catholics sought to grow into an adult faith through "full, conscious and active participation" in the church's liturgical life (SC, 14). NOVA grew up among them. The immediate predecessor of NOVA can be indirectly traced to a group called "The People" in the Washington, D.C. area. This group had been attracting quite large numbers for their lively eucharistic celebrations before they were suppressed by the bishop of Washington. The group and their efforts did not escape the attention of Monsignor Carroll Dozier, later bishop of Memphis, chair of the Richmond Diocesan Liturgical Commission at that time. Dozier was eager to implement the Second Vatican Council's vision and was excited to learn that several members of "The People" were from Northern Virginia. He met with them, eager that liturgy-concerned people in the area "work through the church, rather than have to go underground" (44). Dozier urged them to write a proposal. Although the response of the diocesan commission did not fully endorse the new community, Bishop Russell gave it full canonical privileges as a recognized part of the diocese of Richmond, Virginia, in 1968. However, the new diocese of Arlington was formed in the geographical area of Northern Virginia in 1974 and the NOVA community has no canonical relationship with it.

In introducing the community that has emerged as NOVA, we do so both in continuity with and contrast to Renew. Both initiatives were a direct response to Vatican II's call for the full, active, and conscious participation of the whole People of God in the life of the church. In contrast to the Renew program, inaugurated by a bishop and directed by two diocesan clergy appointed by him, NOVA is the emergent response of grassroots people. The lay, eucharistic community called NOVA came to be in 1968, a fruit of serious reflection and enthusiastic envisioning of another way of being church in the 1960s, the decade of imagined alternatives. The original planners consisted of twelve couples, three single persons, and four diocesan priests. Their intentions were expressed in a proposal to the Richmond Diocesan Liturgical Commission on November 30, 1967.

> We seek creation of a genuine community of Catholic Christians, laymen and women and interested priests and religious, worshipping together in a reverent, living, relevant, creative, joyful, loving liturgy that will unite all in a true community and then (in the words of Archbishop Hallinan) lead us "from the altar to the homes and streets of the city" (45).

The NOVA community, an acronym for Northern Virginia as well as Latin for "new," recently celebrated its thirty-fourth anniversary. It continues to evolve today as a particular people's reflection on and response to Vatican Council II. The community still understands itself as "a genuine experiment," not in relationship to a single element in its life, such as liturgy, but rather in light of the "basic ambiguities, risks and uncertainties of trying to be Christians in an American culture and within an American church." As an experiment, NOVA members attempt to "create a Christian life together within the context of these two institutional bonds" (the American culture and the American Catholic Church) as well as "within the limitations imposed by our geographical dispersion and the mysteries of the 'small group dynamics' through which our community life has been modulated."[4]

NOVA's Community Foundations

From its inception, the NOVA experiment was based on the triple foundation of liturgy, social action, and religious education initiatives for children and adults. As a lay initiative, the group has depended from the beginning on the commitment of priests, both diocesan and religious order. They have never been without these ordained members/friends, who, among other things, provide the community's formal connection with the church universal.

Linked to these foundations is the element of NOVA's size. Though membership has always been open to all, the group believes that it has achieved and sustained a mature level of community life because

> it is small enough for the cultivation of primary, face to face relationships, but large enough to provide room for privacy and choices in friendship. It is small enough to prompt people into a cooperative work style but large enough for an individual's reprieve from overwork. It is small enough for spontaneity, natural warmth and close bonds, yet large enough to require some order and some specialization and diversity of talents.

Ordinary Sunday liturgy attendance hovers between 75–125 persons with a mailing list of some 200, including regular guests. A well-attended general meeting, where community issues are discerned and decisions reached, averages about forty participants. These conditions favored the growth of a vibrant community, but did not guarantee it. Gil Donahue, founding member and community historian, aptly explains, "While we used the term 'community' in our founding proposal, we have only become aware of what that really meant by a progressive revelation over time from our own experience and reflection. And we are still learning, let us hope . . . " (60).

NOVA's Undergirding Ecclesiology

The community has defined its ecclesiology in just this way. "We are a learning community being taught by the Spirit through continuing historical experiences." Foremost among those historical experiences are the social needs that confront a community of faith. More to the point, liturgy and social action are what bind the community together. NOVA has formulated this principle: "If liturgy is successful it will demand social action as a consequence of its celebration."[5] Fidelity to this originating principle has resulted in a four-pronged approach to social action: informational, educational, spiritual, and hands-on.

- The **informational component** consists in ongoing announcements, newsletter articles, networking, and communicating among justice agencies and ecumenical groups and periodic group orientations.

- The **educational component** develops more intensive learning modules, such as discussion series on liberation theology, study groups on the bishops' pastorals on peace and the economy, the project "Simple Christmas"—a re-education program in noncommercial holiday celebrations—a course on gospel economy, and ongoing sessions on group and individual discernment skills.

- The **spiritual component** infuses the liturgy with the concerns of the world, brings the "signs of the times" to the prayer of the church and the illumination of the Scriptures, and raises a prophetic voice when the community needs it most.

- Finally, the **hands-on component** of social action is grouped into meeting of local emergency needs, political action, financial support of church and charitable organizations, participation in national efforts, and global projects.

The community supports both financially and with volunteer services Bethany House, a shelter for battered women, and HEC (Handicapped Encounter Christ), a program that offers spiritual support and community for disabled persons who have little opportunity for religious or social activities. NOVA families include as their "extended" families, several in the "Mississippi Project," providing books, clothing, food, and moral and physical support to poor families in extreme need. The NOVA Food Co-Op has given substantial portions of its bi-weekly food purchase to families in need, such as one young mother who was trying to get her GED while her four children attempted to maintain a healthier lifestyle. NOVA took part in the weekend renovating of an old church in Washington, D.C., which now has a homeless ministry and an ecumenical after-school program for children and the elderly. Likewise, NOVA has offered support to Alderson Hospitality House, a Catholic Worker House of the Washington, D.C. Federal Prison for Women, 150 miles from the capital. The Hospitality House provides food and overnight lodging for families of prisoners coming to visit them. With its ongoing dual focus, the NOVA community has sought to be faithful to its original desire to "be a fully functioning Christian community" by "reaching out to live Christ's message as well as celebrate it."[6]

A COMMUNION OF THE PEOPLE OF GOD

This "new and heady idea" was originally a felt experience of the eucharistic gathering, which upon shared reflection evoked this common meaning. What an inestimable value the community realized in coming to know itself as a communion of the people of God. From such shared meanings and values, the NOVA community found the glue to shape its life together in sustained and enduring ways over the past thirty plus years. The most defining common experience to which the NOVA experiment has committed its energies is the preparation and celebration of its Sunday liturgies. Sonja Donahue describes the "most striking effects of these celebrations" not in terms of "sophisticated liturgical innovations" though indeed there have been some. But rather, the energy invested in preparing and celebrating "engenders within us a heightened awareness theologically speaking of 'communion' or a 'sense of community'" (61).

The community has distinguished three concrete bonds, forged from that "heady idea" or "awareness of communion," that have helped make visible and enduring that liturgical experience and gift of at oneness. The three bonds, identified by NOVA, are their instrumental ties, affective bonds, and ideological commitments (62). In a twentieth anniversary reflection, entitled "The Nova Community: A Study of Lay, Religious Community," Donahue explored some of the interwoven functions of these three ties, associating them with promoting and sustaining the life of this experimental, nonparochial, and catholic community. Together they have helped foster the healthy tension needed to achieve a communal balance.

The instrumental, affective, and ideological functions of community are, of course, interrelated. The ability to get things done depends on both a healthy climate of interpersonal relations and a set of clear values and ties to the Christian ideology (tradition). The affective function, in turn, cannot be authentically achieved unless there is a shared purpose and opportunity for meaningful action. Finally ideology (theology and tradition) requires for its full development, mutual goodwill, and work involvement in the communal enterprise.

Perceiving and valuing these three perspectives is one thing. Balancing them is another. A community intent on merely doing will tend to burn out or get reduced, psychologically, to a service organization. One which overemphasizes feeling may well grow narcissistic and paralyzed by what others think. Or it may become a pseudo-therapy group. An over-fixation on the ideological dimension may result in the strangulation of the communal spirit and create divisiveness, conformity, and rigidity. As a result it would be difficult to elicit cooperation for joint projects while the pressure of absolute values would increase individual isolation for those who do not share such values (60–61).

NOVA's COMMUNITY GOVERNANCE

The need for preserving balance among these communal bonds leads us to question the governance style of NOVA in more direct ways. As a pro-claimed, self-governing body, how does their community function? The answer, as one might expect by now from a group that so consistently understands itself as an experiment, is an amalgam of at least four identi-fiable patterns with strong priority given to a consensus gift model of governance. This governance model supports a structure that is nonhierarchical or overbearing. Governance is itself communal, incorpo-rating everyone's gifts for the good of the whole. It relies on discernment of the Spirit in every particular situation, as well as relying on church tra-dition. It tries to keep its organizational structures congruent with its spiritual values. For example, because the community has come to under-stand itself as "mystical communion" at an experiential level, it has attempted to recast its organizational life to reflect this core value rather than give priority to an institutional model of church governance. To give visible form to the communion they sense, decision making by consensus fits best. More fitting, too, is the understanding of power as personal influ-ence and community-directed talents. Procedurally, this communal model is time consuming, NOVA admits, and it may not work in large groups. It presupposes an informed membership and a high degree of mutual open-ness and commitment.

NOVA'S ADMINISTRATIVE STRUCTURES

There are three traditional administrative elements specified in canon law that NOVA has not incorporated: pastor, building, and financial capital. NOVA works without a pastor. Nor does it depend on a group of privileged elders. Rather it relies for its spiritual life on the discernment of the Spirit, the ongoing faith development and theological education of its members, caring and critical self-reflection processes, and the spiritual counsel offered by its regular priest presiders, who likewise serve as the community's symbolic link with its apostolic roots (34). Leadership in the community is associated with a person not an office; it consists of service and facilitation. While many NOVA officers and committee coordinators have professional backgrounds, they are not chosen for their specialized training but for their interpersonal skills, leadership qualities, and commitment to work for the well-being of the community.

NOVA also has no building. Its weekday meetings all take place in members' homes. Its Sunday worship was located initially in parishes or university chapels, then in various Christian churches and eventually in rented public school facilities. This latest shift was necessitated in part by the length of NOVA's gatherings, problems with church scheduling, and constraints on parish parking lots. Though some have regretted the utilitarian setting of public space, it has heightened awareness of the symbolic meaning of "setting up." Every Sunday liturgy is a challenge, reminding the attentive that community must ever be created anew. The unconstructed nature of most public spaces is also more adaptive to the communal, participatory nature of NOVA's worship.

NOVA has no established financial system of tithing or contribution envelopes. It has a treasurer who keeps the books, writes checks, and submits periodic financial reports. NOVA operates by a spend philosophy that frowns upon accumulations of money and extended bookkeeping efforts that distract from hands-on work. It can afford to be informal, the community insists, because its members are trustworthy. When the communal coffers run low, the individual committee coordinators remind the community of their personal responsibilities that they pledged both in money and work. The periodic financial ebbs force evaluations on the community and prevent routine, complacent giving. Above all, priority is given to a gospel economy. But for all these pros, there are cons to the financial system, pointing out that NOVA has a high degree of patience and a fairly high tolerance for general ambiguity. Members believe that NOVA can govern this way because it has developed successful problem-solving strategies and "has a sixth sense for not biting off more than it can chew" (36).

NOVA is governed by a "community chair," a woman, man, or both as a team, who is "called forth" each year at a general meeting. A treasurer also emerges from this "Calling Forth" meeting. Three standing committees—Liturgy, Social Action, and Children's Education—have a coordinator called forth from this same general meeting. NOVA is supported by a newsletter editor who publishes the monthly liturgy and events calendar and committee reports, disseminates general meeting decisions, and acts as a source of public information. The internal life of NOVA is nurtured by a team of four community life ministers who oversee pastoral care. In no way do they substitute for each NOVA member's responsibility for the care of one another. They step in only when a certain promptness or privacy is needed; otherwise they facilitate the communal ministry in action.

CONCLUSIONS

Whether one looks to the nonhierarchical governance structures of the NOVA community, to the strength of the relational bonds that connect members to one another and to the group, or to the priority given to "the process over the product" in what the community accomplishes, one is struck by the alternative, experimental character of NOVA's presence and actions in the American culture and church over the past thirty-four years. This laboratory of social change must have something important to offer those who search for alternatives to our present crisis of community. The regret that looms large for us is that NOVA, like so many alternative communities, receives so little attention and so little support from the dominant cultures of our churches and our society.

The diversity that such creative communities add to our larger church and society has the potential to enrich us all. As Robert Hovda observed in 1988, "Certainly these extra-parochial communities have a great deal to say to parishes."[7] They call all of the churches to reassess their own movement from being gatherings of passive observers to active participants, from supporting members' understandings of themselves as "going to church to being the church in communion with all the other churches." It was these insights that brought many of these alternative communities into existence and those that have endured have much to teach us of their experience. They have developed, through the crucible of personal and communal experience, some of the structural models we need for growth and development as vibrant communities in the future.

NOVA understands itself as a "learning community." A core member recently reflected on how NOVA anticipated the contemporary appeal to "virtual reality." In some respects, it was that prophetic vision that pressed upon NOVA members to create a new participative form of life together back in the 1960s. As needs have changed over the decades, NOVA is still learning, an experiment still in process. At thirty-four, the community has wisdom born of practical experience to share. Longtime members reflect vividly on the enthusiasm and "hope for change in the ordinary life of the church" that fired their commitments back then. Where those hopes have waned and the vision taken its time in coming, community members suggest that the need for alternatives in the ordinary life of the church may be even more intense today. The NOVA community insists that keeping hope alive is a Christian mandate. While we wait upon the future, we help shape it. To give form to the vision of community, we share NOVA's desire to find more companions, in the form of other learning communities, for the next stretch of the way.

COMMUNITY IN WICHITA, KANSAS

Walking into the 9:30 A.M. Sunday worship service at College Hill United Methodist Church in Wichita, Kansas, is a bright and warm experience. Several hundred people are packed tightly on folding chairs and in massive concentric semi-circles in the church social hall. Some are in suits and dresses, others in jeans and t-shirts, still others in decorative, but alternative styles of clothing. Up front a jazz band is playing. Donuts and coffee are being passed around. The pastor strolls among the people and eventually makes his way up to a bar stool near the jazz band. The pastor has some difficulty in getting people's attention, since so many people are involved in rather intense conversation.

If one came to College Hill an hour earlier or later, much of the same warmth would be there in the more conventional sanctuary worship services. There too the diverse group of people seem to know each other well, and are abuzz with the sense of community. In the 8:30 and 11 A.M. sanctuary worship services the robed choir and organ have replaced the jazz band, but the choir members are also clearly enjoying each other and there is often a dance group that works with the choir.

The worship services at College Hill are central to the sense of community. The prayers and sermons are filled with references to members' ordinary lives. The pastors show their own humanity regularly in the service, confessing to faults and sharing personal stories. Very often worshippers will be encouraged to speak briefly with one another in the service, even though there are hundreds of people there. "We work very hard at making people feel comfortable and welcome, as they enter. The key element in our growth has been the way we have opened up our worship," says Reverend George Gardiner, the church's senior pastor.

When you put Sunday mornings together at College Hill Church, there is an overall sense of aliveness and warmth. A subtle blend of regular church, informality, and commitment communicate belonging. The connections between an astonishingly broad array and number of people seem strong and vibrant. The sense of a lived presence of God through these connections comes to speech regularly among College Hillers.

Ironically it is the conventional shape of this large Protestant congregation that undergirds Christian community at College Hill in very crucial ways. This is ironic, as we will see, because many of the social values College Hill represents are prophetic and exceptional, even though formally much of this church looks completely conventional. With around 2,000 members, the congregation's staffing and governance could not be distinguished from most other churches its size. There is a team of highly trained pastors, support persons, and administrators. A layer of solid citizens—many leaders in their professions—and the city of Wichita itself form the quite traditional set of church boards and committees.

Almost certainly part of the sense of belonging needed in Wichita, Kansas, (and in many other places) is to be a part of a conventional American institution. Part of the glue that holds community together at College Hill UMC is that it looks and acts like a regular church in many respects. For those who feel alone and unrecognized, being a part of a big, successful, and conventional-looking church not only deepens attachment to the other members, but also helps them feel like they belong to the larger society. The traditional church building, the robed choir, those in ties and dresses all make everyone feel a part of the broader American culture. These very conventional symbols of church culture are part of the bonds that hold this specific church community together.

All this reinforces our overall hypothesis that something inherent in American churches provides a powerful force for community formation and maintenance. College Hill UMC may be from this perspective the archetypal example of how church *per se* in America proclaims a gospel of community. There is a blend—at the same time articulate and unstated—of belonging, God, and conventionality.

On the other hand, a closer look at College Hill Church produces a more nuanced picture. Without undermining the importance of College Hill's conventional churchness for community building, this closer look also identifies one major trait that is similar to the other communities we are sampling in this chapter and another major trait that is quite different from some of these communities.

Prophetic Stances in the World that Convene Christian Community

Like St. Vincent Roman Catholic Church and Lancaster Community Mennonite Church (which we will discuss later in this chapter), College Hill UMC's courageous work for justice in its larger social setting has had the effect of forming and maintaining tight-knit community within the church itself. For College Hill this has involved two volatile social issues in America.

In the early 1990s a number of organizations began to attack women's rights in Wichita on a number of fronts. At that point College Hill United Methodist Church went very public with its congregational and denominational position defending women's rights. College Hill church members and pastors were in the forefront of those who stepped forward to debate both the position and tactics of right wing antifeminists.

Although the intention of College Hill Church was simply to take a prophetic stance concerning a volatile issue in Wichita, one of the main results was that a large number of women from the Wichita area began attending the church. Here they found a community that understood the complex factors that go into a woman making choices. In contrast to many religious groups quick to condemn women's rights, here these women found a large group of people who supported them, no matter what their choice. Not only did the College Hill UMC public stance against antifeminist rhetoric attract women to the church, it helped build the sense of belonging these women had to the church as a community. Their prayer together with others in church, their larger life beyond explicitly feminist issues, and their work on other common projects was much more intense because of the church's public support of them over against the rhetoric of others.

In the mid 1990s a very similar set of circumstances emphasized again the power of prophetic stances on societal issues by College Hill to play a formative role in community building. The ripples of College Hill Church's willingness to take public stands over against right wing religion began to capture the attention of gay and lesbian persons in the Wichita area. Some of these people began visiting worship at the church, and liking it. They found at College Hill acceptance in a church in a way that they were not used to. Over a rather short two years the number of gay and lesbian persons joining and attending the church increased rapidly. This development was not without its intra-congregational consequences. Some members left, because of the increasing acceptance of gay and lesbian persons in the church. This precipitated a congregation-wide debate on the subject, in which the vast majority of persons came out strongly for thorough acceptance of gay and lesbian persons in the full life of the church. Similarly, even though less than 10 percent of the congregation was openly gay or lesbian, the church came rather quickly to have a public reputation for its acceptance.

It was surprising to many how deeply this new diversity at the church nurtured community. Many of the rather conventional older women found themselves in important friendships with gay men. Lesbian and gay couples began bringing their children for baptism, and these baptisms became deep celebrations of the church itself and of God's grace and freedom. The pastors of the church—one of whom by this time had come out as an openly gay man—became known in the city for their willingness to perform funerals for those who had died of AIDS. The old church custom of hosting a dinner for the friends and family of the bereaved was transformed as College Hill members bonded together to throw big dinners for the survivors of the AIDS victims. An ongoing adult church school class was formed to discuss issues of homosexuality and faith. The openly gay pastor became the beloved leader of another adult Sunday school class, populated almost entirely by older straight men.

College Hill's prophetic stance is not limited to gender and sexuality related issues. The church has been very instrumental in the establishment of urban ministry in Wichita. College Hill as a congregation is intentionally linked to three other area churches in poor neighborhoods. An African American congregation, a mostly Hispanic church, and a church in the middle of population transition all receive major financial support from College Hill. In addition, all four congregations meet together regularly for worship and study.

Congruent with the centrality of worship is the prophetic preaching stance of the College Hill pastors. That God stands on the side of the poor and oppressed is a message heard regularly in all College Hill services. The community experienced within the congregation extends explicitly both in proclamation and project into the broader arena of justice for Wichita's entire population. Advocacy for women, the poor, people of color, and gay and lesbian persons is accompanied by both long-term action projects and strong assertions of God's presence in these causes.

ADULT LEARNING AS FORMATIVE OF COMMUNITY

Perhaps the most consistent dynamic for community at College Hill UMC is one not encountered nearly so strongly in the other faith communities discussed in this chapter. This is the power of educational groups within the church. For well over the past twenty years College Hill Church has been known for its educational groups. When church enrollment declined in the early 1980s, what kept it going was a set of strong adult Sunday school classes that held members' loyalty even when they were alienated from worship. Since the mid 1980s the church has generated countless long-term and short-term learning groups.

There are long-term adult learning groups of all kinds. One of the older men's Sunday school classes has already been mentioned. Another class of this sort recently celebrated its sixtieth birthday as an ongoing group. Yet another consists of an ongoing membership of young and older women who meet to quilt and talk religion. On Friday evenings there is a singles group that has been meeting for social gatherings and study for years.

In addition there are short and mid-term study groups for adults. Some of these—such as the one that has attracted at least thirty people a year to study "creation spirituality"—last for a year and then disband. In these groups the centrality of God as Creator is emphasized, and the possibility of community not just with one another but with all of God's creation comes starkly into view. A deep sense of connectedness with nature complements people's sense of connection to each other and to God.

Other groups—such as the group that studies Christian mysticism—will run for six to eight weeks and disband. In this case the mystical connection of community is explicitly related to people's connection to God. A relatively recent educational group is based on the national Praxis model, in which the subject of the Sunday worship service is addressed in discussion on Tuesday nights around supper. In these groups about sixty people come together in the evenings, break into small discussion units to deepen their thinking on the Sunday liturgy theme, and then end the evening in the larger group. Additional learning groups focus on life experiences such as grieving, divorce, or parenting.

"When members have the chance to discuss things together, they begin to relate to each other in additional ways," says Reverend Gardiner. Summarizing the centrality of learning for this community of faith, Gardiner adds, "Community comes from the possibility of learning in a nonjudgmental atmosphere. People have got to have something to think about. Our understanding of community bases itself in education."

The learning model is consistent and thorough at College Hill. So many un-churched persons or early church dropouts are coming back to church via College Hill, Gardiner feels that the church must accept people as they are, and then help them think through what they believe and how to develop spiritually. Since community depends on the process of learning together from a variety of points of view, College Hill is careful not to reject people who want to join.

"We have adopted the philosophy of church membership I've heard attributed to Reverend Cecile Williams of Glide Memorial Church in San Francisco," Gardiner says. "In this philosophy there are two questions we ask of each person who wants to join: First, what is your name. Second, how are you doing?"

This astonishing receptivity and lack of discrimination relative to church membership fits closely with the educational emphasis at College Hill. No one needs to know anything special before joining, since it is the process of learning together that binds people together in community. As people start learning together, their lives entwine and their spirits deepen. "In this way we often are creating communities within community. Each learning unit intensifies the individual's sense of belonging," says Gardiner.

This emphasis on education even dominates thinking about worship. Each Sunday is organized around a theme, not an assigned lectionary text. Every service on each Sunday approaches that particular theme in song, prayer, and spoken word. The themes can vary widely: from "what does it mean to confess Jesus as the Christ" to "solidarity with the urban neighborhoods of Wichita" to "Meister Eckhart's four paths" to "the way of the Buddha." Since the College Hill educational emphasis influences even the shape of the worship, the church's liturgy ends up also being its most dramatic moment of learning.

CONCLUSION

College Hill UMC's gripping sense of community consists of a quirky mix of conventional big church Protestantism, powerful prophetic witness, and deep devotion to adult learning. More than any of our other models in this chapter it relies on conventional church forums of Sunday school, large group worship, and public social witness. Its unique contribution to our discussion of what makes churches bearers of community is its thorough-going commitment to an educated faith. Although its powerful social witness is not unique even within the churches discussed in this chapter, College Hill's community moorings are much deeper because of this witness. The almost seamless way both this prophetic witness and educational emphasis are woven into the fabric of a conventional American church places an exclamation point behind our thesis that churches promise community to our society in ways no other institution can.

COMMUNITY LANCASTER MENNONITE CHURCH

Pasted on the cover of her somewhat tattered high school assignment book was a small decal, perhaps an inch tall. Closer examination revealed the decal to be a picture of a colorful parrot. The decal did not scream for attention, nor was it an obvious announcement of affection for a rock group or brand name clothing line. But the teenage girl who put it there was quick to claim and explain it.

"It reminds me that I belong. In the middle of my school day, it helps me remember this church and all that it means to me," Whitney Kulp said. The parrot, it turns out, is the symbol of the Holy Spirit for the Community Mennonite Church of Lancaster in Central Pennsylvania. It is not just found on Whitney's schoolbook. A ten-inch carved wooden parrot, a Ten Thousand Villages product that showed up one Sunday long ago on one of the plants near the pulpit, has become a playful centerpiece at Sunday morning worship, flitting to unexpected perches in the worship space. The church newsletter has the name *The Parrot*, and whenever a congregational member turns fifty, she or he is given a parrot pin.

The colorful quirkiness of the parrot symbol corresponds in many ways with the unexpectedness of Community Mennonite Church of Lancaster itself. CMCL, as the members refer to the church, has burst on the scene in traditional Pennsylvania Amish country with fresh life that claims the loyalty and enthusiasm of a wide range of ages. Founded in 1985, CMCL has grown quickly in this small Pennsylvania city. In the middle of a culture known mostly for its bonnets and horse-drawn buggies, CMCL has become a recognized presence for its artistic and experimental worship, its advocacy for justice and peace, its explicit hospitality of divorced, gay and lesbian persons. In its first fifteen years of existence CMCL grew so rapidly that it required two separate building programs to house the enthusiastic and unusual group.

We have selected CMCL as one of our sample faith communities, however, not because of its exceptional character in its own particular social setting, but because it is actually quite typical of an emerging genre of churches in America. Indeed we know firsthand of one or more of this kind of new church in almost every major urban center in the United States. Although it is not the case that every American city the size of Lancaster has such a church, we are certain there are hundreds of this particular new church type, and that this kind of church is an important development on the American religious horizon. For our purposes we will concentrate on the characteristics CMCL has in common with other newer churches. Without avoiding some of the parrot-like specificities of CMCL,

209

we will focus on the ways it reflects this larger pattern of new community formation.

At the heart of the CMCL experience is worship. At two services on Sunday mornings a total of between 25 and 275 persons gather to sing, recite prayers of joy and concern, listen to a sermon from one of its two women pastors or its many articulate laypersons, and to claim a sense of a greater whole to which they belong. The music is vibrant and eclectic. Without an organ, and often in traditional Mennonite a cappella four part harmony, the congregation sings many international songs, some jazz, bluegrass, and neo-Gregorian chants from the French Protestant monastery Taize and the island community of Iona in Great Britain.

"Singing is our sacrament," said one member. "We feel a unity that goes beyond words when we sing." Art in various and experimental forms in the worship regularly provides connection of people to one another and to God. A large "wailing wall" in the worship room was made available following the attacks of September 11, 2001. This wall contained both visual expressions of grief by a professional photographer as well as a wide variety of graffiti-like scrawling from church members. Often sculpture, paintings, and fabric spring up in the worship space in specific relation to concerns and gifts of the community. Although many of this emerging CMCL type also use dance as a part of their worship, CMCL has been slower to develop a dance element.

The worship does include a monthly communion service and the sacrament of baptism. Children are included in the worship in a very intentional manner. Rituals mark baby dedications and entrance to first grade and the teen years. In addition, each twelve-year-old is matched with a mentor from the congregation and participates with that mentor in a blessing of the relationship in worship. In the monthly celebration of communion, very young children participate in the service by taking a fish or butterfly cracker instead of the communion bread.

The extremely participatory worship expresses a larger and ongoing spiritual search at CMCL. This search is for both a new level of affect and a new level of articulation. The search is clearly not finished. "We are looking for new words. Our worship reflects an openness and struggle for new language of faith that is authentic and that fits with life experience," said Pastor Pamela Dintaman. The worship not only evokes the deep sense of unity in the singing and art, at every worship individual members speak their very personal prayer of concern or joy. "There is a powerful intimacy in our worship," said another member. This affects a sense of acceptance that "you are known and loved by God," according to several members. A sense of spiritual homecoming is nurtured in a variety of settings—annual spirituality retreats for men, women, and members-at-large or by adult education studies on prayer, faith, and practice.

The primary dimension of spiritual search in the worship service points to several larger social characteristics of CMCL and the many new churches of this type. Although more than half of CMCL members come from a Mennonite background, the congregation has in many ways sprung the denominational latch. "I look at this church as part of the dawning of postdenominationalism," said Jeff Hawkes, an active congregant. Even those who have a strong Mennonite background are at least as conscious of their dissonance with some traditions of Anabaptism. "This is the home of the lost sons and daughters of Menno. There are many here who have been deeply injured by our tradition," said Jim Bowman. CMCL also attracts those who have been disillusioned by institutional Christianity in other denominations.

This ambivalence about the Mennonite background is typical of a larger dynamic in American Christianity about loyalty to institutional and historical traditions. One can find very similar resistance in the many new United Methodist, Presbyterian, Lutheran, Episcopalian, United Church of Christ, and Baptist congregations. The resistance is, however, in newer congregations like CMCL almost always accompanied by a need to claim some kind of spiritual legacy. "There is a sense of peopleness that is a part of our attachment to being Mennonite," said pastor Dintaman. "The Mennonite church is full of stories about martyrs and people who stood up for their community. Our members choose to add their stories to this lineage of faithfulness."

CMCL like its sister congregations throughout the country is offering a winsome combination of spiritual openness and a gracious connection to a longer collective memory. This combination appeals particularly to professional people between the ages of thirty and fifty. CMCL's membership consists mostly of college-educated, liberal-minded adults, many of whom work with church institutions and social services. The relatively homogenous congregational constituency and its stable economic and cultural situation provide safety to ask questions. Although many of the members regret that CMCL has not attracted more people of color and poorer people, this safety in homogeneity does allow a broader freedom of expression and an open-ended relationship than people have experienced previously.

Also typical of these emerging congregations, CMCL draws from a fairly broad geographical area. In this way it definitely is a congregation (a coming together of people on a voluntary basis) as contrasted to a parish, where persons come from within relatively prescribed geographical boundaries. Again in this respect the generational and cultural cohesion of CMCL plays a central role in its community cohesion. This Anabaptist community of faith fits then much more closely the type of church renewal happening within certain types of Protestantism, in which the congregating of open-minded, spiritually seeking persons from a broad geography allows a specific community to form. Although our portrait of St. Vincent Roman Catholic Church, which we will discuss shortly, as well as the Church of the Presentation, also fits this Protestant pattern fairly closely, the Roman Catholic Renew model generally assumes the very different and concentrated parish geography as the basis of community renewal. Here CMCL corresponds more closely to the early Christian communities who voluntarily came together across conventional boundaries than to the later and more complex parish structure.

A final major characteristic of CMCL typical of the larger new church trend is a particular set of social commitments in the larger world. Probably for CMCL the commitment felt most acutely is its commitment to peace and nonviolence. Rooted in the long-standing Mennonite tradition of resistance to government conscription for war, CMCL asks every member annually to "practice peacemaking and nonviolence in all areas of our lives." Because of this peace emphasis, the church has a higher-than-usual awareness of international conflict and the huge military expenditures of the U.S. government. CMCL actively translates "peace and nonviolence" in terms of local, regional, national, and international justice. This may include attending peace demonstrations in downtown Lancaster, active conflict mediation work, or occasional trips to Central America, or to Georgia to press for the closing of the former School of the Americas—a government-sponsored training site for foreign soldiers now known as Fort Benning. In April of 2000, a CMCL delegation traveled to Washington, D.C., to demonstrate with other Christians for the cancellation of international debt. Church children attend an annual summer Peace School, which the congregation co-sponsors in the Lancaster community with a neighboring Episcopal church.

The church works with urban poverty near its location in Lancaster itself. With local churches it helps to host meals for the community via "Dinner Out" and morning breakfasts. The church is home to the Life Skills training program of the local intermediate-unit of the Pennsylvania public school system and makes its facility available for regular use by other community-based groups.

Linked to the search for justice in the world is the pledge to "exercise compassionate stewardship of our environment." Although some of the symbols of American materialism—like gas-guzzling cars—can be found in the CMCL parking lot, overall the congregation consciously makes lifestyle choices that are less consumptive than the average American. Several church members work in organic farming, eco-system preservation, and assist the congregation in becoming ecologically aware with both intergenerational and adult studies. Church members regularly cite the colorful parrot symbol as a sign of their resolve to be ecologically aware. Typical of this new mix of social action and spirituality, CMCL links God, community, and justice.

Somewhat less formally, but very much reflective of this faith community's values, are two other CMCL social commitments. "We are definitely a feminist congregation," says pastor Dinteman, "in both practice and biblical interpretation. We interpret Scripture using both women's and men's experiences along with voices from other cultures and traditions. In practice, men and women share leadership and nurturing roles in the church and home." This commitment is evident in a generally "high level of gender consciousness," according to Pastor Pitts, and in specific programs like the ritual blessings of young women and men when they turn thirteen, in monthly men's and women's gatherings, and in the annual men's and women's weekend retreats.

The CMCL Membership Covenant pledges "to face our diverse understandings of the meaning of Christ's lordship with a spirit of openness and love for each other." With the other CMCL social justice commitments, members recognize and face that diversity by addressing controversial issues such as sexual orientation (CMCL has experience as a place of refuge). "I'd never be a Mennonite, if it were not for this congregation," says Rachel Kraybill Stahl as she talks of the importance of her covenanted lesbian partnership. A growing percentage of the congregation is gay, lesbian, bisexual, or transgendered, a characteristic of CMCL that has not gone unnoticed with the Lancaster public.

Such devotion to justice, peace, ecological consciousness, feminism, and GLBT rights do indeed make CMCL stand out publicly. They also represent an important piece of CMCL's own emerging spirituality, one that stands for "the reconciliation of humans to God and of human beings to each other," as the CMCL covenant states. And, although CMCL members experience these social and spiritual commitments as exceptional in their local culture, these same commitments recur over and over again in emerging church types nationally.

Not so typical of the larger genre and in interesting relationship to the Renew faith communities sketched in this chapter, most CMCL members are members of a "house church," as a subunit of their church membership. These groups provide a vital way to express the congregation's social and spiritual commitments. "House church is the place where I can work out how I live my faith," said one member. House churches—about eighteen of them in CMCL—usually meet once or twice a month. The activities of the house churches include "fun, church business, study, service, support, and prayer." They provide a level of personal support and accountability for each church member, and they help form the basic CMCL governance structure in that each house church is represented on the church council. Some churches are based on geographical proximity, others on common special interest, and still others on informal relational networks.

CONCLUSION

The parrot says it all. CMCL is its own bright and colorful self in a black and white landscape. But CMCL is not really alone at all. Seeing itself in the parrot is a way of this new church saying that it belongs to a larger order beyond its particular social exceptionality. It belongs to the new movement of socially progressive, spiritually interested churches. It belongs to the bigger world of ecology and nature. It belongs to the long-standing Mennonite traditions of peace and justice advocacy. It belongs to a fresh celebration of God's own connective power.

A PARISH BECOMES A PEOPLE

"So, how are we doing?" The question reaches out to greet us as we walk through the large, wooden doors of the church on Sunday morning. The question hangs from large panels forming an extensive timeline of carefully framed events and experiences of the past four years. The chart refers very specifically to a "Covenant of Racial Healing" that the community made in 1997. Holding themselves accountable to one another is a significant component in how this parish community "keeps on keepin' on." "What have we done well; what has helped advance our goals; what mistakes have we made and what can we learn from them?" The questions are not asked lightly; they are not cosmetic but integral to the community, as it seeks to realize more of the dream that they believe God has for it. But St. Vincent's parish dream was not always so clear, so communal, so inclusive, so justice-minded as it is in 2002.

St. Vincent de Paul Church in Philadelphia is an inner-city Catholic parish, in the Vincentian tradition, located in the historic, but run-down Germantown area of the city.[8] Because of economic decline and white flight,

St. Vincent's became a small, financially strapped parish of older Catholics after 1960. For most of the 1960s, leadership of the parish was in the hands of an ex-Navy chaplain. During those years, parishioners recall that "the rectory was off-limits to parishioners," the associate pastors were forbidden to "even talk to the laity who worked in the rectory," and the "cooks all in uniform were summoned to the dining room by pressing a buzzer attached to the underside of the table" (19).

A Community-Centered Pastor

The fire of community at St. Vincent's was hardly more than a flicker until the arrival of "Bud" (Father August H. Englert, CM) in 1977. Bud's personal power was vested in his relentless conviction that "we are strong together." As pastor, Father Englert's goal was to live into the vision of Vatican II, where the church is seen as the whole "People of God" (*Lumen Gentium*, II). But how does one begin to open up the whole environment of a parish strapped for so long in a clerical straightjacket to promote a new spirit of belonging?

Father Bud decided to begin with the parish staff.

> If we're going to ask the parish to be a people, with a mutual bond, acceptance, forgiveness, trust, faith-sharing, I felt we had to start with us in the staff. If the staff could exemplify Christian community, it might spread out in concentric circles. We on the staff would have to pay the price of struggling with each other, not walking away when there is disagreement, being willing to forgive, acting as a regular family would. Then when we would draw others in, maybe, they would feel it, not just hear it. They would see us working on it.

Beginning with this inner circle of staff formation, people began to notice the rippling effects. Before long, they were able to articulate the following staff goals:

- to develop a new attitude in the people so that they could move from "going to church" to "being church,"

- to encourage lay ministry, helping people to recognize their responsibility to share their gifts in service,

- to encourage people to know one another, to share faith and life with one another.

An active concern for peace, justice, and service to the poor became strong at St. Vincent's during Bud's pastorate. But Bud was clear. "In social justice work, I saw too many people burn out and get eaten up with anger. They had no core of loving people they could fall back on. I decided instead to try to 'form a people.'"

GETTING PEOPLE CONNECTED

Bud's formation work consisted primarily in "getting people to feel connected" (25). In contrast to being off-limits, the rectory's kitchen became "a hearth, a space where people could share bread and soup, talk things over, let their hair down after a job painting, fixing the roof, or working on a committee." Sitting together around the big kitchen table, members of the early community at St. Vincent's were reminded of how often Jesus broke bread with his disciples.

Wednesday evening liturgies were followed by simple suppers around the kitchen table. The gift of those Wednesday evening sharings still provides rich fare for gratitude and growth as the community remembers together. Nora Concannon recalls her first Wednesday liturgy and the get together that followed. "As people shared their day's experiences around a pot of soup, I could feel the concern and caring. I knew this was a special place and that I belonged among the St. Vincent's people."

Retreat weekends deepened connections, evenings and days of prayer and reflection, each included the power of personal sharing. This component became integral to life at St. Vincent's. The intimate circle of community, begun with a staff willing to "pay the cost of struggling together and not walking away when there was a disagreement" widened into ever expanding circles.

Before long, Father Englert formed a "Community Life Conference" to learn what the neighborhood needed. Sensitive to the hopes and needs of African American parishioners, he worked with them to create the first Black History celebrations, listening compassionately to people's feelings of displacement. As needs of the larger community became better understood, seeing just how much needed to be done posed a danger. Lynne Horoschak recalls how Bud's stress on the necessity of "getting to know one another" first, before getting to work, shaped the life of the community. This community formation priority prevailed, despite Lynne's and others' practical leaning toward doing the task. Lynne recalls continual reminders from many, who repeated Bud's message about the importance of connecting first. Anyone can do a task, Kathy Nolen Edwards explains, "we are trying to build community. We evolved an ABC approach to all parish meetings. A) we pray, B) we share, C) we do the work." "And everything gets done," the practical Lynne attests (29).

Community Trials and Errors

Not every effort at promoting community at St. Vincent's has endured the test of time, but none has been inconsequential. For example, St. Vincent's devoted several years to forming neighborhood groups, dividing the parish eventually into seventeen areas, "by observing where our parishioners were clustered and recognizing some natural boundaries." Back in the early 1980s, this was Bud's vision of the parish as "a community of communities," thinking of them as "little parishes where people connect and develop deeper relationships" (29). Some groups caught on immediately, while others lagged. Often leaders, subsequently called coordinators, remarked that they felt insecure and uninformed. The parish staff committed itself to more formation for leaders. Over a three-year period, the neighborhood groups never attracted more than 40 percent of the parish folks, usually about 25 percent. Recalling the "neighborhood groups" effort, even though the movement did not enjoy long-term success, people attest to what they learned. Here, they learned to pray together, to learn more about being church, to celebrate and ritualize their faith and their life, to feel connected, and to reach out in service to the hurting.

Liturgy Forms a People

By 1983, St. Vincent's parish had undergone significant changes toward becoming a people, a community of faith reaching out in service to its neighborhood and world. One of the sources of its enduring power undoubtedly came from the community's strong, liturgical life. St. Vincent's has long understood itself primarily as a eucharistic community trying to become what it celebrates. There's an ancient principle that says that the praying church is the believing church (*lex orandi, lex credendi*). How a people prays tells you best what a people believes. It's there in a community's worship that one ought to search for the community's faith convictions. The weekly event of St. Vincent's parish community at worship is rich and fertile ground for uncovering this community's faith.

"Let justice roll like a river and wash all oppression away. Come God and take us, move and shake us. Come now and make us anew, that we might live justly like you." As the community belts out its prophetic rendition of these lines from Amos and Micah, there's a palpable feeling that these people believe this and really want it to happen to them.

The liturgical ministry at St. Vincent's is integral to the faith formation of the community. No music is tangential but woven finely into the tapestry of the whole faith experience. The assembly seems finely tuned and alert to every ritual action; sustained periods of silence before and after the Word is proclaimed, common gestures of raised hands, held hands, outstretched hands over one another in blessing, in petition, in thanksgiving; sung and said, communion lines that move slowly and reverently toward raised cups and baskets of baked bread. The order is beautifully disrupted by the sending forth of the community's children for their own Liturgy of the Word and by their return.

"Hospitality will take place after Mass in our parish center." This announcement is repeated week after week. But one might well argue that hospitality has been going on from the moment you come through those big doors. The Gathering Rite includes "doing the work of hospitality." The assembly is invited to "get out of your pews and go to meet people you do not know yet." This takes time week after week. The work of hospitality is never over and never omitted. The Word is piercing but so is the silence. The community commitment to racial healing is often prayed about and examined in homilies and reflections, in bulletin inserts and intercessions. This particular community's commitment to the work of racial healing reminds them, at times painfully, that as God's people, they are "unfinished and needy," dependent on God's mercy and the forgiveness and help of one another.

The unfinished character of the community is visible still again as one gazes around the gathered assembly. Purple stoles worn around the necks of men and women are easily recognizable. They are a symbol of lament, a people crying out to God about the injustice suffered by women in the Roman Catholic Church, who are denied priestly ordination because of their gender. The pain is worn on many shoulders; the protest is silent and public.

Public also is the awareness that this "House of Vincent" desires to be a reconciling presence for all who have felt marginalized by the churches, especially by the Roman Catholic Church. Its gay and lesbian community is one of many "communities within the community" that shines out as a beacon of welcome and inclusive love for the entire parish and neighborhood.

The liturgical assembly itself provides the context for paying attention to diversity, not in evenly measured proportions, but a diversity that, nevertheless, clearly defines this community. The communion line itself reveals the "many-membered body of Christ" as abled and disabled, infants in fathers' arms and elderly on adult children's arms, black and white, resident scholars and street people, gay and straight, poor and rich, clergy—religious and lay—families and singles come to the table. The center of gravity and creative energy upholding and drawing together the diverse social construction of this House of Vincent is, as members affirm in unison, its eucharistic self-understanding. Repeatedly, the words of St. Augustine are spoken as invitation and challenge. "Receive who you are and become what you eat." This work of becoming goes on where the work of liturgy ends.

A COMMUNITY WORKS FOR JUSTICE

One concrete sign of the work going on is the vitality of "Inn-Dwelling," a name initially given to an old boarding home on nearby Coulter Street, which St. Vincent's opened in 1981. It began as a center for poor and mentally ill elderly people, under the pastoral ministry of Brother Al Smith. Parishioners fondly describe Brother Al as "the hands of Christ for the poor" long before the rest of the folks realized that they were Christ's Body. After 1984 with the donation of a house, Inn-Dwelling expanded as a ministry committed to renovating houses and working with low-income persons who rent them. As of today, Inn-Dwelling has renovated more than thirty houses in Germantown and is helping to create small businesses and employment cooperatives for low-income persons and families in the city.

The circle of community is expanded for the House of Vincent through their sister parish of Las Anonas de Santa Cruz, in El Salvador. The bonds of communion, connecting local communities with a larger church, become more concrete by this vital link. The early churches' commitment to letter writing and visits, prayers of concern and sharing of goods continues between the community of St. Vincent's and of Las Anonas de Santa Cruz. The sister parishes visit and work together, receiving one another as guests, sharing resources and partnering in prayer and life.

A COMMUNITY OF MEMORIES AND HOPE

As an unfinished people "on the way," the community has acknowledged its need for touchstones. The parish of St. Vincent's has celebrated and retold the story of its past, especially the past twenty-four years of community formation. At the same time, this faith community anticipates the future by earnest preparation and envisioning. At a recent parish forum, a regular event, where the community gathers for open-mike discussion of its life together, the evening was devoted to envisioning the parish ten years from now. For busy, efficiency-driven North Americans, this very exercise can feel nonproductive, but for people of faith, it helps form a community of shared hopes. Once again a vision of a world where people care for each other, where justice is experienced in relationships of equality and mutuality, leads this community back to the work of racial healing right here and now in their own neighborhood. Here, the community is confronted by its worship life again. The House of Vincent gathers for worship with a membership, still 80 percent white, in a neighborhood that is 85 percent African American. There are unmet needs and unreconciled pain in the community outside its large, wooden doors, despite the inclusive WELCOME SIGN on its lawn.

Discovering a Community's Atoning Deed

The community members, lay and clergy, challenge each other to stay at this work of reconciliation. The task takes concrete shape for the forseeable future in the "parish's unflinching commitment to racial healing." The House of Vincent has articulated its goal of creating

> a Christian community where all people find a safe environment to examine and overcome their prejudices and where those who suffer racial prejudice and discrimination feel truly welcomed and accepted, have their gifts and culture valued and included, and find solidarity in their struggle for equality (African American Leadership Ministry, May 1997).

In the early twentieth century, Josiah Royce's vision of the "Beloved Community" was dependent upon each particular community's discovery and doing of its own "atoning deed" in the present. The deed is intended to atone for an act of betrayal that had broken the community originally, resulting in the plight of lost individuals. Only communities can participate in this saving of the lost individual and be healed of its brokenness in the process. Royce's theory remains simply that, without concrete communities to attest to his speculation. The atoning deed, Royce claimed, is such that its achievement brings about new life, a quality of life that would not have been possible had the act of betrayal not taken place in the first place. For the community of St. Vincent's, the work of racial healing may well qualify as such "an atoning deed." It is, for sure, integral to their self-understanding of God's dream for a Beloved Community, broken by the terrible divide that is racism right there in Germantown, Pennsylvania.

Signs of hope line the road to healing for this community, in stories shared by whites and blacks, meeting together in small "racial healing communities." The stories tell of fear and ignorance faced, forgiveness and repentance dared, understandings sought and misunderstandings acknowledged, awakenings to white privilege and new awareness of oppression, blessings counted and burdens lightened. Despite setbacks and personal limitations, there remains, above all, a willingness to stay at the table together. Without ever speaking directly about an atoning deed, the community of St. Vincent's asks: "how are we doing?" The words of Micah the prophet come to mind. You're "doing justly, loving tenderly, walking humbly" (6:8). Keep on keepin' on . . .

CONCLUSION

Early on in the faith formation work of the House of Vincent, members realized that they were about more than doing good work. They were building community for which some simple ABC's were thought to be solid building blocks. A) we pray, B) we share, C) we do the work (of justice). The formula has not changed greatly but the momentum has grown and the stakes themselves may be increasingly higher. An urban community seeks to heal itself of its racial divide in order to be a healing presence for the larger world. They see this as integral to God's dream and commit themselves to the doing of this "atoning deed." Community is for them both a means to their goal and, in an ultimate sense, the final goal itself. In the meantime, a deep liturgical life keeps them at it. We raise up St. Vincent de Paul parish in Germantown as reflective of many other urban church communities that are making a significant commitment to their neighborhoods and cities. To communities such as these we have turned for the enthusiasm and hope that inspire this project.

GOOD NEWS IN SPECIFIC AND DIVERSE FORMS

These five examples of new Christian communities are nothing short of spectacular. Although only five communities have been profiled, they illustrate a much deeper truth about the brilliant possibilities for community already being embraced in American churches. These new developments in American church life truly do express the root meaning of gospel as good news.

This sampling of communities is offered along with two liberating truths for those willing to re-imagine life together in America:

1. There are hundreds of additional examples of such communities throughout the United States. The good news is not just about these five communities. It is about an identifiable pattern in the current church landscape.

2. These communities—in some contrast to other lock-step religious programming efforts—reflect a broad and gracious diversity. A new gospel of community is breaking loose across denominational boundaries and in a variety of social settings. These emergent communities are diverse demographically and geographically. They are occurring in urban, suburban, and rural settings. Perhaps at least as striking is the obvious trend that within the particular communities, diversity is prized. Most of our sample communities have shown commitment to racial, gender, economic, social, cultural, and sexual orientation reconciliation.

Part 3 pointed out the wasteland of individualism in America, and was daunting. In an explicit and energized fashion, the church communities sampled in this chapter provide needed inspiration to address the disheartening forces and claim a new gospel of community.

Chapter Twelve

BUILDING COMMUNITY:
EXPLORING A METAPHOR

As Miguel and his three young children sweep the barn and relocate chickens and their coops, one can feel the significance of the work in progress. It is Wednesday and the Bonino family is preparing for the gathering of church. The base community of Santa Maria de la Cruz on the outskirts of Buenos Aires, Argentina, will meet in the barn later that evening. Moving the chicken coops literally helps build the church space. A sign was hung earlier in the week in the center of town to announce where church would meet. The Bonino barn serves as a place for the church to gather. There is no confusion in any one's mind. The barn is necessary for church to come together, and moving the chicken coops helps construct church space. But the more essential building blocks of church are the people who are being built up into one body. This church is the tired and fiery, young and old, struggling and searching people who gather, needing each other and finding God in their midst. The construction of church community is social, and as such, a human and divine project. It is this kind of re-imagining life together that the churches throughout the Americas need to be about.

COMMUNITY AND THE METAPHOR OF CONSTRUCTION

Community does not just appear. Like reality itself, community is constructed. It is not as if one day it can be decided that community should happen, and the rest occurs automatically. Nor does community exist in some pure or abstract form. The emergence of community depends on an extended process. It is the product less of romantic longing than intense and prolonged passion, decision, and commitment.

Building community requires a variety of resources as well. In fact, a metaphor of "construction" helps recapitulate the meaning of this book. As in any building project, the development of community involves:

1. a vision

2. a feasibility study

3. the laying of a foundation, and

4. the drawing up of specifications for the various dimensions of the structure itself.

Each stage of building and each set of resources require in themselves focused efforts that anticipate and promote the grander dynamic to come. Building community, similar to other construction projects, begins with a number of basic natural resources and, through human engagement of these resources, produces a new entity. At the same time, our use of this building metaphor is not meant to infer that the realization of community is simply a human project. As noted throughout this book and as will be reiterated in this chapter, the building of community depends directly on deeper, inherently connective resources underneath and simultaneous with the human endeavor. God constructs group life as initiator, companion, and goal. We are in this together.

Nevertheless the necessity of human resolve, initiative, passion, and persistence in all building does justice to this book's emphasis on real decisiveness and commitment to the construction of community in America through church dynamics and institutions. Indeed, we do mean this book to be a manifesto with a double edge. We call directly upon the spectrum of wistful, apathetic, and/or searching individuals to wake up to the real sense of purposeful and open-ended belonging inherent in the churches. The other edge is our insistent challenge to the churches to take seriously the disaster of American individualism and the resources within church structures and traditions for the reconstruction of more genuine life together.

A RE-IMAGINING OF AMERICAN COMMUNITY

All building begins with a vision of something not yet in existence. It might emerge as a creative imagination of a daring and beautiful structure. Beauty is recognized as both the source and goal of such a construction. Or, it might be a simple recognition of a desire for additional space. One builds for the sake of some perceived advantage. Vision is often born of an identified need and a way to meet it. No matter where along this spectrum one places the building of community, everything that is built begins in vision.

The vision that Americans can live in sustained structures of belonging comes perhaps most poignantly from the acute sense across a broad swath of both population and history that this framework of togetherness no longer exits. It needs to be re-imagined. We have seen in the introduction, chapter 8, and chapter 9 how deep the void of community is in America. The collective sympathies and supportive structures that undergird civility, family, governance, and other basic patterns of human coherence are severely lacking in the United States. More suburban sprawl and urban flight, more cars with less people in them, intense competition within and between businesses, more single living units than ever before and countless other trends highlight the difficulties Americans have in coming together in any sustained manner. Even though the historical drama of the individual American pioneer conquering the wild frontier has long played itself out, the recent research of Robert Bellah and Robert Putnam has shown that Americans are more isolated than ever. Underneath all this aloneness, an ache for connections and belonging surfaces intermittently, partly as angst and neuroses, partly as a deeper vision of that which ought to be but is not. Indeed in survey after survey of the last decade, community ranks as a primary spiritual value sought by Americans.

But the well-documented wistful American longing for community is only part of the vision that has emerged in this book. Complementing it and shoring it up is the long tradition of community within Christianity. Even though these traditions of group life have only with fits and starts expressed themselves in American society, they nevertheless are present in American consciousness, if only as combination of lure, experiment, and occasionally effective church. Such a collective memory—even when uneven and socially dislocated—makes the vision of building community much more promising than just the wistful American search for sustained group life. It is true that many European and some early American configurations of community from church history dance at the edge of American consciousness as ethnic and denominational heritage. But even these vestiges of community, geographically sporadic but important in our past, seem to have almost entirely disappeared in the present.

But experiments in building community by early Christians, as sketched in part 1, do serve here to fill out the vision for a contemporary construction of American community in particularly critical ways. That the early Christian groups emerged out of existing, at least implicitly communitarian, impulses such as the Greco-Roman voluntary associations and the Jewish synagogues attaches a distant plausibility to the vision of churches helping build American community. That these same early communities saw their relationship to God and to one another in tight tandem gives specific credence to the vision of religious bodies helping infuse America with a commitment to group life. That the development of first and second century Christian communities thrived on diversity resonates with vision for the increasingly diverse American society. Most visionary for the endemic American lack of belonging is the creative way the early Christians fashioned community in the midst of Roman oppression of many traditional communal forms.

THE FEASIBILITY OF CHURCHES BUILDING COMMUNITY IN AMERICA

In addition to providing a vision of American community, this book has examined in a sustained way the feasibility of church life making a significant contribution to the building of such community. Like other construction, the vision of community building promoted here has needed to be tested relative to whether the churches have the kind of resources necessary for a substantial building of community.

Whether churches have a thorough enough set of social structures, theological and ethical principles, and spiritual traditions to energize the complex process of community formation across a wide range of American society has deserved a close look. Such a feasibility study has formed a substantive part of this work. On it depends any positive conclusions we may proffer. Given the strong American individualist legacy and present-day technological and economic reinforcements of it, no vision of community in America could appear as more than a pipe dream without such a serious study. In parts 2 and 4, respectively, we have tested the vision's feasibility from both theoretical and practical perspectives. Especially from the perspective of local churches designing ways to promote community on a more sustained basis, the in-depth treatment of these sections provides frameworks of preparation. In this regard much of part 2 needs to be regarded both as the demonstration of the theoretical feasibility of Christian community and the blueprint for how local churches can lay out their own community building plans.

For instance, from a Roman Catholic starting point, but by no means stopping there, the twentieth-century movement to "return to the sources" discussed in chapter 4, proposed a clear priority and framework for Christian community. While the Second Vatican Council was still decades away, the three visionary theologians studied in chapter 4 were busy doing a feasibility study of why the Roman Catholic Church needed to rebuild itself for the sake of the world and how it could respond to such a call. The historical links that DeLubac, Congar, and Rahner make between theology and community practice, the inclusivity of church, and the social character of salvation itself provides a framework for Christian group life. And, any contemporary church weighing its feasibility to nurture group life for Americans today needs to ask the same pressing questions about its ability to integrate theology and practice, to advocate inclusivity, and to challenge privatistic notions of salvation. In many ways, these theological voices have still more to say about what is feasible for the churches today out of "dangerous memories" (ones that have a future intent) from the church's past. An historical and theological "return to the sources" provides a wellspring into which churches in America can tap.

In an even more comprehensive fashion chapter 6's review of the thinking of Josiah Royce and Bernard Lonergan demonstrate the contemporary coherence of Christian conceptions of community. In a clear and systematic way both these thinkers outline the intersection of Christian self-expression and the dynamics of group life. Together Royce and Lonergan contribute a detailed elaboration of the main elements of Christian social belonging in our day.

In drawing the strands of this book together through the metaphor of building community, we recall two particular formulations of the structure of group life in Royce. First, he lays out three conditions of the individual self that allow a community self to exist. Second, he develops three criteria for this community self. Each of these sets shows the theoretical viability of Christian community and provides an assessment tool for churches planning initiatives in this regard.

Royce's criteria for community take deep spiritual themes of Christianity and frame them in terms of contemporary group life. He does so by explaining that members 1) are actively open to working for the unity of all persons, 2) love each other in a way that affirms loyalty to the community itself, and 3) perform atoning deeds that triumph over betrayal in community. These criteria bring to clear consciousness the important ways that Christian faith calls for personal dynamics that emphasize group life. For instance, the way Royce appropriates the Christian belief in atonement in order to address the key issue of betrayal in group life shows in a pointed way the power of Christian expression in forming community.

That all communities experience persons betraying one another is obvious. That communities are an integral part of a larger society where betrayal has broken its social fibers is also evident. The way Royce frees atonement vocabulary from stale dogmatic formulations and claims them as a lens to help specific people in a group to heal and become one is both surprising and liberating. The way he calls communities to take seriously their healing role in society is likewise surprising and demanding.

Similarly Royce's outline of the three conditions needed within each individual to allow the formation of a community self demonstrates on another level the feasibility of Christian tradition to provide basic building blocks for group life. He enumerates his conditions as: 1) the individual self's capacity for extension in an idealizing projection into both the past and future, 2) the necessity for a number of distinct selves capable of social communication, and 3) the sharing of some individual idealizations of the past and future among those distinct selves. Although phrased within Royce's vocabulary of social philosophy, this sequence of how particular individual self-understanding makes group dynamics possible can also be illustrated straightforwardly in less technical terms. A first example is the way various Christian individuals extend their understanding of themselves by identifying with characters in past stories found in the New Testament gospels. By thinking of themselves as the Syrophonecian woman seeking healing for her child, the disciples struggling to understand parables, the woman in the parable of the leaven, or Jesus himself being transfigured, contemporary Christians extend their understanding of themselves and life itself. But the decisive formation of what Royce calls a "community self" takes place when specific individuals, who have extended themselves into the gospel stories, and who can communicate socially about differences, hold in common some ways they identify with these figures. This common identification becomes part of a shared story. The example also reveals the socially formative power of Christian tradition in group life. One could easily trace how other dynamics of Christian life such as the hope for a world to come or the claiming of the life of a particular saint can similarly aid in the feasibility of Christian community through Royce's three-fold explanation of individual and community selfhood.

Chapter 6 likewise describes Royce's understanding of community and the time process of memory and hope, his outline of the three roles within a community of interpretation, and his characterization of two major twentieth-century obstacles to community. Each of these dimensions can be seen similarly as demonstration of and help for the feasibility of the church's crucial contribution to the development of community in America.

Similarly, Bernard Lonergan's theologically grounded, understanding of community as a dynamic achievement of shared meanings and values and his dialectic of community recommend the vision to churches building twenty-first century community. That American churches can provide arenas for shared experiences, understanding, judgment, and actions (Lonergan's four levels), in ways that few other institutions in America can, indicates real plausibility for the vision. Noticing how these levels of community consciousness engage specific thirsts of people today is also promising. There are few places where groups of people can take time simply to share experiences. Even educational settings rarely provide the opportunity for groups to develop common understandings of specific experiences. The clash of values in families and neighborhoods only illustrates the paucity of settings in which common values can be affirmed by a group of people. The short-term volunteerism described in Wuthnow's *Loose Connections* (cf. chapter 8) makes clear that Americans rarely find a place where they can take action together in a sustained manner. Lonergan's four levels of community consciousness show from a different angle the feasibility of the church's formative role and provide a framework for local churches to map out strategies of community formation.

Portions of part 4 have confirmed the feasibility of building community in America through churches in a more practical way. Especially chapter 11's sampling of five different contemporary communities of faith can be seen as signaling several prototypes for this vision. The metaphor of "feasibility study" names very accurately the way we see these already existing new church examples of American group life. First, this is so because these specific communities of faith actually are functioning and therefore confirm the viability of much of what this book proposes. Second, the "feasibility study" metaphor is telling because these five examples do form a certain set. Although they were chosen to a great extent for their differences, taken together they form the outlines of new Christian community in the American landscape. Each of them is in some tension with more static, institutional church life. Each of them is marked by concern for justice, both in church and secular settings. Each of them shows sparks of new spirituality and creative worship. Group life in most of them concentrates on units of less than 200 people, in contrast to older parish structures or current mega-church models. Finally, the "feasibility study" metaphor best characterizes what chapter 11's sample communities signify because these communities do not yet represent a significant shift in the way most Americans do (not) experience group life. Although we have limited ourselves to five community portrayals here—and indeed we estimate modestly that there are several thousand communities meeting these feasibility criteria—it is not yet true that most Americans perceive churches as a renewed source of social belonging. Nor is it the case that anywhere near the majority of American churches look like these examples. The better part of this work is yet to be done. Chapter 6 provides a theoretic form for the vision and chapter 11's examples only signal viability of the vision, not its achievement.

A Foundation for Community

With a vision to impel and a feasibility study to direct, any construction still needs a foundation. For after the vision is articulated and its feasibility is determined, a foundation to support every structure and elaboration must be in place. This book hopes to have laid such a foundation.

The foundation is clearly theological. That is, the new feasible community we envision grounds itself in God. In parts 1, 2, and 4, we have continually returned to the intimate connections between who God is and who we can be in community. Especially in chapters 1 (where the social and spiritual character of first-century Christian communities is described), 3 (where the theological notion of communion is central), 4 (where twentieth-century theologians reclaiming of social meaning is charted), and 6 (where Lonergan and Royce both detail the connections between community and the basics of life), God and group belonging merge. Holding all of these together, chapter 5's discussion of the work of John Zizioulas in many ways needs to be seen as the theological hinge pin for our thesis of building community in America. Combined with chapter 7's discussion of the work of Elizabeth Johnson, our focus on Zizioulas lays claim to relationality as primary category for God. Both Zizioulas and subsequently Johnson frame this divine relationality in terms of the persons of the Christian Trinity. Since God is relationship above, before, and beyond all other attributes, we propose that the basic relational nature of community is a subset of God's own basic relational character. Grounded in the careful patristic study of Zizioulas, God's relationality becomes the text and context of human community.

Since this relational thesis about God and community has been detailed in a variety of explicitly theological categories throughout the book, we take care here to make this same theologically foundational proposal also in implicitly theological language. Another way of saying that the foundation for community building lies in God is to note that relationality is the primary building block of all life. That is, being itself seems to consist of the coming together into relatively small group constellations of distinct individual units. Cosmologist Brian Swimme, in characterizing what he calls the "fundamental order of the universe," names three principles on which the universe operates. Each of these three principles relates directly to what might be called the character of community at the very heart of the universe. These principles are differentiation, communion, and interiority. Differentiation is the abiding tendency of the universe to create an endless variety of entities and processes. The universe is always, Swimme says, producing new elements, species, and energies. At the same time, according to Swimme, the principle of communion is operative. This is the ongoing characteristic of everything in the universe to connect to something else. That is, everything tends to develop multiple relationships. Put together, these two principles of the universe make for an endless set of differentiated relationality. Or, in our terms, community as a group relationship is a subset of the universe's tendency to bring differentiated entities and processes into relationship. The third characteristic of the universe, interiority, names that dynamic center of uniqueness and mystery inherent in all life, in even the smallest particle. In more explicitly spiritual language, this dark center of mystery, present in everything that is, radiates as the divine spark of life. The principle of interiority provides another way of understanding a sacred presence at work even in cosmic formulations of community. Community, then, as a human endeavor, is both within and greater than our grasp. Community is in the very nature of the universe.

That the foundation of all community is God allows this book's proposals about the churches to build group life for America in important ways to rest not just on our arguments, but on the very nature of creativity. In proposing this foundation we do not mean to say that our project is unusually godly or that our work is divine in ways that other projects are not. We simply celebrate the underlying universal power on which this project rests.

SPECIFICATIONS FOR BUILDING COMMUNITY

Once the vision, feasibility, and foundation for building have been provided, specifications for the actual structure need to be drawn up. This gives the building a particular character, and begins to show its place vis-à-vis all other structures. This book has also engaged the stage of community building that entails specifications. Because of the provisional character of new church community in America, the list of specifications is not extensive, although some of this needed work has been done. These specifications are present mostly in chapters 7 and 10.

That the character of community needs to express itself as liberating is a hallmark of chapter 7. All communities need to attend to issues of justice. The level of specifications here is somewhat vague in that different communities face different justice concerns. It depends on the location of the community as to whether racial justice, economic justice, or gender justice are to be engaged. But every community needs to face particular justice concerns. This specification of justice is not an arbitrary choice by us as authors. Rather justice is necessary in every community in order that the connections within the community be genuine. If a community does not attend to justice, its own structures will collapse in disarray or implode upon its self-enclosed members.

Such attention to justice—even the relative to the particular location of each community—has been specified in chapter 7 to a certain degree, where the dynamics of awakening to justice, the structural dimensions of justice, the accounting for genuine difference in community, and the need for a variety of creative approaches and social disciplines are explored.

The way many contemporary experiments in community have pointed to the necessity of specific relational dynamics has been treated in chapter 10. Mainly through a series of personal stories the requirement of communities to exercise hospitality, to foster forgiveness, to take time to reflect on each individual's faith journey, to promote everyone's inner life, to address broader societal needs outside the community, and to construct power dynamics in a relational fashion is specified there. Again here it is not accidental that these specifications are articulated in the context of real and personal examples. The practice of community, where it actually does occur in American church settings, has made clear that all communities must have these specific dynamics, if they are to continue.

CONCLUSION

This project is then on one level a handbook for building community. It contains in some detail the vision, the feasibility studies, the foundation, and some specifications for a sense of social belonging for a broad range of isolated Americans. As such it beckons to these individualist Americans to consider seriously loyalty to church as their primary community. Similarly it encourages churches to claim a central role in American society and the lives of individual Americans by reclaiming the heritage of Christian community and meeting some of the most desperate needs of the American people. As a handbook, this guide to community building is of use only as a response to a deeper call, one that we do not accept full authority for issuing.

CAVEATS

Two reservations we have about the task of community building cannot be avoided. These caveats to our overall, wholehearted proposal that American churches become an important means by which Americans learn to live together are not meant to detract from the proposal, but to refine it.

The first is an acknowledgment that community, as local and concrete, is not the be-all and end-all of human existence, even though we have claimed that communion is. Once again, it is important to note the distinctions between communion and community described in chapter 3. Communion is the invisible gift of Spirit by which community becomes a significant achievement of human consciousness and endeavor. But it remains a dynamic process in social organization. It is never fully achieved in human history. Related to, but distinct from community development, lies the development of human societies, which contain within them various communities. Societies are larger, more complex and more powerful human organisms than communities. We want to emphasize that the quality and character of societies often depend to a large extend on the character of communal life. For instance, American society is clearly more impersonal and often more violent than many other human societies, just because its ability to form communities is so underdeveloped. Nevertheless, communities, as concrete human constructions, remain a subset of societies. Their place in God's final communion life is part of a larger mystery.

Only recently have humans become conscious of another level of social organization beyond both community and society. Mostly through the discovery of the earth's place in the larger universe, humans have noted that they are a particular species on a particular planet. There is now a vague awareness of a larger communion in life; that community is not only a subset of society, but that both community and society are subsets of the human species as a planetary whole. Life in communion opens us exponentially into still greater wholeness and diversity.

The danger in missing this larger context of community development involves the reduction of all consciousness to that of human communities. There are many places in which isolated groups, posing as communities, do try to replace or deny the larger world. In these cases community becomes sectarian. The terms themselves are contradictory, even though sects often name themselves communities. Instead of expanding human consciousness, sectarian community limits it. It is important to note that sectarian groups are often self-consciously religious. Religious language often helps such pseudo-communities pretend that the larger societal and species-wide issues do not exist by applying cosmological religious language to the community *per se*. In such sectarian communities, the community sees itself as representing all of society, the whole human race, or even the universe itself.

This book dramatizes the quest for community, not because we can attain it in the universal sense of God's ultimate dream. Communion as final achievement lies always beyond our grasp, an important reminder for Americans whose spirit of acquisition keeps mounting. Community cannot be added to a long list of sought-after possessions. But, we do see the quest for community as absolutely crucial for human development in our particular American context. This is so primarily because Americans have so drastically neglected and ignored community. Such ignorance of community in America has made America a caricatured society. Unless Americans learn to live in community, they cannot participate fully in the further developments of society and species.

The second caveat addresses another implicit danger, not directly treated in the book. This danger is the active and crushing opposition to community coming from American social life itself. It is true that in chapters 8 and 9 we examined what we call the American disaster of individualism and lack of community. But those chapters did not treat the social forces in our country that actively undermine American community and continually thwart the influence of the churches.

In America two major and very different social forces actively vie for allegiance over against community. They attack the possibility of community from very different angles. The two forces are an obsession with the nuclear family and the competitive business ethos.

The stereotypical nuclear family makes overwhelming and untenable claims on the American psyche. In nostalgia for a nonexistent past, many individuals and organizations promote the organization of American society around the private home unit of mother, father, and children. High-pitched rhetoric proposes that Americans give priority to the social and economic stability of this small unit. This results in many social ills, including the withdrawal from neighborhood and civic involvement, environmental damage through the sprawl of the single family dwelling over vast expanses of nature, neglect of the extended family with its intergenerational needs and gifts, and high rates of divorce due to the overblown expectations of marital partnership. The community virtues proposed and described throughout this book cannot be fostered in families being formed in environments threatened by demands for continuous indulgence and immediate self-gratification. Family ills compete with other social ones, as early sexual activity, rampant drug use, hypertension, and depression drain families and youth of participating vitally in a larger social context. Most crucial to our hypothesis, the American nuclear family, as stereotypic and enclosed, is the main countermovement to real community consciousness. The promotion of such a closed family system causes many Americans to limit drastically their investment in community building. Despite the clear historical precedence that humans have, for the vast majority of their history, lived in communities that are larger and more complex than the nuclear family, Americans are continually barraged with the injunction to be loyal primarily to this singularly, self-contained unit.

Business culture with its pervasive promotion of competition undermines in major ways the possibility of Americans developing community. This competitive business ethos reinforces American individualism by encouraging Americans to see their economic success as dependent on competition. It not only endorses rivalry between companies, it also promotes employees within corporations to view themselves as adversaries of one another. Because this business culture has so dramatically raised the level of American affluence, many Americans understand it to be divinely ordained and natural. Such a pervasive mentality actively discourages Americans from raising the question of how to commune and cooperate with one another. The move from competitive isolation to cooperative community will ask that new levels of social commitment based on shared meanings and values be lived out.

The Construction of Community as America's Primary Spiritual Calling

The damage done by American individualism to individuals themselves, to the society's ability to function in less violent and alienated ways, to entire peoples in other parts of the world who suffer from American individualist greed, and to the earth's own ecospheres is enormous. Despite these obstacles and qualifications, the hope of community for Americans is vivid and prophetic. The ability for churches to contribute to more social belonging is visionary, feasible, grounded, and specific.

That American history, geography, the nuclear family, and capitalist culture array themselves against any effort to be in community simply raises the stakes. That movements exist within the churches themselves that threaten to divide and polarize rather than promote unity in diversity only increases the need for genuine community development. As persons who have spent the last three decades in church-based incubators of American community, the end of this writing sojourn brings us back to our beginning. We return to the words from Scripture with which we began part 1: "What we have seen and heard, we proclaim to you as well, so that you yourselves may have community with us. This community of ours is with God and God's son Jesus Christ" (1 John 1:3). The building of community in America is our primary spiritual calling; through it we share the very life and work of God.

NOTES

1. These trends are discussed at length in part 3.

2. As we have written this book, only one major terminological disagreement has remained between us as separate co-authors. This disagreement is about the constellation of terms: church, Church, the Church, churches, established church, local church. With regard to these terms our separate positions are as follows:

Cathy Nerney has wanted to use all of the above terms in different contexts. In distinction from Hal Taussig, however, she thinks that one can refer to "the Church" as an overarching reality, even while also speaking of various kinds of particular churches in that all-inclusive category of *the Church*. For Nerney, *the Church* exists as the body of Christ within and beyond all particular churches. For her, *the Church* is a universal and particular reality that includes what she would call "the established church" of history, but is not limited to this established church. The theological or sacramental reality of *the Church* as an entity beyond all the particularities of history and social setting is essential to Nerney. That is, for Nerney who *the Church* is cannot be disconnected from who God is. However, for her *the Church* can never exist outside of a particular social setting in history. The Church remains always mystery or sacrament—both concrete in particularity and beyond the corruptions of any one particularity. To abandon the symbolic nature of the Church allows it to slip into a relativity disconnected from God's transcendent existence (a sociological reductionism) while to abandon the concrete nature of the Church fosters an abstraction and the potential for absolutist claims that negate the need or capacity for historical and social critique (a theological reductionism).

For Hal Taussig it is also necessary to be able to talk about the idea of *a Church* that expresses a general notion of "churchness" beyond each particular church community. But for Taussig, it is impossible to speak of *the Church*. The combination of a capital "C" and a definite article ("the") makes for Taussig an unjustifiable assumption that there is a particular church perspective that is privileged above the others. When anyone means *the Church* simply to refer to the absolute, ideal, or incorruptible character of church, that person deludes her/himself in not recognizing that such use at least unconsciously privileges the point of view of the speaker. To preserve some notion of a general idea of churchness and at the same time avoid the establishment of an un-self-critical generalization, Taussig prefers the terms "a Church," "Church" (without any article), or "churches." This allows some generalization at the same time as it relativizes the inevitable privileging that occurs when generalizing. The theological intention of this resistance to what seems to Taussig an un-self-critical privileging of *the Church* of a particular speaker's is to honor God's perspective, which always outstrips any particular human expression.

As two authors, we are aware that this terminological tension between us can be typified in two well-known categories. Nerney's position is after all much more Catholic and Taussig's much more Protestant, corresponding to our actual ecclesial roots and loyalties. Nerney's position is both more classically theological and more modern than Taussig's, whose position exhibits stronger characteristics of postmodern thought.

For the better part of a year, we creatively sought some term which would respect both our positions and continue to carry our common enthusiasm for Church/church as crucial in building an American sense of community. But we were unable to find such a term. The result is twofold: 1) each of us has critically re-read the material in this book for which we were directly responsible, and tried to recognize as much as possible the other author's point of view in those sections of the book; 2) where, however, the tension has remained, we have allowed the individual co-author to maintain their particular Church/church vocabulary. This, of course, does then make for some inconsistency in presentation. But as co-authors—even in this particular disagreement—we trust that this honest difference may enrich the book by keeping alive two opinions of integrity.

3. In fact, we stand over against those who would privilege Christianity over other religions. The tendency of Christianity throughout the majority of its history to consider itself the best and the only valid faith has left churches with a terrible legacy of arrogance, intolerance, and prejudice. The continuation of this privileging of Christianity over other religions today poisons the self-understanding of many well-meaning and deeply committed Christians. It also undermines the possibility of mutual relationships between Christians and members of other faiths in a

time when such mutuality is desperately needed. This is not to say that we as authors think that all religions and/or faiths are equal in merit and insight. Over against a rising and rather undifferentiated contemporary tide of opinion that holds all faiths are the same, we think that a much more nuanced evaluation is in order.

In other words, we are of the opinion that in many regards for many different human social locations Christianity may be indeed the religion above all others that we would recommend. On the other hand it is also clear to us that Buddhism, Islam, or Judaism, for instance, are to be most highly recommended to certain other people coming to faith. Very often it makes a great deal of difference which faith expression a person embraces.

And, today there are increasing situations in which such responses are being made. Even to begin to sort out this more nuanced evaluation of faith traditions would need more colleagues, a great deal of time, and at least another book. In the meantime we hold that such decisions/ choices about which is the best faith tradition for particular people are meaningful, complex, and deserving of attention. But we reject the two different positions of most Americans: 1) that Christianity is categorically and globally superior or 2) that all faiths are the same.

4. The most recent survey work on this front is being done in a massive manner by the Social Capital Community Benchmark Survey of the Saguaro Center on Civic Engagement in America at Harvard University's Kennedy School of Government. See also similar work and results in the DDB Life Style, available through DDB World Wide of Chicago, the Comprehensive Social Capital Index described on pages 290–91 of Robert Putnam's *Bowling Alone*, and the Roper Social and Political Trends Archive at the Roper Center for Public Opinion Research at the University of Connecticut.

5. In Bellah, *America*, 13.

INTRODUCTION TO PART ONE
A GOSPEL OF COMMUNITY IN EARLY CHRISTIANITY

1. In quoting 1 John, we have intentionally translated *koinonia* as community. We will differentiate/connect our use of communion/community in chapter 3.

CHAPTER ONE

THE EMERGENCE OF CHRISTIAN COMMUNITY IN THE HELLENISTIC
MEDITERRANEAN

1. See the work of Burton Mack for some of the clearest discussions of this. Cf. his *Who Wrote the New Testament?* and *The Christian Myth*.

2. For a recent survey of this scholarship, see John Kloppenborg and Stephen Wilson's *Voluntary Associations in the Graeco-Roman World*. This study summarizes the most recent scholarship, places some focus on its relationship to early Christianity, and provides a very comprehensive bibliography for the last century of study. A similar study exists in the recent encyclopedic survey of Greco-Roman meals in Mattias Klinghardt's *Mahlgemeinschaft und Gemeinschaftsmahl* (loosely translated Community in Meals and Meals of Community). The term *voluntary association* does not come from the ancient documents themselves, but is a designation for a cluster of groups, which act in similar ways.

3. Examples of such new Roman cities are Corinth, in which there was an association with which Paul wrote, and Sepphoris, a major "Greek" city just three miles from Nazareth, Jesus' home town.

4. In the last thirty years many New Testament scholars have identified this passage as one that Paul most likely took from those who were in the Christ movement before him. The suggestion is that these phrases may have been a part of a baptismal formula used by the very early pre-Pauline Christian groups. For a summary of these positions, see Dennis MacDonald, *Male and Female* and Hans Dieter Betz, *1 Corinthians*.

5. In a clear reference to the ongoing question in the hellenistic Mediterranean of whether men and women could eat together, Gospel of Thomas 612–14 reads: "Salome said, 'Who are you, mister? You have climbed onto my couch and eaten from my table as if you are from someone.' Jesus said to her, 'I am the one who comes from what is whole. I was granted from the things of my Father.' 'I am your disciple.'" (Salome said.) And Gospel of Thomas 114 reads: "Simon Peter said to them, 'Make Mary leave us, for females don't deserve life.' Jesus said, 'Look I will guide her to make her male, so that she too may become a living spirit resembling you males. For every female who makes herself male will enter the domain of heaven.'" Although these references do not necessarily supply answers to the questions we have today about mutuality of the sexes, they do reflect an active debate about such matters in the first century.

CHAPTER TWO
FIVE EARLY CHRISTIAN COMMUNITIES

1. It is important to note that the larger movement of contemporary biblical scholarship toward a social understanding of early Christianity and its texts is constantly being qualified and updated. Of particular note in this regard are some very recent responses to works such as Wire's, Brown's, and Mack's. On the one hand the National Society of Biblical Literature is sponsoring a major, long-term seminar ("Ancient Texts and Modern Myths of Christian Origins") which is mapping out in detailed terms a number of early Christian communities. On the other hand, some literary critics have hastened to qualify the entire notion that an ancient text can correspond on a one-to-one basis to a particular community. This point—with which the authors of this book are sympathetic—notes that the relationship between early Christian texts and the exact communities is probably more complex. That is, some of the texts may represent minority points of view within particular communities, others (a perfect example are the works of Ignatius of Antioch) may represent a sometimes forced combination of beliefs and practices of several communities, and still others may represent several different points of view within a particular community artificially brought together in a text. In this regard, one could view this chapter as oversimplified. The nontechnical character of this presentation for a more general public certainly has had to forgo certain nuances in its presentation. The overall point, even with the justified reservations of the literary critics, remains. Early Christian texts manifest their roots in particular social processes, the best characterization of which is "community."

2. Robert Tannehill's several volumes on Luke are seen as classic articulations of the Lukan milieu. Cf. his two volume *A Literary Introduction to Luke-Acts* as well as his Abingdon Press commentary *Luke*. The role of women in Luke's milieu is well summarized in Turid Seim's essay in *Searching the Scriptures*, volume II, edited by Elisabeth Schüssler Fiorenza and in her own book *A Double Message*. In this regard, cf. also (two Liturgical Press volumes). Two recent volumes complement each other tensively in reinforcing the complexity of Seim's thesis: Barbara Reid's *Choosing the Better Part?: Women in the Gospel of Luke* and Loretta Dornisch's *A Woman Reads the Gospel of Luke*.

3. We take this name from the technical use of the Greek term *klasis artou* by the Gospel of Luke, which occurs in Luke 24:30, 34 and Acts 2:46. The term literally means the "rupturing of bread," and appears to be

the name of the ceremonial meal in the Lukan community.

4. Scholarship generally credits Paul Achtemeier with the identification of the "miracle catenae," a group of miracle stories written prior to the existence of the first narrative gospel, Mark. Cf. his studies. Burton Mack, both in his study of Mark and in *Who Wrote the New Testament?*, has popularized and extended Achtemeier's proposals. In Hal Taussig's "Dealing Under the Table: Ritual Negotiation and the Syro-Phonecian Woman Pericope," in *Re-Imagining Christian Origins*, he has paid particular attention to the ways meals may have functioned for this Congregation of Israel and to the roles women played at those meals.

5. The pivotal study of the Corinthian milieu is Antoinette Wire's *The Corinthian Women Prophets*. Karen King, professor of New Testament and Early Christianity at Harvard Divinity School in her lectures has taken Wire's work and applies it to a more general understanding of women's prophetic roles in several early Christian communities.

6. Thomas is the only gospel of the first century that actually within the body of its text mentions its "author" Thomas. All the canonical gospels "titles" or attributions to Matthew, Mark, Luke, and John do not occur within the gospel text itself, but are later superscriptions added by copiers of the documents.

7. Scholarship on the Thomas movement is nicely summarized in Ron Cameron's *The Other Gospels* and John Dominic Crossan's *Four Other Gospels*. One of the early studies of Thomas, which is still recognized as significant is Stevan Davies' *The Gospel of Thomas and Early Christian Wisdom*. For a short summary portrait of the Thomas community see pp. 60–64 of Burton Mack's *Who Wrote the New Testament?*

8. In a technical sense most scholars now think that the Corinthian Christ cult and the Congregation of Israel communities also thought of themselves as Jewish. This, of course, had its own ironies, since most probably the majority of people in the Christ cults and the Corinthian groups were gentiles, and the larger part of the Congregation of Israel were people excluded from certain parts of regular Jewish life by virtue of purity laws and practices. But if one would have asked the people in these groups whether they "belonged to Israel," they would have most likely answered in the affirmative. (The term *Jew* is not used consistently in the first century to designate a member of the Jewish religion or people. The term *Israel* seems to be the most predominant operative term of identity.) It is less likely that the Lukan groups thought of themselves as Jewish.

9. Cf. David Balch, ed. *Social History of Matthean Christianity.*

10. The connection between Matthew and the Didache, written ten to thirty years later, is striking.

11. Mid-twentieth-century New Testament scholarship produced the notion of the early Christian community. In this new understanding, scholars produced a synthesis of much of their research from the previous one hundred years. This synthesis suggested that within early Christianity there was a new vitality, meaning, and community allegiance. The early Christian community, this scholarship suggested, was gripped by a moving and alive sense of the presence of the risen Christ. Often described as the Easter event, this new awareness and commitment to life with God in the postcrucifixion community of Jesus' followers was expressed in the language of both resurrection and the presence of the Holy Spirit. Taking the descriptions of a dynamic community of disciples in Jerusalem after the death of Jesus in the Acts of Apostles (2:42–47; 4:32–35) at face value, but seeing the stories of Jesus' resurrection as symbolic of that renewed sense of Jesus' presence, this mid-twentieth-century view provided many with a religious and reasoned understanding of how Christianity began.

    The last three decades have both honored and challenged that scholarly proposal. It still makes a great deal of sense that much of the ecstatic and life-affirming language of the early Christian scriptures comes from a dynamic experience of community. The experience of a resurrected presence of Jesus, the new stories and sayings of Jesus in the generations after Jesus' death, and the powerful early Christian assertions of new globally relevant ethics all still seem to point to inspired community experiences in the first century.

    But closer examination of the texts have revealed many different enthusiastic Christian communities, not one generative community. The deep diversity of these communities, as illustrated by this chapter's sampling of five, clearly could not have come from one common "resurrection" experience. Rather there appears to have been a deeper flow of community inspiring energy across a broad spectrum of ethnicities and geography.

12. An extended example of how contemporary churches can appropriate different early Christian models exists in chapter 5 of *Many Tables: The Eucharist in the New Testament and Liturgy Today* by Dennis E. Smith and Hal Taussig.

1. Some examples of the tension among first century Christian communities are the competition between Paul and Peter, the rivalry between the
Johannine and Thomasine movements, the controversy between Paul
and James, the enmity between the Markan community and Peter, the
tension between Paul and Apollos, the strident Johannine attack on a
group that separated itself from Johannine circles and called itself "the
Antichrist," the dispute between Paul and the Corinthian leaders, and
the striking difference about the Law between Paul and Matthew. Many
more could be cited and studied.

2. For a careful treatment of the connections between the Spirit of Christ
and the gift of communion, see the work of John D. Zizioulas, *Being as
Communion* (Crestwood, N.Y: St. Vladimir's Seminary Press, 1985), 81–
83, 130–32. Zizioulas insists that "It is not insignificant that since the
time of Paul, the Spirit has always been associated with the notion of
communion. It is because of this . . . that it is possible to speak of Christ
as having a body, i.e. to speak of ecclesiology, of the Church as the body
of Christ" (131).

3. We are indebted to Anne Casavecchia, a 2002 graduate of Chestnut Hill
College, who read our manuscript. She offered her journal reflection on
the trapped miners as a connection she made in response to learning
about communion as "a tie that binds us." See also *The Philadelphia
Inquirer*, July 28, 2002, 1.

4. John Zizioulas, *Being as Communion* (Crestwood, N.Y.: St. Vladimir's Seminary Press, 1985), 207.

5. Two additional clarifications of this "community/communion" vocabulary need to be acknowledged here. The word *communion* can be used to
describe the Christian act of sharing bread and cup, also called "eucharist"
or "the Lord's supper." Our use of "communion" does not directly reference this sharing of bread and cup. As is noted throughout the book,
common Christian meals and rituals of bread and cup are very important to the Christian sense of communion/community. But our use of
the word "communion" does not imply a direct synonymy of "communion" and the Christian sharing of bread and cup. It is true that the
conflation of these two uses of the word is very meaningful in many
Christian rituals, but for the sake of thoughtful clarity in this book,
some distinction needs to be maintained.

Similarly, it is important to note that this distinction between community and communion is not functioning in this book until chapter 3. In the introduction and chapters 1 and 2 we use the term *community* to connote all of the meanings chapter 3 assigns to both. We do this for two reasons: 1) as noted in the beginning of chapter 3 the larger connections among Christian communities were not functioning much during the first one hundred years of Christianity, the period covered by chapters 1 and 2; and 2) the elaborate distinction and overlap between "community" and "communion" would have broken up the content of the material in the introduction and chapters 1 and 2 in confusing ways.

6. Ibid., 134, speaking about Basil of Caesarea who says that "the unity of God is in the communion of the Persons."

7. In the letters of Ignatius, there are five references to altar/table (Greek, *trapeza*), three references to bread (one of which uses the unique Lukan terminology of "breaking of bread"), two references to eucharist, two references to cup, and one reference to *agape*. There is one additional reference which uses the root word for eucharist, but it is almost always translated "thanksgiving," since it is used here as a literary pair with "glory (Greek, *doxa*)." Since the root word "eucharistis" literally means "thanksgiving," such a translation makes the most sense. However, the same passage does refer to "meeting" in thanksgiving and glory, so the root word of eucharistis here is associated with a gathering, and might have a secondary meaning of eucharistis as an event.

In the two references to "eucharist" as a meal gathering, Ignatius uses the definite article, clearly suggesting a singular unit, conceptuality, and event, among all Christians. However, of specific interest is that Ignatius only uses the term *eucharist* to denote Christian meal celebration in two of his seven letters (Philadelphia, Smyrna), whereas he refers to Christians eating together in six letters.

But in the other letters Ignatius in similar fashion consistently uses either the definite article or the word "one" adjectivally with reference to other words referring to Christians eating together (e.g., bread, cup, table/altar) to imply that there is only one singular unit, conceptuality, and event among all Christians.

In Smyrneans 8:2–4 Ignatius forbids holding either baptism or "love feast (Greek, *agape*)" without the bishop. Here with the word "agape" he is clearly referring to what he sees as the central Christian community act of eating together, by virtue of its parallel with the central Christian initiation act of baptism. Understanding Ignatius' terminology becomes additionally difficult here, however, in that this is the same letter in which he refers to the central Christian act of eating together as "the eucharist."

There are two major references (disparaging and critical) to Christians who are not eating correctly. In Traillians 6:1 there is a strong objection to the way a group of Christians eat and the meaning they give to it, but there is no reference to or contrast with "eucharist." In Smyrneans 7:1 there is criticism of those who "remain aloof from the eucharist and prayers because they do not confess that the eucharist is the flesh of our savior." Here the criticism seems to be that these particular Christian opponents are eating with a different set of terms and meaning for their meal together.

There is a history of scholarship of identifying several traditions of "eucharist" in Ignatius (cf. von Wetter and Bartsch). Although this scholarship does not attend to the ambiguity of Ignatian terminology about Christian meals discussed here, it corresponds to it in that it detects several different ways in Ignatius of understanding "eucharist" (used as a scholarly term to denote early Christian ceremonial eating). It is also standard in Ignatius scholarship to note that he does not link the passion of Jesus with the meal (cf. Schoedel), no matter what term is used.

How does one then make sense of what Ignatius means with reference to these terms and various Christians eating together? And, what can we deduce about the meal practices themselves and the meaning different Christians connected with Ignatius attributed to them?

It is possible to read in these texts the following twenty-first century conventional conclusions: All the Christian communities Ignatius encountered were celebrating the same kind of meal and using the same terminology. They all generally thought of their meal together as the "eucharist," and they used other terms such as cup, bread, *agape*, table/altar as alternate ways to describe this one type of meal with one general meaning. The groups that had different practices or different meanings were indeed exceptional, dangerous, and out-of-line. Ignatius' writing simply reflects and appeals to what is already a unified Christian meal practice and meaning about the meal practice.

The difficulties with this conclusion, however, are substantial. That Ignatius only uses "eucharist" in two letters, one of which also uses another central term for the Christian meal, raises questions about whether the term "eucharist" itself is an overarching term for all Christian meals (this position corresponds to the great variety of terms for Christian meals in other early Christian literature of Ignatius' time, very few of which use the term *eucharist* as the central term for Christian meals). The variety of meal terms used in both Ignatius and Christian literature contemporary with him hints strongly at a plurality of practices and meanings at meals in Ignatius' time. That certain central notions of the eventual Christian consensus on eucharistic practice do not exist in Ignatius (e.g., the connection between meal and Jesus' passion), but do exist in other early Christian literature (in the case of the passion-meal, Paul and Luke both show this connection) indicate that Ignatius' own synthesis was different from both future consensus and other roughly contemporaneous Christian writers. Ignatius' own disparaging reports of Christians doing meals differently with different meanings suggests that he himself was experiencing a variety of practices and meanings, which he saw—especially in his mission to express Christian unity—as problematic. Ignatius' overall message in all his letters that unity is central represents his own interest in linking different Christian communities, at least in the minds of himself and his readers. This could mean that his interest in unity might be served by overlooking differences in the specific communities' meal practices and understandings thereof.

An alternative reading of the above observations in Ignatius' letters, highlighting Ignatius' contribution to the notions of Christian community and communion, while taking seriously the above problems, follows:

As noted in the body of this text, Ignatius' experience of various Christian communities had shown him that they all ate together and experienced in those meals together connection to each other, God, and Jesus. This insight of Ignatius became important to him in his quest for Christian unity. He passionately pursued the good news that throughout his travels Christian communities were holding a similar meal and seeing meaning in it. Although actually these communities were not using the same terms (as each other or Ignatius) necessarily for the meaning of their meals together, Ignatius' own emphasis on unity overlooks this. Only when there are glaring differences in meaning from his own is Ignatius willing to acknowledge this variety. It is possible that Ignatius may have used various terms for the way the similar early Christian meal celebrations demonstrate a larger unity through strategic application of terms to specific communities. So, it may be that his use of "eucharist" only in two letters reflects his knowledge that those communities used the term centrally for what they were doing, whereas his use of "breaking bread" for another letter reflects his knowledge of what that community's terminology was. Ignatius is therefore using a small range of meal-related terms to pursue his message of Christian communion. His use of these terms as connoting the same thing (and therefore representing real Christian unity) moved many Christians to adopt similar meal practices, terminology, and meaning as a reflection of unity/communion. His use of terms does not, however, reflect anything near unanimity of meal practice and meaning in the communities to whom he wrote.

9. The term *episkopos* translated "bishop" does not exist in many Christian documents of this period. It appears that different groups and groups of groups had different forms of governance (in others the terms of *elder* and *prophet* have central authority. In still others there seems to be fluid and informal authority structures).

Pagan writers, such as Pliny in the early second century, did not perceive Christians as part of a worldwide community. Christian groups existed in some forty or fifty cities within the Roman Empire, groups quite small, some numbering several dozen people, others numbering several hundreds. The total number of Christians may have been less than fifty thousand, which was quite insignificant in a society of some sixty million persons. The five to six million Jews far outnumbered them. See Michael Fahey, "The Catholicity of the Church in the New Testament and Early Patristic Period," in *The Jurist* 52 (1992): 1, 44–70.

10. For a fuller study of the demand for unity in doctrine as an external criterion for communion, see the essay of Bernard Prusak, "Hospitality Extended or Denied: *Koinonia* Incarnate from Jesus to Augustine," in James H. Provost (ed.), *The Church as Communion* (The Canon Law Society of America, 1984), pp. 89–126.

11. Bishops came to determine who was included or excluded from the communion of the churches, visibly expressed by communion in the eucharist. That excommunions were more often than not the result of disagreement in doctrine is evident in the writings of Justin Martyr (*Dialogue with Trypho*), Irenaeus (*Adversus Haereses*), Tertullian (*De Prescriptione Haereticorum*), and Cyprian (*De Ecclesiae Unitate*). By the mid-third century, Cyprian, bishop of Carthage, serves as spokesperson for a growing consensus that a worldwide communion of local churches is achieved by the communion of bishops with one another. As the church expands geographically and it becomes more and more difficult for bishops to meet regularly face to face in synods, letters of communion serve to testify that the bishop named in the letter has been validly elected and is a teacher of orthodox doctrine. As Ludwig Hertling observes in his careful study, *Communio: Church and Papacy in Early Christianity,* the communion of the bishops does not depend on friendship but on their

mutual concern about "the growing problem of sectarians" (49). Cyprian, bishop of Carthage from 249–258, refers to the practice of excluding the name of a bishop from the lists (dyptychs) of names for whom prayer were said during a eucharist. See Werner Elert, *Eucharist and Church Fellowship in the First Four Centuries* (St. Louis: Concordia, 1966).

12. By the time of the Constantinopolitan Creed in 381, the adjective "catholic" came to be used as a shorthand designation for a community's relationship to the triune God which formed a communion with other Christians no matter how widely distributed geographically or temporally these communities might be. "This is the meaning that appears with one, holy, catholic and apostolic church" (Fahey, 49).

13. Robert Payne, *The Holy Fire: The Story of the Fathers of the Eastern Church* (New York: Harper and Row, 1957), 115.

14. Long Rule of Basil, Answer to Question #9. Migne, *Patrologia Graeca* 31, 917. Quoted in Peter Phan, *Message of the Fathers of the Church: Social Thought*, vol. 20 (Wilmington: Michael Glazier, 1984), 122.

15. Quoted in John Meyendorff, *Byzantine Theology* (New York: Fordham University Press, 1974), 175.

16. Philip T. Weller, ed., *Selected Easter Sermons of St. Augustine* (St. Louis: B. Herder Co., 1959), 101.

17. See Augustine's "Communion in 1 John," Migne, *Patrologia Latina* 35: 2055–2066, quoted in Bernard Prusak, "Hospitality Extended or Denied: *Koinonia* Incarnate from Jesus to Augustine," in James Provost (ed.). *The Church as Communion* (Washington, D.C: Canon Law Society of America, 1984), 121.

18. By the time of Augustine the ramifications of the Manichaen mythology became complex, but the teaching of Mani (216–276) was simple. Mani believed there were two principles, Light and Darkness, and three moments: Past, Present, and Future. Light and Darkness were eternally contrasting realities, which originally were separate. But in the Past, Darkness invaded the Light and mingled with it as it does in the Present. The purpose of existence was to distill the Light from the Darkness so that in the Future, Light and Darkness will be separate again and the universe restored or saved. The true Manichaen was an ascetic who did no work, for work participated in the Present, where Darkness invaded Light. The bodily needs of a true Manichaen was attended to by his followers, the second grade of Manichaen, called the Hearers. These accepted the teaching of Mani but continued in their professions and even

married. Augustine had belonged in his early years to this second order of Hearers. See W.H.C. Frend, *The Rise of Christianity* (Philadelphia: Fortress Press, 1984), 314–18; also, Joseph A. Komonchak, Mary Collins and Dermot Lane (eds.), *The New Dictionary of Theology* (Collegeville: Liturgical Press, 1987), 623.

19. Augustine, *On the Morals of the Catholic Church* 30: 62–64, quoted in Jaroslav Pelikan, *The Mystery of Continuity: Time and History, Memory and Eternity in the Thought of Saint Augustine* (Charlottesville: University Press of Virginia, 1986), 91.

20. Cf. the recent work of Margaret Aymer at Union Theological Seminary in New York City on the ways the longer term Roman oppression of North Africa affected the Donatist controversies. Her public lecture at Union on December 17, 1999, on "Collective Memory and the History of Early Christianity" summarized recent scholarship on the Donatists and brought into sharp focus the long term effects of Roman rule in North Africa. Aymer's work is not yet published.

PART TWO
THE COMMUNITY OF GOD:
TWENTIETH CENTURY THEOLOGICAL AND PHILOSOPHICAL CONTRIBUTIONS

CHAPTER FOUR
A CHURCH CALLED BACK TO ITS ROOTS

1. Emmanuel Lanne, "Perspectives: Unitatis Redintegratio Voies vers la communion des Eglises," in *Unitatis Redintegration 1964–1974: The Impact of the Decree on Ecumenism.* Gerard Bekes and Vilmos Vajta, eds. (Rome: Editrice Anselmiano, 1977), 119–40.

2. The Final Report," *Origins* 15, no. 27 (December 19, 1985), 448.

3. The Council of Trent (1545–1563) was called by Pope Paul III in response to the need for reform of the church, articulated in the various propositions of the Protestant Reformation. The Council met in twenty-five sessions over this eighteen year period, presided over by three popes, Paul III, Julian II, and Paul IV. The juridical and confrontational nature of the Council of Trent was determined by the purpose for which it was called. As stated in its opening paragraph, that purpose included: "the uprooting of heresies, the peace and unity of the church, the reform of the clergy and the Christian people, the crushing and complete removal of the enemies of the Christian name." See Norman P. Tanner (ed.),

Decrees of the Ecumenical Councils, Vol. II. (Washington, D.C.: Georgetown University Press, 1990), 656–799.

4. *STPD Dieu*, 715—MacPartlan, 8.

5. The term *neoscholasticism* describes a nineteenth century theological movement that was institutionalized by Pope Leo XIII in 1879 with his papal encyclical *Aeterni Patris*. Leo XIII recommended that scholasticism, especially as taught in the theories and methods of Thomas Aquinas, be the only philosophy and theology used in Catholic seminaries. It was Leo's hope that the "old" theology of the scholastic doctors could clear up the confusion between nature and grace, faith and reason that the newer methods of Cartesian and idealist philosophy had introduced into Catholic theology. The problem came with the misconception that there ever was a common scholasticism shared by St. Thomas and other thirteenth century scholastic doctors. By the mid-twentieth century, disagreements between scholastics on one side and exegetes, historians, and patristic scholars became irreconcilable. The research of Henri DeLubac revealed that the Post-Tridentine (Council of Trent) teaching on nature and grace that neoscholastics attributed to Thomas Aquinas had never been taught by him. Diversity was much more prevalent even among the scholastics than the neoscholastic manuals allowed.

6. See the study of Dennis Doyle, *Communion Ecclesiology*, 61.

7. Von Balthasar, *The Theology of Henri deLubac: An Overview.* Trans. Joseph Fessio, S.J. and Michael Waldstein (San Francisco: Ignatius Press, 1983), 28.

8. Chapter 3 of his book *Diversity and Communion*, entitled "Diversity Has Always Been Accepted in the Unity of Faith," summarizes his conviction (23–33).

9. Lanne, ibid., 119–40.

CHAPTER FIVE
AN EASTERN ORTHODOX CONTRIBUTION TO UNDERSTANDING COMMUNION: THE WORK OF JOHN ZIZIOULAS

1. Zizioulas uses the term *individual* only to refer to an isolated monad, not as others may use it to refer to a differentiated human being.

CHAPTER SIX
SOCIAL PHILOSOPHERS AS CONVERSATION PARTNERS ABOUT COMMUNITY

1. Two important scholars of Josiah Royce to whom we are indebted are John E. Smith and Frank M. Oppenheim, S.J. Details of the early life of Royce are taken from John E. Smith (ed.), *Josiah Royce: Selected Writings* (New York: Paulist Press, 1988), 3–4.

2. Lonergan frequently uses the term *heuristic* from the Greek *heurisko* meaning "principle of discovery." We use it here to denote a dynamic process that has a desired end, a horizon toward which it moves.

3. The work of Robert Doran, S.J., a Lonerganian scholar and psychologist who directs the Lonergan Institute in Regis College, Ontario, Canada, offers further elaborations of affective conversion and makes his own important contribution of psychic conversion. Doran has devoted much of his own study to the application and ongoing development of Lonergan's theories to the fields of psychology and spirituality. See his essay, "From Psychic Conversion to the Dialectic of Community," in *Lonergan Workshop* 6 ed. Fred Lawrence (Atlanta: Scholars Press, 1986).

CHAPTER SEVEN
COMMUNION AND LIBERATION: THE CONTRIBUTION OF LIBERATION AND FEMINIST THEOLOGIANS TO UNDERSTANDING COMMUNION

1. Anne E. Patrick, "Authority, Women and the Church," in *Empowering Authority: The Charisms of Episcopacy and Primacy in the Church Today.* Eds. Patrick Howell and Gary Chamberlain (Kansas City: Sheed and Ward, 1990), 20, and Margaret Farley, "New Patterns of Relationship: Beginnings of a Moral Revolution," in *Woman: New Dimensions* ed. Walter Burghardt (New York: Paulist Press, 1977), 52.

PART THREE
THE CONTEMPORARY NORTH AMERICAN SOCIAL SITUATION AS CRISIS OF COMMUNITY

CHAPTER EIGHT
THE AMERICAN DISASTER

1. Jennifer is an actual person, but the name is fictionalized.

2. Friday, March 1, 2002, *USA Today*, Hal Bodley's "On Baseball"column,16C.

3. Richard Madsen, William M. Sullivan, Ann Swidler, and Steven M. Tipton co-authored the work, published initially by the University of California Press, and subsequently by Harper and Row. Bellah's voice seems to be the integrative one, while much of the book depends on extensive sociological research projects by Madsen, Sullivan, Swidler, and Tipton.

4. It would be a misrepresentation of Bellah *et al.* to characterize individualism as completely negative. The authors' preferred term for the positive dimensions of individualism is "individuation," which was "necessary to free us from the tyrannical structures of the past," (277) but which now is a caricature of itself and threatens to turn into its opposite (277). For the longer appreciation and critique of individualism cf. 142–56.

Chapter Nine
The Crisis of Community in the Christian Churches of America

1. The 2002 crisis in the Roman Catholic Church, centered in the clergy sex abuse and episcopal cover up, has been named by many as a crisis of authority. In its wake, a new lay-directed movement of reform has emerged. Called Voice of the Faithful (See www.VOTF.com) this group originated in the local church of Boston, where shocking numbers of abuse cases and their cover up by the local bishop, Bernard Cardinal Law, has shaken millions of Catholic laity, clergy, and religious with disbelief, dismay, and determination. After a gathering of more than four thousand people—lay, religious and clergy—in Boston on July 20, 2002, to listen and clarify the purpose and goals of the movement, Voice of the Faithful continues to form local chapters in dioceses throughout the country. As a social body in the church, it is committed to advocate for the healing of victims/survivors of sexual abuse by clergy, support clergy of integrity, and work for structural change of the church. These newly emerging local chapters understand prayer and spiritual conversion to be at the heart of their purpose and method. We await their further development as hopeful possibilities in our re-imagining project.

PART FOUR
A GOSPEL OF COMMUNITY FOR THE TWENTY-FIRST CENTURY

CHAPTER TEN
THE EMERGENCE OF CHRISTIAN COMMUNITY IN CONTEMPORARY AMERICA

1. The full article, "Parish Turns Murder to Grace" by Robert McClory, appeared in the *National Catholic Reporter*, November 7, 1997.

2. Cf. chapter 5's treatment of the thought of Josiah Royce.

3. See the studies of Bernard J. Lee, S.M., in *The Catholic Experience of Small Christian Communities* (New York: Paulist Press, 2000), 139–42. See also, Michael Cowan and Bernard Lee, *Risk and Conversion* (Maryknoll: Orbis Books, 1997), 11.

4. See Bernard Lonergan's heuristic structure of community in chapter 7 for fuller information on data for understanding and judging provided by sources of Christian tradition or other classic truth claims. Understanding and judging are never done in a vacuum but in conversation with a larger body of meanings and values, striving to approach Ultimate Meaning and Value Itself.

5. Bernard Loomer, a process philosopher, has distinguished unilateral from relational power in a most insightful correlation entitled "Two Conceptions of Power," in *Process Studies* 6 (1976), 5–32.

CHAPTER ELEVEN
ENCOUNTERING DIVERSE "FORMS" OF CONTEMPORARY CHRISTIAN COMMUNITIES

1. Renew materials, used by facilitators and participants, include a ritual/prayer format, scripture texts, reflections on the scriptures, questions for sharing, and outreach/justice suggestions. For resources and information, contact: Renew International, 1232 George Street, Plainfield, New Jersey 07062.

2. For more information about the parish as a community of communities, see Kleissler, LeBert, and McGuinness, *Small Christian Communities: A Vision of Hope for the Twenty-First Century* (New York: Paulist Press, 1997), especially 59–74.

3. All direct quotes of Father Walter Plominski's are the result of ongoing telephone conversations with him in May 2001.

4. Gil Donahue, *The Social Context of Nova's Origins* (unpublished manuscript, May 1987), 58.

5. See "Attachments" in Nova Community's "Educating Ourselves for Social Justice,'" (June 1999).

6. Ibid., 8.

7. Robert Hovda, "The Amen Corner," *Worship,* vol. 62, no. 4 (July 1988), 53–359, at p. 356.

8. In honor of its 150th anniversary, St. Vincent's recently chronicled its history in a book entitled, *God's Love Is Fire: A Parish Becomes a People* (Philadelphia: Richard K. Taylor, 2000).

WORKS CONSULTED

Arrupe, Pedro. *La Vie Chretienne*, June 1975.

Balch, David, ed. *Social History of Matthean Christianity.* Minneapolis: Fortress Press, 1991.

———. *Ecclesiogenesis: Base Communities Reinvent the Church.* Maryknoll, N.Y.: Orbis Books, 1986.

Bellah, Robert. "Reforming our Institutions of Meaning." In *Fugitive Faith: Conversations on Spiritual, Environmental, and Community Renewal.* Edited by Benjamin Webb. Maryknoll, NY: Orbis Books, 1998.

———. "Religion and the Shape of National Culture." *America*, July 31–August 7, 1999.

Bellah, Robert, et al. *Habits of the Heart: Individualism and Commitment in American Life.* New York: Harper and Row, 1985.

———, et al. *Individualism and Commitment in American Life: Readings on the Themes of Habits of the Heart.* New York: Harper and Row, 1988.

Bettenson, Henry, ed. *The Later Christian Fathers.* New York: Oxford University Press, 1956.

Betz, Hans Dieter. *1 Corinthians.* Philadelphia: Fortress Press, 1983.

Boff, Leonardo. "Trinitarian Community and Social Liberation." *Cross Currents*, Fall 1988.

Brock, Rita Nakashima. "What Is Feminist: Strategies for Change and Transformation of Consciousness." In *Setting the Table: Women in Theological Conversation.* Edited by Rita Nakashima Brock, Claudia Camp, and Serene Jones. St. Louis: Chalice Press, 1995.

Brown, Raymond. *Community of the Beloved Disciple: The Life, Loves, and Hates of an Individual Church in NT Times.* New York: Paulist Press, 1979.

Cameron, Ron. *The Other Gospels.* Philadelphia: Fortress Press, 1983.

Carr, Anne. *Transforming Grace: Christian Tradition and Women's Experiences.* San Francisco: Harper Collins, 1988.

Congar, Yves. *Divided Christianity.* London, 1939.

———. *Diversity and Communion.* Mystic, CT: Twenty-Third Publications, 1985.

———. *The Mystery of the Church.* Translated by A.V. Littledale. Baltimore: Helicon, 1969, 160.

Davies, Stevan. *New Testament Fundamentals.* Santa Rosa, CA: Polebridge Press, 1996.

DeLubac, Henri. *Catholicism.* London: Burns and Oates, 1950.

———. *The Motherhood of the Church.* San Francisco: Ignatius Press, 1982.

Dornisch, Loretta. *A Woman Reads the Gospel of Luke.* Collegeville, MN: Liturgical Press, 1997.

Doyle, Dennis. *Communion Ecclesiology.* Maryknoll, NY: Orbis Books, 2000.

Crossan, John Dominic. *Four Other Gospels: Contours on the Canon.* San Francisco: HarperCollins, 1987.

Egan, Harvey. *Karl Rahner, Mystic of Everyday Life.* New York: Crossroad, 1998.

Farley, Margaret. "New Patterns of Relationship: Beginnings of a Moral Revolution." In *Woman: New Dimensions.* Edited by Walter Burghardt. New York: Paulist Press, 1977.

Faus, Jose Ignatio. "Sin." In *Systematic Theology: Perspectives from Liberation Theology.* Edited by Jan Sobrino and Ignacio Ellacuria. Maryknoll, NY: Orbis Books, 1996.

Fedwick, George. *The Church and the Charisma of Leadership of Basil of Caesaria.* Toronto: Pontifical Institute for Medieval Studies, 1990.

Freie, John F. *Counterfeit Community: The Exploitation of Our Longings for Connectedness.* Lanham, MD: Rowman and Littlefield, 1998.

Greeley, Andrew. *The Catholic Myth.* Berkeley, CA: University of California Press, 2000.

———. *The Catholic Imagination.* Berkeley, CA: University of California Press, 2001.

Gregson, Vernon, ed. *The Desires of the Human Heart: An Introduction to the Theology of Bernard Lonergan.* New York: Paulist Press, 1988.

Gutierrez, Gustavo. Homily, February 16, 1979. In *The Violence of Love: The Pastoral Wisdom of Archbishop Oscar Romero*. Translated by James R. Brockman. San Francisco: Harper and Row, 1988.

———. *A Theology of Liberation: History, Politics, and Salutation*. New York: Orbis Books, 1988.

———. *We Drink from Our Own Wells*. New York: Orbis Books, 1984.

Hines, Mary. "The Church: Community for Liberation." In *Freeing Theology*. Edited by Catherine Mowry-LaCugna. San Francisco: HarperCollins, 1993.

Johnson, Elizabeth. "Redeeming the Name of Christ." In *Freeing Theology*. Edited by Catherine Mowry-LaCugna. San Francisco: HarperCollins, 1993.

———. "Let the Symbol Ring Again." *Theology Today* 54, October 1997.

Kirkpatrick, Frank G. *The Ethics of Community*. Malden, MA: Blackwell, 2001.

Klinghardt, Mattias. *Gemeinschaftsmahl und Mahlgemeinschaft*. Tübingen: Francke, 1996.

Kloppenborg, John, and Stephen Wilson, eds. *Voluntary Associations in the Graeco-Roman World*. New York: Routledge, 1996.

Komonchak, Joseph. "The Return of Yves Congar." *Commonweal*, July 15, 1983.

———. "The Church and the Mediation of the Christian Self." Unpublished manuscript. Catholic University of America, Washington, D.C., January 1991.

Lanne, Emmanuel. "Perspectives: Unitatis Redintegratio Voies vers la communion des Eglises." In *Unitatis Redintegration 1964–1974: The Impact of the Decree on Ecumenism*. Edited by Gerard Bekes and Vilmos Vajta. Rome: Editrice Anselmiano, 1977.

Lonergan, Bernard. "Healing and Creating in History." In *A Third Collection: Papers by J. F. Lonergan, S.J.* Edited by Frederick E. Crowe, S.J. New York: Paulist Press, 1985.

———. *Insight: A Study of Human Understanding*. New York: Philosophical Library, 1957.

———. "The Mediation of Christ in Prayer." *Method: Journal of Lonergan Studies* 2, no. 1 (March 1984).

————. *Method in Theology.* New York: Herder & Herder, 1972.

————. "Natural Right and Historical Mindedness" in *A Third Collection: Papers by J. F. Lonergan, S.J.* Edited by Frederick E. Crowe, S.J. New York: Paulist Press, 1985.

————. *A Third Collection: Papers by J. F. Lonergan, S.J.* Edited by Frederick E. Crowe, S.J. New York: Paulist Press, 1985.

Louth, Andrew. *Maximus the Confessor.* New York: Rutledge, 1996.

MacDonald, Dennis. *Male and Female.* Cambridge: Harvard University Press, 1987.

Mack, Burton. *The Christian Myth.* New York: Crossroad, 2001.

————. *The Lost Gospel.* San Francisco: HarperCollins, 1995.

————. *Who Wrote the New Testament?: The Making of the Christian Myth.* San Francisco: HarperCollins 1996.

MacPartlan, Paul. *The Eucharist Makes the Church: Henri De Lubac and John Zizioulas in Dialogue.* Edinburgh: T and T Clark, 1993.

Maximus the Confessor. *The Mystagogia of St Maximus the Confessor.* Translated with historical notes and commentary by Dom Julian Stead, O.S.B. Still River, MA: St. Bede's Press, 1982.

Mowry-LaCugna, Catherine. *God for Us: The Trinity and Christian Life.* San Francisco: HarperCollins, 1996.

————. "Reconceiving the Trinity as the Mystery of Salvation." *Scottish Journal of Theology* 38 (1985).

————. "God in Communion with Us." In *Freeing Theology: The Essentials of Theology in Feminist Perspective.* Edited by Catherine Mowry-LaCugna. San Francisco: Harper, 1993

O'Neill, Mary Aquin. "The Mystery of Being Human Together." In *Freeing Theology: The Essentials of Theology in Feminist Perspective.* Edited by Catherine Mowry-La Cugna. San Francisco: Harper, 1993, 139–60.

Patrick, Anne E. "Authority, Women, and the Church." In *Empowering Authority: The Charisms of Episcopacy and Primacy in the Church Today.* Edited by Patrick Howell and Gary Chamberlain. Kansas City: Sheed and Ward, 1990.

Puebla Documento. "Final Document of the Third General Conference of the Latin American Bishops." In *Puebla and Beyond*. Edited by John Eagleson and Philip Sharper. Maryknoll, NY: Orbis, 1979.

Putnam, Robert. *Bowling Alone: The Collapse and Revival of American Community*. New York: Simon and Schuster, 2000.

Quinn, John. "The Exercise of the Primacy." *Commonweal*, July 12, 1996.

Rahner, Karl. *Faith in a Wintry Season: Interviews and Conversations with Karl Rahner in the Last Years of His Life, 1982–1984*. Edited by Hubert Biallowons, Harvey D. Egan, S.J., and Paul Imhof, S.J. New York: Crossroad, 1990.

———. *Foundations of Christian Faith*. New York: Crossroad, 1978.

———. *The Love of Jesus and the Love of Neighbor*. New York: Crossroad, 1983.

———. "New Image of the Church in Vatican II." *Theological Investigations 10*. New York: Herder and Herder, 1973.

———. *The Practice of Faith: A Handbook of Contemporary Spirituality*. Edited by Karl Lehmann and Albert Raffelt. New York: Crossroad, 1986.

———. *Theological Investigations 7*. Baltimore: Helicon, 1967.

Reid, Barbara. *Choosing the Better Part?: Women in the Gospel of Luke*. Collegeville, MN: Liturgical Press, 1998.

Romero, Oscar. Homily, February 16, 1979.

Ross, Susan. "God's Embodiment and Women." In *Freeing Theology: The Essentials of Theology in Feminist Perspective*. Edited by Catherine Mowry-LaCugna, San Francisco: Harper, 1993, 185–210.

Royce, Josiah. *The Problem of Christianity*. Chicago: University of Chicago, 1968.

Ruether, Rosemary Radford. "Goddesses and Witches: Liberation and Countercultural Feminism." *Christian Century* 98 (1980).

———. *Sexism and God-Talk*. Boston: Beacon Press, 1993.

———. *Women-Church: Theology and Practice of Feminist Liturgical Communities*. San Francisco: Harper and Row, 1985.

Ruether, Rosemary Radford, and Eugene C. Bianchi, eds. *A Democratic Church*. New York: Crossroad, 1992.

Schüssler Fiorenza, Elisabeth. "Hermeneutics of Oppression: Socio-Cultural Analytics." Graduate Spirituality class. Chestnut Hill College, June 1998. Handout.

———. *In Memory of Her: A Feminist Theological Reconstruction of Christian Origins*. New York: Crossroad, 1983.

———. *Searching the Scriptures*. Vol. II. New York: Crossroad, 1996.

Seim, Turid. *A Double Message*. New York: Crossroad: 1999.

Smith, Dennis E., and Hal Taussig. *Many Tables: The Eucharist in the New Testament and Liturgy Today*. Philadelphia: Trinity Press International, 1990.

Swimme, Brian, and Thomas Bery. *The Universe Story: From the Primordial Flaring Forth to the Ecozoic Era: A Celebration of the Unfolding of the Cosmos*. San Francisco: HarperCollins, 1992.

Tannehill, Robert. *A Literary Introduction to Luke-Acts*. Minneapolis: Augsburg-Fortress, 1992.

———. *Luke: A Commentary*. Nashville, TN: Abingdon, 1998.

Taussig, Hal. "Dealing Under the Table." In *Reimagining Christian Origins*. Edited by Elizabeth Castelli and Hal Taussig. Valley Forge, PA: Trinity Press International, 1996,

Thunberg, Lars. *Man and the Cosmos: The Vision of St. Maximus the Confessor*. New York: St. Vladimir's Seminary Press, 1985.

de Tocqueville, Alexis. *Democracy in America*. New York: Doubleday, 1969.

Vatican Council II. *The Basic Sixteen Documents*. Edited by Austin Flannery, O.P. Northport, NY: Costello Publishing, 1996.

Von Balthasar, Hans. *The Theology of Henri deLubac: An Overview*. Translated by Joseph Fessio, S.J. and Michael Waldstein. San Francisco: Ignatius Press, 1983.

Von Campenhausen, H. *The Fathers of the Greek Church*. New York: MacMillan, 1959.

Vorgrimler, Herbert. *Understanding Karl Rahner: An Introduction to His Life and Thought*. New York: Crossroad, 1986.

Whitehead, Evelyn Eaton, and James D. Whitehead. *Seasons of Strength: New Visions of Adult Christian Meaning*. Garden City, NY: Doubleday and Co., 1984.

Wire, Antoinette. *The Corinthian Women Prophets*. Philadelphia: Fortress Press, 1983.

Wuthnow, Robert. *Loose Connections: Joining Together in America's Fragmented Communities*. Cambridge, MA: Harvard University Press, 1998.

———. "Mobilizing Civic Engagement," cited on p. 77 of Putnam's *Bowling Alone*.

Zizioulas, John. "The Unity of the Church in the Holy Eucharist and the Bishop during the First Three Centuries." Oxford University diss,. 1965

———. *Being as Communion*. New York: St. Vladimir's Seminary Press, 1985.

INDEX

sense of, 4, 7, 8, 9, 10, 15, 39;
  as contemporary role model,
  20, 21, 31–32, 226; and
  diversity of, 9, 15, 16, 17, 18,
  19; and Jews, 14; and social
  character of, 19–20; and
  synagogues, 14; and urban
  life, 46; and voluntary
  associations, 11, 13; and
  women, 17
Edwards, Kathy Nolen, 216–17
Egan, Harvey, 70
Egypt, 29
Egyptians, 11
Einstein, Albert, 127
Eleusis, 13
Elijah, 15, 27
Elisha, 27
Elmer Gantry, 152
Englert, August H. ("Bud"), 215,
  216, 217
Enlightenment, 127; and
  individualism, 64
Ephesians, 51
Ephesus, 40
Eucharist, 80–82
Evangelicalism, and community
  building, 157; and
  individualism, promotion of,
  160

Fedwick, George, 48
Feminists, 129, 130. *See also*
  Women-Church.
Feminist theologians, 114, 117,
  123, 126; and sexual
  discrimination, 117
Feminist theology, 116, 117, 121,
  122, 125, 131; and sin, 119–20
Food Shuttle of Western New
  York, xxi, 177
Formalism, 156–58, and
  churchgoing, 156; and social
  alienation of, 157
Fort Benning, 212

"Friends of the Night," xxi
Funeral associations, 12

Gardiner, George, 203, 207, 208
Gerety, Peter L., 186
Glide Memorial Church (San
  Francisco), 208
Gospel of Luke, 17, 18, 32
Gospel of Mark, 17, and women,
  17
Gospel of Mary (Magdalene), 17
Gospel of Matthew, 30–31
Gospel of Thomas, 17, 28–30; and
  baptism, 29; and Jesus, 29;
  and women, inclusion of, 29
Grace, 118, 121, 122; and small
  group communities, 188
Greece, 7
Greeley, Andrew, 161, and
  sacramental imagination, xix
Gregory of Nazianzus, 44, 65, 84
Gregory of Nyssa, 44, 65, 84
Gutierrez, Gustavo, 115, 116, 117,
  118, 128–29, 131

Habits of the Heart (Bellah), xv,
  139, 140, 141
Handicapped Encounter Christ
  (HEC), 198
Happiness, and churchgoing,
  xviii; and community, lack of,
  138
Hawkes, Jeff, 211
Hiroshima, 135
Horoschak, Lynne, 216–17
Hovda, Robert, 202

Ignatius, 36, 39–42, 44, 50, 81
Individualism, and the common
  good, 178; religious aspect of,
  149
Insight (Lonergan), 101
Iona (Scotland), 210
Irenaeus, 50, 65, 69, 81
Isis, 13, 24